ENVIRONMENTAL GEOMORPHOLOGY AND WATERSHED MANAGEMENT

About the Author

M.S. Rawat obtained his Master's Degree in Geography in 1984 securing first position in Kumaun University followed by Doctoral Degree in 1990 in Environmental Geomorphology and Hydrology. With over 25 years of research and teaching experience, he is presently working as Associate Professor in the Department of Geography under School of Sciences, Nagaland (Central) University, Lumami. His areas of interest are geomorphological, hydrological processes and watershed management. He has contributed several scientific research papers and is recipient of many prestigious awards as well as honours.

Environmental Geomorphology and Watershed Management

A Study from Central Himalaya

M.S. Rawat

CONCEPT PUBLISHING COMPANY PVT. LTD.
NEW DELHI-110 059

ISBN-13: 978-81-8069-758-6

First Published 2011

Published and Printed by

Concept Publishing Company Pvt. Ltd.
Regd. Office :
A/15-16, Commercial Block, Mohan Garden
New Delhi-110059 (India)
Phones : 25351460, 25351794, *Fax* : 091-11-25357109
Email : publishing@conceptpub.com,
Website : www.conceptpub.com

Editorial Office :
H-13, Bali Nagar, New Delhi-110 015, India.

Cataloging in Publication Data--*Courtesy:* D.K. Agencies (P) Ltd. <docinfo@dkagencies.com>

Rawat, M. S., Dr.
Environmental geomorphology and watershed management : a study from central Himalaya/ M.S. Rawat.
p. cm.
Originally presented as the author's thesis (Ph. D.--Kumaun University, 1990) under the title: Physical landscapes and their degradational processes in the Nana Kosi Basin : a study in environmental geomorphology.
Includes bibliographical references (p.) and index.
ISBN 9788180697586

1. Environmental geomorphology--India--Nana Kosi River Watershed. 2. Watershed management--India--Nana Kosi River Watershed. 3. Land degradation--India--Nana Kosi River Watershed. I. Title. II. Title: Physical landscapes and their degradational processes in the Nana Kosi Basin.

DDC 551.410954 22

Preface

Wise management of land and water resources in the geodynamically sensitive and tectonically active domain like the Himalaya requires knowledge of the interrelations within the environment and numerous controlling physical processes, i.e., pluvial, fluvial, tectonic and anthropogenic. Geomorphologists have traditionally studied physical processes of landscapes by analysis of individual degradational processes—measurement of water and sediment yield at one or more points within a drainage basin or watershed, and stratigraphic analysis of deposits. These approaches, however, have rarely been used collectively to provide a framework for understanding water and sediment movement through watershed. Many current problems in the environmental geomorphology and landscape ecology can be better addressed when placed in the broad, conceptual framework provided by the analysis of all the degradational processes of the watershed. Such analysis provides an understanding of geomorphic systems, just as similar studies have been fruitful in analysis of nutrient cycling, hydrology, and other complex systems.

Geomorphology is the study of landforms and in particular of their nature, origin, processes of development and material composition. In this investigation the author has tried to bring together geomorphological materials that has been, or could be of value in environmental management and watershed management for sustainable development. The study includes all the aspects of applied geomorphology of a Central Himalayan watershed and provides a useful introductory survey for those interested in exploring practical applications of geomorphology and for those who require a geomorphological component in their study or practice of environmental management/watershed management for sustainable development. The main thrust of the book—anthropogenic degradation of the physical landscape is important in view of the widespread ecological impalance being caused in the fragile mountain ecosystems by the headlong academic development in recent years.

To the physical geographer, this study offers a fresh look at parts of the subject, of the using material that has not previously appeared in environmental geomorphology texts of the Himalaya. It is hoped that the display of techniques degradational problems caused by pluvial, fluvial, tectonic and anthropogenic processes, and environmental relationship may be of value of environmentalists, physical geographers, geologists and other natural scientists with an interest in geomorphology. To social scientists, planners, decision-makers, and others who increasingly have to consider the natural environment, this study may serve to introduce these aspects of geomorphology central to some of their problems. It is fully realized that these are ambitious aims and that any introductory investigation of this kind must have many shortcomings. The present book is a vital part of the author's Ph. D. Thesis entitled *"Physical Landscapes and their Degradational Processes in the Nana Kosi Basin : A Study in Environmental Geomorphoogy"*.

The study has been divided into four parts. In the first part, the author has dicussed briefly, major objectives, methodology and some of the broader aspects of this study in environmental geomorphology (Chapter 1) and embraces physical (Chapter 2) and morphometric personality (Chapter 3) of the experimental watershed. Subsequent parts are of two major types. Part second is concerned with identification, mapping analysis of landscapes (i.e., tectonic, Chapter 4, structurally controlled, Chapter 5; pluvial and fluvial, Chapter 6; and anthropogenic, Chapter 7) and their associated landforms.

Part third deals with identification, quantification and analysis of pluvial and fluvial processes (Chapter 8), mass-wasting, anthropogenic and technogenic transformation of geomorphic processes (Chapter 9). The last part provides considerations on the watershed in environmental management, regeneration strategies for watershed management and recommendations for the conservation of land and water resources of the experimental watershed (Chapter 10); and embraces major conclusions of this study (Chapter 11).

M. S. Rawat
(msrckr@rediffmail.com)

Acknowledgements

I wish to record my deep sense of gratitude to my mentors Prof. J.S. Rawat and Dr. S.C. Joshi, Department of Geography, Kumaun University for their guidance and encouragement. I am thankful to Prof. H.S. Bisht and Prof. O.P. Singh for providing all the Departmental facilities. I am also thankful to all the members of the Department of Geography, Kumaun University campus Almora and Nainital for their help and cooperation. I am indebted to Prof. K.S. Valdiya, F.N.A., Jawaharlal Nehru Centre for advanced Scientifc Research Bangalore and Prof. Martin J. Haigh, Oxford Brookes University, Oxford, U.K. for their kind help, guidance and blessings.

I am grateful to D.S.T. Government of India, New Delhi for the financial assistance in the form of J.R.F. and S.R.F. under a multidisciplinary research project funded to Prof. J.S. Rawat and Prof. H.S. Bisht, Department of Geography, Kumaun University, Almora.

Presently, the author is working as Associate Professor in the Department of Geography, School of Sciences, Nagaland (Central) University, Lumami. During the publication work of this book I was much encouraged and blessed by Prof. K. Kannan, Vice Chancellor, Nagaland University, Prof. G.D. Sharma, Former Vice Chancellor, Nagaland University, Prof. P. Lal, Former Dean, School of Sciences, Nagaland University, Prof. T. Lanusosang, Head, Department of Geography Prof. N.S. Jamir, Dean School of Sciences and Dr. S.K. Chaturbedi, Head Department of Botany, Nagaland University.

Contents

PART B

LANDSCAPES AND LANDFORMS

PART C

DEGRADATIONAL PROCESSES AND THEIR MEASUREMENT

List of the Tables

List of the Figures

List of Plates

PART A

INTRODUCTION AND PHYSICAL BACKGROUND

1

Introduction

Environmental Geomorphology may be defined as the practical use of geomorphology for the solution of problems where man wishes to transform or to use and change surficial processes. Many scholars have dealt with Environmental Geomorphology, in the discussion of both specific topics and the various applications of geomorphology in the form of Applied Geomorphology which involves the issues and themes such as (1) The study of geomorphological processes and terrain that affect man, including hazard phenomena such as floods and landslides. (2) The analysis of problems where man plans to disturb or has already degraded the land-water ecosystem. (3) How the science of geomorphology can be used in environmental planning and management. Much of the current knowledge concerning the effectiveness of different geomorphic processes, particularly mass movement processes, has been gleaned from field observations in high mountains. Precise measurements of actual geomorphic processes remained a rarity. The variability of major geomorphic events in time and space, the present data base is completely inadequate for determination of actual rates of activity of the various processes affecting the land surface. The efforts for determination of the impacts of human intervention, including deforestation, land-use changes, and manipulation of water flow, and their differentiation from the natural processes as a proportion of the total rate of change is urgently required in the mountain environment especially in the Himalaya.

Few studies have been conducted to map the Himalayan physical landscapes, and to identify and monitor their degradational processes. Nossin (1971) presented a geomorphic outline of the Dehra Doon valley which includes the geomorphic mapping of the physical landscapes and portrays tectonic and fluvial landscapes of the Doon Valley. Significant results of his study embrace as how the tectonic activities are changing the Himalayan physical environment specially due to regional as well as differential tectonic movements. Similar works have been undertaken by Nakata (1972) in the Himalayan foothills and Valdiya, *et al.* (1984) in the Balia Valley along the Main Boundary Fault in district Nainital.

Although there are few studies (Das, *et al.*, 1967; Chakrabarti, 1969 and 1971; Anonymous, 1970 and 1977; Sharma and Biswas, 1972; Patnaik, 1977 a and 1977 b; Tejwani, 1978 and 1979; Haigh, 1979 a and 1979 b; Rawat, 1979, 1985 a, 1985 b, 1987 and 1988; and Joshi and Rawat, 1982 *et al.*) on the Himalayan basin directed towards identification and monitoring sediment delivery but none of these includes the identification of all the degradation forms such as degradation by rain-water, viz., sheetwash or surface flow (pluvial), degradation by running water (fluvial), forms of degradation by various mass-wasting processes and degradation of physical landscape by man himself (anthropogenic). The fundamental aim of the present investigation is to study various physical landscapes and to map their components as well as to identify various forms of degradational processes and to monitor some of the important degradational processes related to rain-water (i.e. sheetwash erosion) and running water (i.e. suspended and dissolved load erosion). A drainage basin, encompassing an area of 55 sq.km from the Central Himalaya, viz., the Nana Kosi Watershed has been employed as a natural laboratory for the present investigation. In recent years, watershed management has been identified as a key for planning and management of natural resources in the mountain ecosystems. It provides an ecologically sound economic base for the watersheds and its people. In any management and development activities the watershed approach is more scientific because the inherent potential of soil, water and forest resources in a particular area is controlled by various factors such as physiography, geological base, geomorphology, soil characteristics, climate, land use and socio-economic aspects, etc.

The Study Area

The Nana Kosi Watershed extending over the crystalline rocks of the Almora Nappe, lies between 29°37′ 30" and 29°43′ 40" N Latitudes and 79°31′ and 79°37′ 40" E Longitudes in the District Almora, Central Himalaya of India, Uttarakhand (Fig. 1.1). It encompasses an area of about 55 km^2, supporting a population of about 53095 (Census, 2001) which, mainly depends on agriculture. The agricultural land account only for 33.52 per cent of the total area. The area is quite accessible as the Almora-Ranikhet and Majkhali-Golchhina roads traverse through the catchment area from its south-western and north-eastern ridges, respectively. A newly constructed road, i.e., Kosi-Korichhina (Majkhali), runs along the Nana Kosi river from mouth to reach (Fig. 1.1).

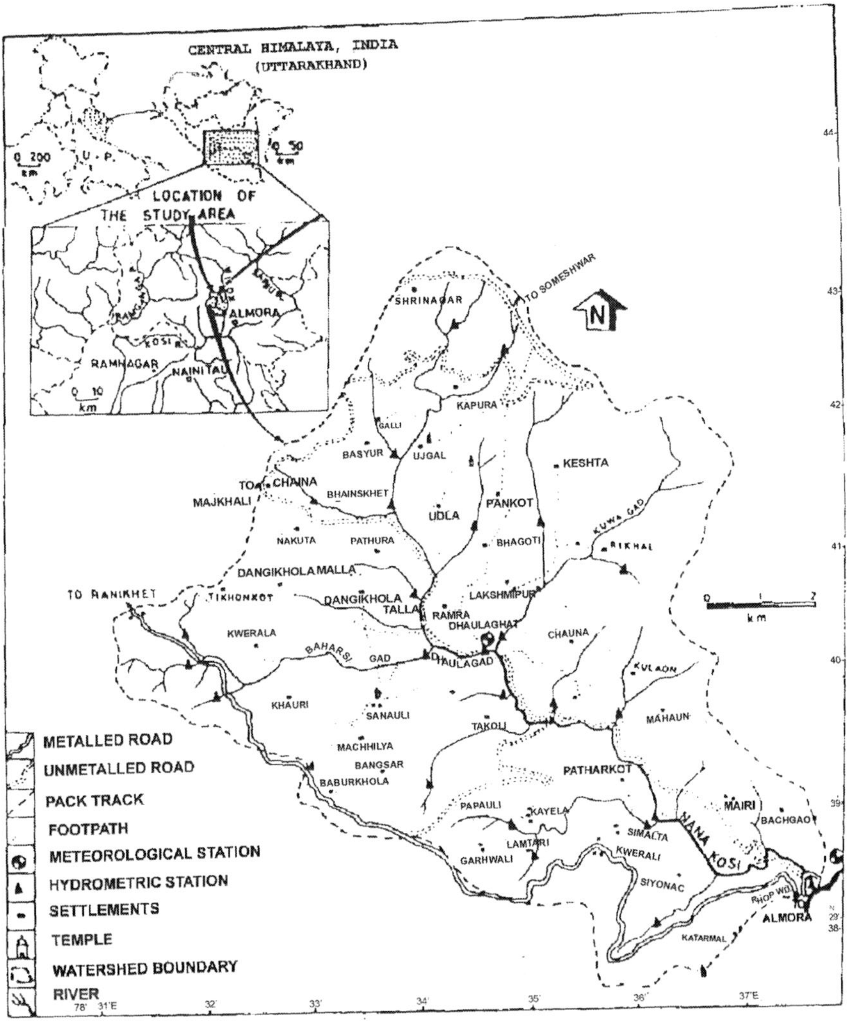

Fig. 1.1 : The location and index map of the Nana Kosi Watershed, Central Himalaya, India

Definition of the Problem

The geodynamically active and ecologically sensitive Himalaya is facing two major problems having bearing geohydrology (i) slope failures and accelerated erosion, and (ii) drying up of springs and reduced river discharges. Besides, some sectors are prone to hazards from earthquakes and neo-tectonics. Although the vulnerability to erosion of certain areas is the consequence of peculiar geodynamic conditions, the damage to the ecological balance is primarily man-made, or due to human negligence. The alarming development in the region is the drying up of springs and their becoming seasonal. This is discrenible in the areas where the watersheds have been deforested.

Degradation of natural resources is a major concern of livelihood, poverty alleviation and environmental services. Environmental and natural resources sustainability are relatively more important in the Himalayan region. It is necessary not only to halt further exploitation and degradation but also to actively restore and rehabilitate the degraded ecosystems through appropriate scientific strategy and approaches like environmental geomorphology as well as applied geomorphology for sustainable development. As an integral part of sustainable development, environment and resource management programmes are taken up on watershed basis as the shape of the watershed controls the natural resources like soil, water and productivity of land for successful implementation of environmental management and eco-restoration programmes. Soil and water are critical natural resources. The careful management of these resources is essential to food security and environmental protection. Watersheds are increasingly being employed in various resources management and development programmes like soil and water conservation, environmental management, water resources management and development etc. Watershed management is an integration of technologies within the material boundaries of drainage area for optimum use and development of land, water and forest resources to meet the basic minimum needs of the people in a sustained manner. Projectisation of the scattered programmes of soil conservation, afforestation, water resources development and management, minor irrigation, animal husbandary and other rural development activities into well prepared watershed projects based on a study of climate, land, water and forest resources on the one hand and man and animal resources on the other offers hope for bringing about sustained natural resources development based on principles of ecology, environment, economics, employment generation and energy conservation. Watershed management aims at optimizing the use of land, water vegetation, man, animal and environment to prevent soil erosion, moderate floods, improve water availability, increase food, fuel, fodder, fibre and timber production on a sustained basis. There are three main parts of this study as follows—

(1) The study of different landscapes such as *tectonic, fluvial* and *anthropogenic.*
(2) The identification of various degradational processes such as block failure, rock fall, debris flow creeping and gully erosion, etc., and monitoring of some of the major and fast degradational processes, viz., hillslope erosion by rainsplash and sheetwash, and channel erosion in the form of suspended and dissolved load flow.

3. Formulation of watershed management strategy for the Nana Kosi Watershed of the Central Himalaya.

Objectives

The specific objectives relevant to above three major parts of this study are as follows :

(1) To obtain channel and relief morphometry of the study area.
(2) Identification and mapping of various tectonic landforms such as fault scarp, triangular fault facets, subsequent valley, abandoned valleys and abandoned channels, etc.
(3) Identification and mapping of various fluvial landforms such as river terraces, meanders, flood plains, channel cross-section geometry, etc.
(4) Identification and mapping of various anthropogenic as well as technogenic landforms such as deforested and agricultural land, roads, settlements, watermills and quarrying, etc.
(5) Identification and mapping of various masswasting forms such as block failure, rockfalls, debris falls, gullying, slumping and creeping, etc.
(6) Monitoring of road induced landslide erosion.
(7) Monitoring of hillslope runoff.
(8) Monitoring of hillslope erosion.
(9) Monitoring of channel runoff.
(10) Monitoring of channel erosion in the form of suspended load flow.
(11) Monitoring of channel erosion in the form of dissolved load flow.
(12) To formulate strategy for the watershed management of the Nana Kosi Watershed.

Methodology

Geomorphology, as a physical science is concerned primarily with the development of landforms and testing of theories that attempt to explain and analyse the spatial distribution and evolution of terrain elements and locations of various geomorphological attributes of earth surface.

Such a statement might be regarded as an adequate definition of the field geomorphology (Bloom, 1979). The idea is just to analyse the form of the above statement. A cursory examination of the statement reveals that it can be divided into two parts, firstly, it concerns with "how" we should go about studying geomorphological phenomena and in particular it is concerned with two operations, i.e., testing of theories and explanation and analysis. The second part is concerned with "what" we should study;

it identifies a domain of objects and events to which the operations of analysis and explanations should be applied. For convenience, we shall refer to the second part of the statement as the goals or sustaintive "objectives" of geomorphological study. The first part can be referred to as the "method" of the study.

Geomorphological methods are essentially based upon "the logic of justification" rather than with the philosophical understandings of our beliefs with respect to the nature of geomorphology. The philosopher and methodologist, therefore, have rather different tasks. The former is concerned with speculation with value judgments, with inner questing regarding what is or is not worthwhile, the latter is concerned primarily with the logic of explanation and discussion, with ensuring that our arguments are rigorous, our inferences are reasonable and our method is internally coherent (Harvey, 1976). To explain the rigorous arguments in geomorphology, the internally coherent methodology requires the use of materials, selection of scale of measurement, data recording and analysis and confined cartographic techniques.

Material used—Survey of India Toposheet ($53\frac{0}{10}$) with 1 : 50,000 scale, has been used to measure the morphometric elements of the study area such as drainage and relief morphometry. For mapping of landform components of different landscapes, i.e., tectonic, fluvial and anthropogentic, the drainage basin area was enlarged six times from the topographic sheet by using 'Pantograph'. Thus large scale map (3 cm = 250 m) was used to record the micro geomorphic forms.

Field instruments like 'Altimeter', 'Pedometer', 'Brunton Compass', and 'Measuring Tape' were used for geomorphic mapping.

A 'Pigmy Current Meter' was used to monitor channel runoff. To monitor suspended and dissolved load flows 'Plastic Bottles' of one liter were used to collect water sample. Detailed methodology of runoff suspended and dissolved load determination techniques are presented in Chapter VI and VIII respectively.

'Gerlech Troughs' (20 × 10 × 10 cm) were used to monitor hillslope runoff or surface runoff and hillslope erosion or sheetwash erosion. Detailed methodology is discussed in Chapter VIII.

Scale of Measurement—The basic kind of measurement of scales are nominal, ordinal, interval and ratio scales (Doornkamp and King, 1971). The nominal scale of measurement deals with the most generalized values which may be placed in the classes like low, medium and high. The ordinal systems of measurement ascribes a rank order to a series of qualitative expansion. Interval scales consists of measures for which there are equal intervals between each discrete measurement. Ratio scale implies when a true zero-exits. The present investigation deals with the intensive use of interval and ratio scales. The morphometric parameters and runoff data have been widely analysed by using interval scale wherein the length measurements of streams, sheetwash erosion, suspended load erosion data have been analysed by using ratio scale.

Data Collection

(1) Channel and relief morphometry data presented in this study were derived from topographic sheet by using map measures and planimeter.
(2) Identification of various mass-wasting forms was done by conducting field surveys.
(3) The hillslope runoff and sheetwash erosion data (Chapter VIII) were collected in sample sites during rainy season.
(4) The channel runoff, suspended, dissolved load and the meteorological data were collected under an interdisciplinary research project funded by Department of Science and Technology, Government of India.

Data Analysis—The different components of landforms have been explained presenting their genetic interpretation. Statistical techniques such as central tendencies and correlation analysis have been used to obtain the nature of different morphometric, runoff and erosion data. All the data have been diagrammatically illustrated or thematically presented by using appropriate cartographic techniques.

Concept and Approach Adopted

Among the various approaches (Gregory and Walling, 1979) the open system approach has been adopted in the present geomorphic study of the Nana Kosi Watershed. The drainage basin receives a continuous energy supply from above its surface and endogenetic processes from below its surface. The watershed loses energy through the water and sediment loss (Rawat, 1985). Gregory and Walling (1973) have aptly remarked that the advantage of the open system approach arises from the fact that it places emphasis upon adjustment and upon relationships between degradation and processes, between landform and processes, upon the multivariate character of the many surface phenomena and upon the total physical environment which includes even the consideration of the influence of man.

Scope

The study presented in this book is useful for teaching, research and judicious planning purposes as follows.

Teaching—The study adds the knowledge on the subject matter in different aspects of "geomorphology" such as *tectonic* geomorphology, *fluvial* geomorphology, *pluvial* geomorphology and *anthropogenic* geomorphology in particular, and "Environmental Sciences" in general. The study is based on a widely accepted unit, i.e., drainage basin or watershed. The drainage basin has been considered as a natural laboratory for environmental studies by various workers (Rawat, 1985 and 1988). It has specific laws of environmental composition and geomorphic character and demonstrates association among all the environmental systems and embodies entire the environment.

Research Communities—The outcomes of this study may be useful for various research communities (for further research), such as, hydrologists, geomorphologists, ecologists, geologists, botanists and environmental scientists—particularly engaged in Himalayan studies.

Decision-Makers—Wise management of land and water resources requires such kind of geomorphic study through watershed management. The present study is proposing a scientific strategy of planning for comprehensive watershed management in the Nana Kosi Watershed of Central Himalaya.

REFERENCES

Anonymous, 1970 : An evaluation of ravine reclamation programme in U.P., Planning Research and Action Inst., Lucknow.

Anonymous, 1977 : Flood and their control in India, Cent. Water Comm. Min. Agr. Irrig., New Delhi.

Bloom, A.L. 1979 : *Geomorphology : A systematic analysis of late cenozoic landforms*, Prentice-Hall of India Private Limited, New Delhi, pp. 1-54.

Chakrabarty, D.C. 1969 : Investigation on erodibility and water stable aggregates of certain soils of Eastern Nepal, *Jourl. Indian Soc. Soil Sci.*, 17, pp. 465-470.

Chakrabarty, D.C. 1971 : Investigation on erodibility and water stable aggregates of certain soils of Eastern Nepal, *Jourl, Indian Soc. Soil Sci.*, 19, pp. 441-446.

Das, D.C. *et al.* 1967 : Rainfall intensity energy and erosion index, *Jourl Indian Soc. Agric. Engg.*, Vol. 4 (2), pp. 9-18.

Doornkamp, J.C. and King, C.A.M. 1971 : *Numerical analysis in geomorphology*, London, p. 9.

Gregory, K.J. and Walling, D.E. 1973 : *Drainage basin form and processes*, Londona, Edward Arnold, p. 9.

Haigh, M.J. 1979a : Landslide sediment accumulation on the Mussoorie, Tehri Road, Garhwal Lesser Himalaya, *Indian Jourl. Soil Conserv.*, 7 (1), pp. 1-4.

Haigh, M.J. 1979b : *Environmental geomorphology of the Landour-Mussoorie,* Mussoorie area, U.P., Himalayan Geology, 9, pp. 657-688.

Harvey, D. 1976 : Explanation in geomorphology of the Landon, p. 3.

Joshi, S.C. and Rawat, J.S. 1982 : Channel morphometry indices and stream discharge, *Geogrl. Rev. India,* 44 (2), pp. 248-253.

Nakata, T. 1972 : *Geomorphic study and crustal movements of the foothills of the Himalaya.* Inst. Geography Tohoku University, Sendai, pp. 39-77.

Nossin, J.J. 1971 : Outline of the geomorphology of the Doon Valley, Northern U.P., *India, Z. Geomorph.* N.F. Suppl. Ed. 12, pp. 18-50.

Patnaik, N. 1977a : Floods and National Flood Commission : Its Scope, Structure and terms of reference. *Soil Conserv, Digest,* 5 (1), pp. 52-57.

Patnaik, N. 1977b : *Floods and role of soil conservation,* address Delivered at the Cent. Soil Water Conserv. Res. Trng. Inst., Dehradun.

Rawat, J.S. 1979 : A quantitative morphometric analysis of the Stratigraphical formations in the Lower Ramganga Catchment, District Pauri and Almora. *Himalayan Geology,* 9 (II), pp. 701-715.

Rawat, J.S. 1985a : Hydrometric implications of morphometry and geology : a study of Lower Ramganga Catchment, *J. Geol. Soc. India,* 26 (10), pp. 734-743.

Rawat, J.S. 1985 : The drainage basin as a unit for physical Environmental Studies, In : *Environmental Regeneration in Himalaya—Concept and Strategies* (ed) J.S. Singh, Nainital, pp. 427-434.

Rawat, J.S. 1987 : *Modelling of water and sediment budget : Concept and strategies,* Geomorphological Models, Theoretical and Empirical Aspects, CATENE, Supplement-1, pp. 147-159.

Rawat, J.S. 1988 : Anthropogenic transformation of channel network capacity : an experimental study in Kumaun Himalaya. *Proc. Ind. Nat. Sci. Acad.,* 54 (4), pp. 605-615.

Sharma, R.R. and Biswas, N. R. 1972 : Erodibility of hill soil of Sutlej Catchment area in H.P., *Indian Jourl. Agric. Sci.,* 42, pp. 161-169.

Tejwani, K.G. 1978 : Soil erosion and watershed management in Ganga basin. Presented at the workshop on integrated development of Ganga-Brahmputra-Barak Basin, New Delhi.

Valdiya, K.S. *et al.* 1984 : Geomorphic development across the active main boundary thrust : an example from the Nainital Hills in Kumaun Himalaya. *J. Geol. Soc. India,* 25 (12), pp. 761-774.

2

Physical Background

Climate

Climate is one of the two major sources which provide energy to regulate all the physical systems (Rawat, 1987). The drainage basin is not an exception. To define and correlate the degradational processes with environment, it is essential to monitor and quantify that how much energy is being provided by the climate to the drainage basin (Fig. 6.3). The principal elements of climate include radiation from sun and sky, temperature, wind direction and speed, humidity, evaporation, cloud and sunshine, precipitation and atmospheric pressure (Monkhouse and Wilkinson, 1971). Among these elements, long-term rainfall and temperature data are available for Almora which lies 12 km south-east of the study area. These rainfall and temperature date (Table 2.1) suggest that climatically, the drainage basin falls into cool temperate climatic region. The climatic records at Almora reveal that in the months of December and February the average temperature never rises more than 10°C, and in May, June and July it is always less than 25°C. January is the coldest (average 8°C) and June is the hottest month (average 24.1°C). The average annual (1972-1988) temperature stands at 17.8°C (Table 2.1). The rainfall records show that it is a region of moderate rainfall where the average annual rainfall (1972-1988) stands at 997 mm. July is the month of heaviest rainfall (average 262mm). About 76.33 per cent of the total annual rainfall is contributed by summer monsoon.

Table 2.1 : Mean monthly temperature (in °C) and rainfall (in mm) at Almora, 1972-1988.

	Months												
Para-meters	*Jan*	*Feb*	*Mar*	*Apr*	*May*	*Jun*	*Jul*	*Aug*	*Sep*	*Oct*	*Nov*	*Dec*	*Annual*
Tempe-rature	8.0	11.5	14.4	17.8	22.3	24.1	23.2	22.8	22.3	19.2	16.8	10.8	17.8
Rainfall	43	41	40	23	49	138	262	238	123	28	6	6	997

Source : Vivekanand Parvatiya Krishi Anusandhanshala, Almora.

For detailed temperature, rainfall, humidity and evaporation characteristics of the study area, climatic data (Tables 2.2, 2.3 and 2.4) were obtained from the meteorological stations established in 1986 at the centre of the Nana Kosi Watershed viz., Daulaghat, under Department of Science and Technology, Government of India project and at Hawalbagh—operated by Vivekanand Parvatiya Krishi Anusandhanshala, Almora near the mouth of the study area (Fig. 1.1). A brief account of rainfall, temperature, humidity and evaporation recorded during the study period is given below.

Table 2.2 : Rainfall and evaporation data recorded during the study period (1986-88) at the centre (Daulaghat) of the Nana Kosi Watershed, Central Himalaya

Months		*Rainfall*		*Evaporation*	
		Total (mm)	*Intensity (mm/day*	*Total (mm)*	*Average (mm/day)*
February	1986		Not recorded		
March	1986		Not recorded		
April	1986		Not recorded		
May	1986	96.50	3.11	131.70	4.24
June	1986	178.90	5.96	83.50	2.78
July	1986	499.05	16.09	86.50	2.79
August	1986	133.30	4.30	102.70	3.31
September	1986	59.70	1.32	82.90	2.76
October	1986	0.0	0.0	117.00	3.77
November	1986	1.96	0.06	43.90	1.46
December	1986	7.50	0.24	38.80	1.25
January	1987	23.00	0.74	33.57	1.08
February	1987	27.50	0.98	44.80	1.60
March	1987	25.00	0.80	62.57	2.02
April	1987	49.50	1.65	135.00	4.50
May	1987	36.20	1.16	153.81	4.96
June	1987	36.50	1.21	198.40	6.61
July	1987	58.35	1.88	197.00	6.35
August	1987	81.50	2.62	129.90	4.19
September	1987	69.50	2.31	130.70	4.36
October	1987	10.48	0.34	137.08	4.42
November	1987	7.08	0.24	103.00	3.42
December	1987	18.50	0.59	67.80	2.18
January	1988	11.60	0.37	38.50	1.24

Rainfall—Table 2.2 reveals the rainfall data recorded at the centre of the basin during study period. It suggests that there is much variation in rainfall of different months. In 1986-87 about 49.90 per cent of the total annual rainfall was received in only one month, i.e., July (499 mm). Winter rainfall is insignificant (i.e. 3.25 per cent of the total annual). In the study year 1987-88 (which was the drought year) the maximum rainfall (81.5 mm) was recorded in the month of August which was about six times lower than that of the maximum rainfall of the previous year (499 mm). Hyetographs (Fig. 2.2 B) shows the month-wise distribution of rainfall recorded at Daulaghat and Hawalbagh.

The rainfall intensity ranges in between 0 to 16.1 mm/day in 1986-87 and 0.24 to 2.62 mm/day in 1987-88.

Temperature—Temperature data of Daulaghat and Hawalbagh (Table 2.3) have been used to compute the mean monthly temperature for the study period. Figure 2.1 A and 2.2 A depict the temperature characteristics of different months. It reveals that during the study period :

(1) The mean maximum temperature ranges in between 9.75°C and 27.48°C at the centre of the basin; and 16.6°C and 29.76°C near the mouth of the basin (Table 2.3);

Table 2.3 : Monthly characteristics of temperature during study period (1986-88) at the Centre (Daulaghat) and near the mouth (Hawalbagh) of the Nana Kosi Watershed, Central Himalaya

Months		*Temperature (°C)*				
		Mean	*Mean*	*Average*	*Extreme*	
		Maxi.	*Mini.*		*Maxi.*	*Mini.*
			Daulaghat*			
February	1986		Not recorded			
March	1986		Not recorded			
April	1986		Not recorded			
May	1986	21.48	19.04	20.26	33.5	10.0
June	1986	26.22	24.05	25.13	35.5	14.0
July	1986	24.68	23.40	24.04	35.5	18.0
August	1986	25.73	23.97	24.85	36.0	16.5
September	1986	22.93	21.14	22.03	32.0	16.5
October	1986	16.34	14.33	15.33	27.0	3.0
November	1986	11.82	9.60	10.77	23.5	1.0
December	1986	11.37	8.97	10.17	24.0	1.0
January	1987	11.82	9.75	10.78	22.0	1.0
February	1987	14.14	12.01	13.07	25.0	1.0
March	1987	19.12	16.64	17.88	32.0	7.0
April	1987	23.84	21.35	22.59	33.0	11.0
May	1987	25.18	23.72	24.75	26.0	13.0
June	1987	25.54	23.11	24.32	34.0	12.0
July	1987	27.48	23.09	25.28	35.0	20.0
August	1987	26.24	24.61	25.43	35.0	14.0
September	1987	26.51	24.81	25.66	34.0	19.0
October	1987	18.55	15.45	17.00	28.0	10.0
November	1987	13.05	10.00	11.52	24.0	5.0
December	1987	11.58	8.45	10.01	21.0	2.0
January	1988	9.95	7.75	8.85	19.0	1.0

(contd. Table 2.3)

(contd. Table 2.3)

Months		*Temperature (°C)*				
		Mean	*Mean*	*Average*	*Extreme*	
		Maxi.	*Mini.*		*Maxi.*	*Mini.*
			Hawalbagh**			
February	1986	20.13	3.07	11.60	23.5	0.2
March	1986	22.50	6.10	14.30	28.2	1.0
April	1986	28.60	9.90	19.25	32.5	4.0
May	1986	27.60	12.80	20.20	32.9	8.5
June	1986	31.10	17.90	24.50	39.9	12.5
July	1986	27.72	20.26	23.99	31.5	17.5
August	1986	29.26	20.13	24.69	32.7	19.6
September	1986	29.76	19.80	24.78	30.6	18.2
October	1986	25.40	15.80	20.60	26.5	14.0
November	1986	20.80	11.35	16.07	23.6	9.5
December	1986	17.66	9.30	13.48	20.9	6.0
January	1987	18.24	7.55	12.89	20.9	1.5
February	1987	19.18	8.12	13.62	20.7	4.0
March	1987	25.00	8.00	16.50	30.6	4.5
April	1987	27.45	12.56	20.20	30.8	8.0
May	1987	27.45	17.51	22.48	35.6	15.6
June	1987	34.52	17.54	26.03	36.8	13.5
July	1987	30.59	20.89	25.75	36.7	18.2
August	1987	30.08	20.53	25.30	32.8	17.4
September	1987	30.15	18.03	24.09	31.5	12.4
October	1987	28.58	9.62	19.10	30.5	3.8
November	1987	27.00	4.95	15.95	28.3	4.1
December	1987	19.60	5.00	12.30	22.5	2.9
January	1988	16.60	1.55	9.07	18.0	1.5

* *Source* : Rawat and Bisht (1986 and 1987-88)

** *Source* : Vivekanand Parvatiya Krishi Anusandhanshala (ICAR), Almora

(2) The mean minimum temperature ranges in between 7.75°C and 24.05°C at the centre; and 1.55°C and 20.89°C near the mouth of the basin (Table 2.3);

(3) The average temperature ranges in between 8.85°C and 25.13°C at the centre; and 9.07°C and 26.03°C near the mouth of the basin (Table 2.3).

(4) The extreme maximum and minimum records stand at 36°C and 1°C at the centre; and 39.9°C and 0.2°C near the mouth of the basin (Table 2.3).

Humidity—Table 2.4 contains the humidity data recorded at the centre of the basin, viz., Daulaghat. It reveals that during the study period (1986-88) :

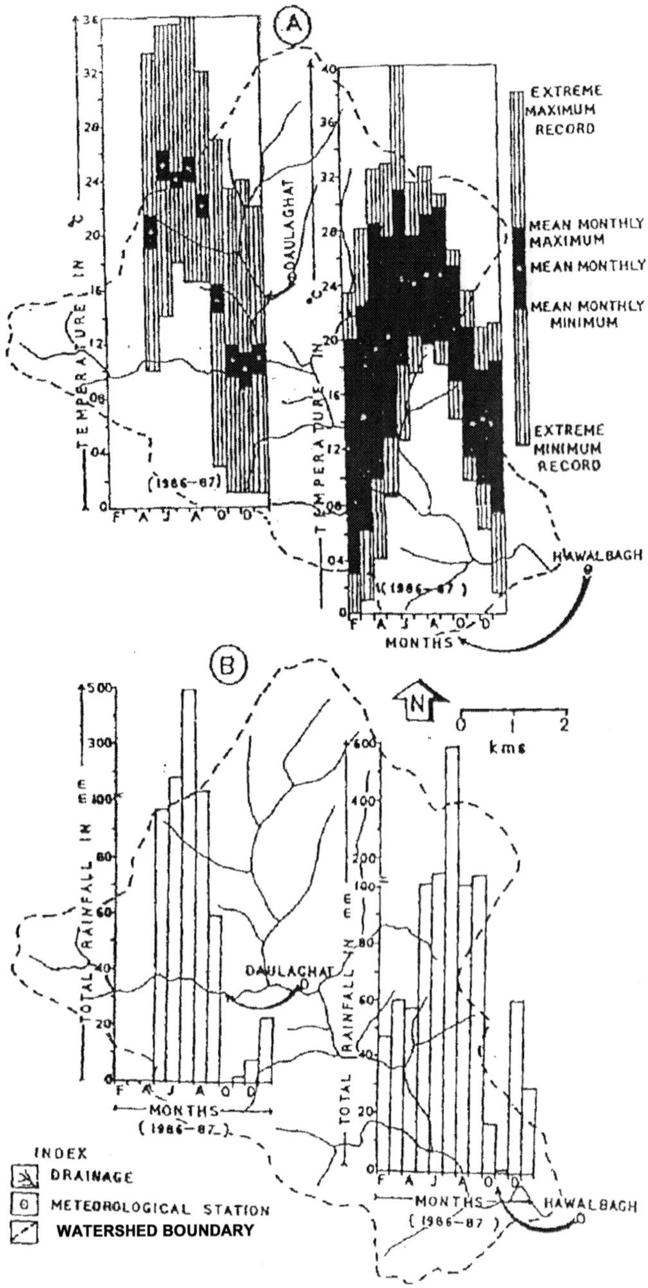

Fig. 2.1 : Located columnar compound thermographs showing the temperature variations (A), and located simple columnar hyetographs showing monthwise distribution of rainfall (B), during 1986-87 in the Nana Kosi Watershed, Central Himalaya, India.

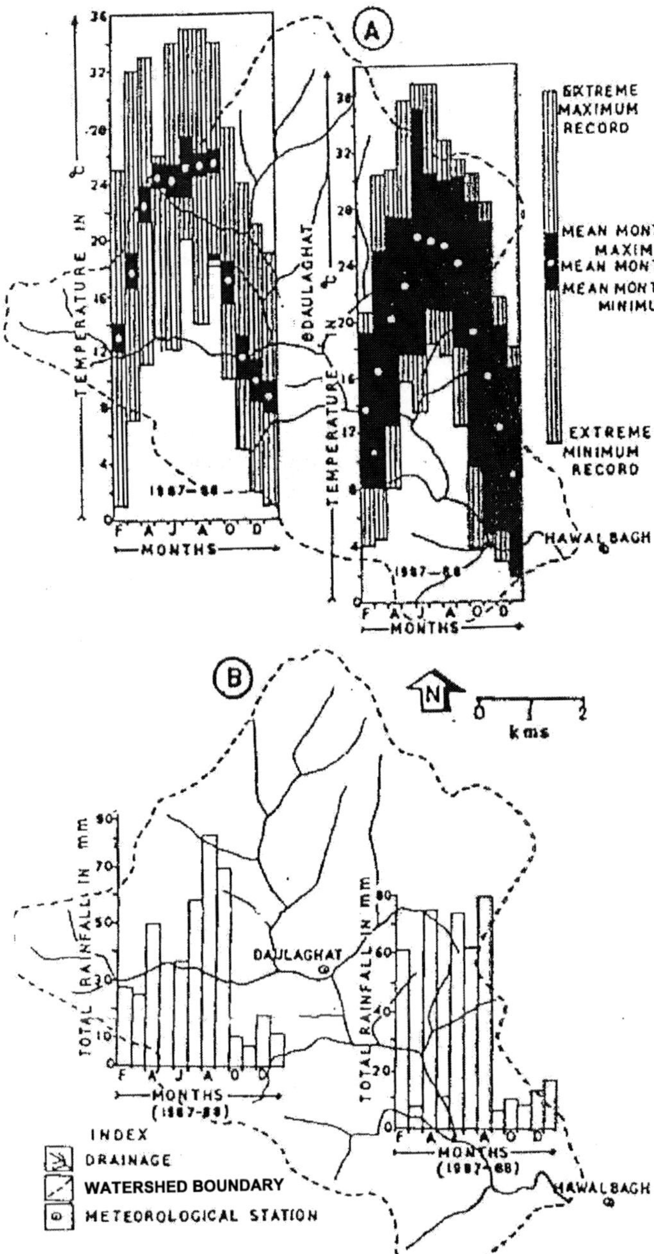

Fig. 2.2 : Located columnar compound thermographs showing the temperature variations (A), and located simple columnar hyetographs showing monthwise distribution of rainfall (B), during 1987-88 in the Nana Kosi Watershed Central Himalaya, India

(1) the mean maximum humidity ranges in between 52.33 per cent and 83.82 per cent;
(2) the mean maximum humidity ranges in between 49.33 per cent and 74.59 per cent; and
(3) the average humidity ranges in between 53.79 per cent and 78.67 per cent.

Table 2.4 : Humidity data recorded at the centre (Daulaghat) of the study area during study period (1986-88)

Months		*Humidity (in %)*		
		Mean maximum	*Mean minimum*	*Average*
February	1986		Not recorded	
March	1986		Not recorded	
April	1986		Not recorded	
May	1986	58.25	49.33	53.79
June	1986	60.86	53.41	57.14
July	1986	80.35	74.59	77.47
August	1986	75.14	66.65	70.89
September	1986	80.75	71.67	76.21
October	1986	73.00	50.47	61.73
November	1986	71.36	60.38	65.87
December	1986	71.61	61.54	66.57
January	1987	73.53	61.33	67.43
February	1987	67.28	54.02	60.65
March	1987	71.70	59.05	65.37
April	1987	75.59	66.71	71.15
May	1987	62.44	54.39	58.41
June	1987	52.33	47.33	49.83
July	1987	75.42	65.49	70.45
August	1987	78.92	70.43	74.67
September	1987	83.82	73.52	78.67
October	1987	79.56	68.50	70.03
November	1987	71.45	65.00	68.22
December	1987	65.85	59.08	62.46
January	1988	60.95	54.25	57.60

Source : Rawat and Bisht, 1986 and 1987.

Evaporation—Table 2.2 contains the evaporation data recorded at the centre of the basin. It reveals that during the study period :

(1) the total evaporation of different months ranges in between 33.57 mm and 198.40 mm;
(2) the evaporation rate ranges in between 1.08 mm/day and 6.61 mm/day; and

(3) the mean rate of evaporation for the study period stands at 3.3 mm/day.

Natural Vegetation

Table 2.5 shows the distribution of forest area in the geographical entity "Kumaun" and the Nana Kosi Watershed. It reveals that the study area is highly deforested (i.e. 68.76%) in comparison to other parts of the region. In district Almora about 73.25 per cent area (of the total districts) falls under forest while in the Nana Kosi basin, which constitutes a part of Almora district, only 31.24 per cent area is covered by forest (Fig. 2.3). Joshi (1988) has classified the vegetation of the Himalayan zone of Kumaun in five major groups. These are :

- Himalayan Chir Pine Forest (750-2000 m)
- Himalayan Moist Temperate Forest (1900-2100 m)
- Himalayan Dry Temperate Forest (2300-3200 m)
- Sub Alpine Forest (3000-3500 m)
- Moist Alpine Scrubs (above 3500 m)

Table 2.5 : Distribution of forest area in Kumaun

District/basin	*Geographical Area (km²)*	*Forest Area (km²)*	*Forest Area (% of the total geographical area)*
District Almora	5385	3944.32	73.25
District Nainital	6794	4026.40	59.26
District Pithoragarh	8856	3302.89	37.30
Total Kumaun	21035	11273.61	53.60
The Nana Kosi Basin	55	17.18	31.24

Source : Joshi, 1988 and Rawat, 1988.

The vegetation of the Nana Kosi Watershed falls in the first group, viz., Himalayan "Chir" Pine Forest. This is the most important forest types of the Himalayan zone on a scale from 750 m to about 2000 m and ascending higher whenever adverse conditions prevent the survival of temperate forest. The height of the study area ranges in between 1200-1900 m where the major vegetation is chir pine (Plate 2; 9, above; 11 above and 12, below). At few places specifically on northern hill slopes such as at Golchhina, Charpathar, Paikham, and north-western hillslopes, Kathpuria, Durarsaun, Gulli, Basur and Korechhina, Laudar, Pankot and Patharkot, chir pine is remarkably mixed with "Banj" (Quercus incana), "Burans" (Rhododendron arboreum) and "Kaphal" (Myrica supidea) etc. (Plate 13, and 29, above).

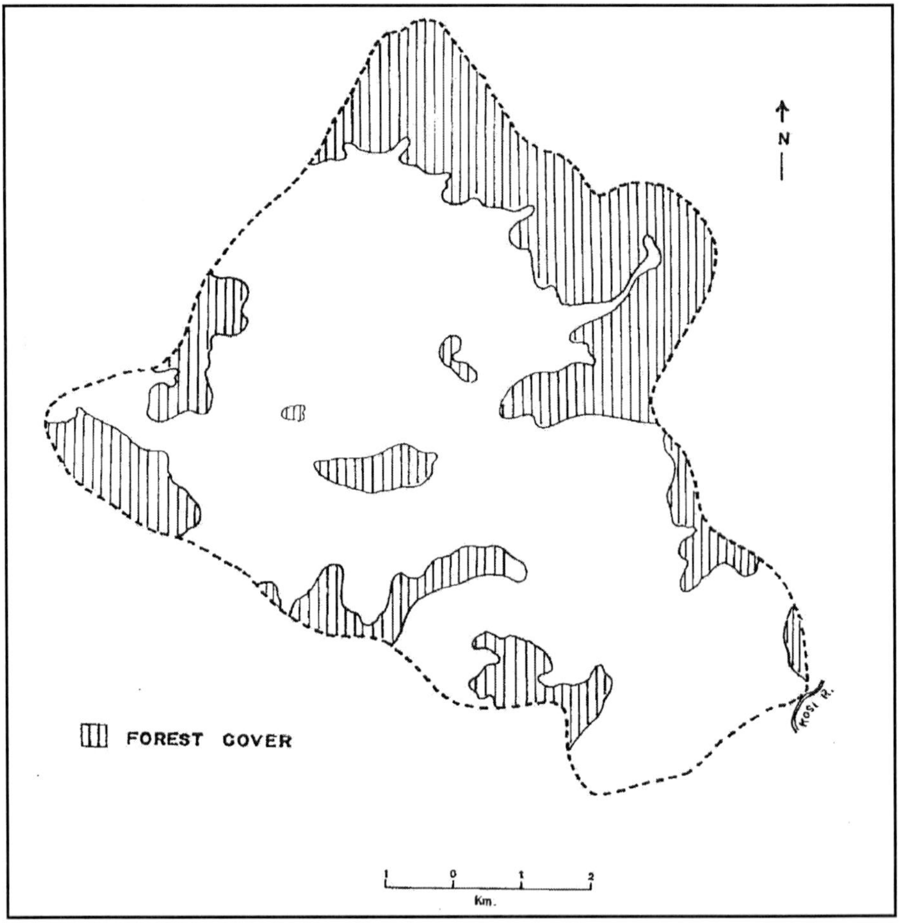

Fig. 2.3 : The vegetation cover in the Nana Kosi Watershed, Central Himalaya, India (*Source* : District Forest Office, Almora) in the year 1985.

Geology

South of the extremely rugged topography, viz., the Great Himalaya, and north of the highly dissected terrain of Siwalik Hills lies the Lesser Himalayan terrain. The study area lies in the central part of the Lesser Himalayan tectonic unit (Fig. 4.2 B). The area is far away from the zones of geodynamically sensitive and severe mass-movements and erosion which are mainly concentrated along the Main Central Thrust in the north, Main Boundary Fault in the south and along active transverse faults (Valdiya, 1981). Thus, geodynamically the study area lies in the most stable zone of the Himalaya which is geodynamically known as zone of moderate erosion and landsliding (Valdiya, 1981).

Stratigraphy

Stratigraphically, the Nana Kosi Watershed falls in Almora crystalline unit known as the Almora Nappe (Heim and Gansser, 1939; Gansser, 1964; Pande, 1963; Misra and Sharma, 1966; Valdiya, 1963, 1980, 1988; Misra and Kumar, 1965; Sharma and Kasyap, 1971). The rocks of the Almora area have been further divided into different stratigraphical units by Valdiya (1980). These are as follows :

(1) Saryu Formation
(2) Pilkholi Formation
(3) Chausali-Dyoli Formation
(4) Barsima Formation
(5) Almora Granite
(6) Gumalikhet Formation
(7) Kalmatia-Kapharkhan Formation

The rocks of the Nana Kosi drainage basin belong to the last two formations, i.e., Gumalikhet and Kalmatia-Kapharkhan. A brief account of the rocks of these formations is given below.

Lithology

Gumalikhet Formation—Figure 2.4 depicts the distribution of different rock types of the study area which reveals that except a small part in Chauna area, entire the basin falls under Gumalikhet Formation. According to Valdiya (1980), the Gumalikhet Formation is composed of coarse-grained garnetiferous mica-schist and schist and micaceous quartzite. Detailed field investigation in the Nana Kosi Watershed (Rawat, 1989) have shown that the rocks of the Gumalikhet Formation in the Nana Kosi basin are divisible into three rock types (Fig. 2.4). There are—

(1) Mica-schist, garnetiferous mica-schist,
(2) Weathered mica-schist,
(3) Quartzites.

The major part of the study area is composed of mica-schist. At places, such as particularly on Papoli, Patharkot ridge and at Golchhina, there are small areas of garnetiferous mica-schist. A large part in the upper courses of the basin—specifically at Bainskhet, Gulli, Basur, and in the lower courses in village Patharkot, Manoun is composed of wethered mica-schist.

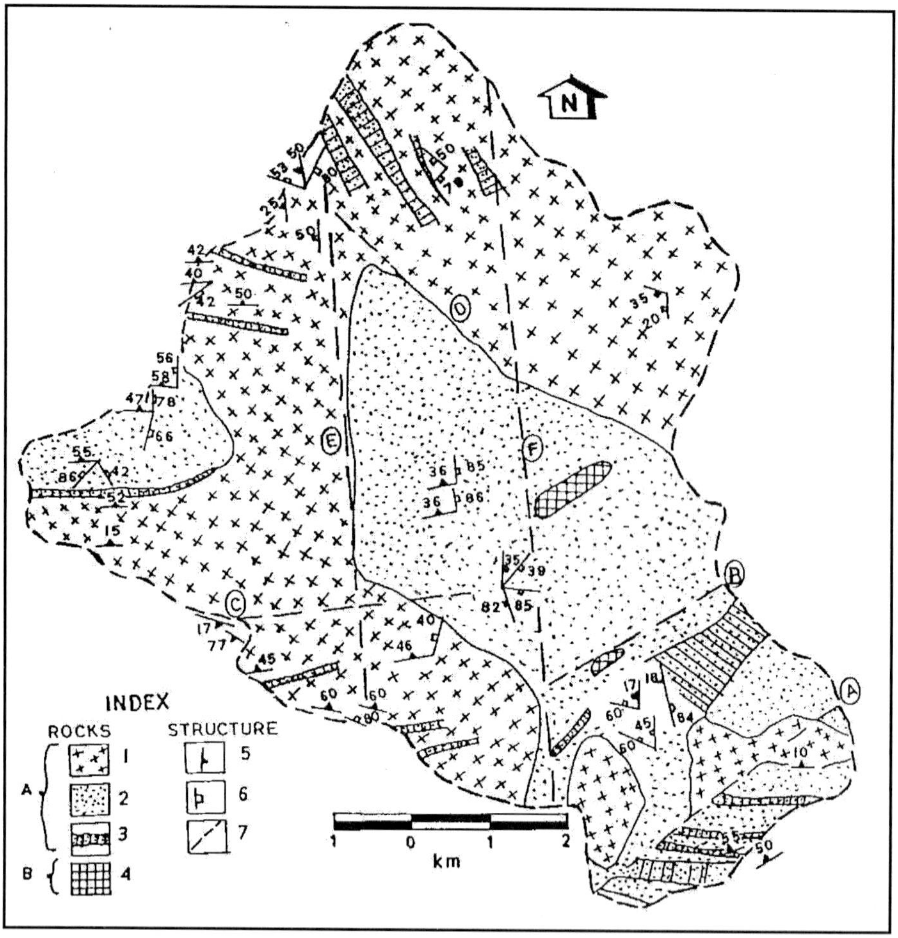

Fig. 2.4 : Geological map of the Nana Kosi Watershed, Central Himalaya showing the lithological formations (A- Gumalikhet, B- Kalmatia Kapharkhan rock-type (1- Mica-schist, 2- Weathered mica-schist, 3- Quartzites, 4- Greywach quartzites) and structure (5- Rock-dip, 6-Joints, 7- Faults). (A) Pajgaon-Jyoli Reverse Fault, (B) Patharkot-Kayela Reverse Fault, (C) Baburkhola-Burisia Reverse Fault, (D) Basyur-Chauna Transverse Fault, (E) Golchhina-Kathpuria Transverse Fault, (F) Kwerali-Paikham Transverse Fault.

The mica-schist in the Nana Kosi basin is interbedded with a thin bed of quartzites (Fig. 2.4). The major beds of quartzites are discernible particularly at Jyoli, Katarmal and near Gazol.

Kalmatia-Kapharkhan Formation—The Kalmatia-Kapharkhan formation is made-up of greywack quartzite with very common lentils of graphitic/carbonaceous schist within the schistose horizon (Valdiya, 1980). Small patches in village Chauna and patharkot falls under this lithological formation (Fig. 2.4).

Structure

Heim and Gansser (1939) were the pioneer, who investigated that the rocks of the Almora crystalline are in the form of a Nappe, delaminated by Almora Thrust (Fig. 4.2B). The root lies at the base of the Great Himalaya implying that it is the prolongation of the Munsiari Thrust. Heim and Gansser (1939) have named the two flanks of this asymmetrically synformal thrust as North Almora Thrust (NAT) and South Almora Thrust (SAT) (Fig. 4.2 B).

Detailed structural studies of the Almora Nappe (Valdiya, 1963, 1981, 1988; Gansser, 1964; Mishra and Kumar, 1965; Misra and Sharma, 1966; Sharma and Kasyap, 1971) reveal that the rocks of the Almora crystallines dipping mainly towards northeast (average dip 20°), represent three generations of superimposed folding. The earliest isoclinals recumbent to reclined folds plunging NNE are folded again into NW-SE trending asymmetrical to slightly overturned folds, and the few sets were finally folded along the roughly NE-SW axes giving rise to culminations and depressions and swinging of the earlier folds (Valdiya, 1980). Misra and Sharma (1972) have suggested that three type of folds of different styles have developed during the folding of Almora Nappe known as F_1, F_2 and F_3 folds.

Detailed geomorphological investigation conducted during the course of the present study reveals that the Almora crystallines is multiply splitted by various reverse and transverse faults (Fig. 2.4 and 4.5) due to the under thrusting of Indian Plate under the Himalaya (Fig. 4.2). A brief geomorphic account of these faults is presented in Chapter-four.

REFERENCES

Gansser, A. 1964 : *Geology of the Himalayas,* Inter-science Publisher, London, p. 289.

Heim, A. and Gansser, A. 1939 : Central Himalaya. Denks. Schweiz., *Nat. Gessel.,* 73, pp. 1-245.

Joshi, D.P. 1988 : Forest resources and wildlife of Kumaun. In : *Kumaun Land and People,* Valdiya, K.S. (ed.), Gyanodaya Prakashan, Nainital, pp. 223-240

Misra, R.C. and Kumar, S. 1965 : An outline of the stratigraphy and tectonics of Ganai area distt. Almora, U. P. Summary of the *procee. and abst. Him. Geol., Seminar,* Lucknow, p. 59.

Misra, R.C. and Sharma, R.P. 1966 : *Metamorphic rocs of Devidhura area,* distt. Almora U.P., Pub. Cend. Adv., Stud. Geol., Punjab University, 3, pp. 1-12.

Monkhouse, F.J. and Wilkinson, H.R. 1971 : Maps and diagrams. London, p. 191.

Pande, I.C. 1963 : The Magnatities of Kumaun Hills, U.P. India, *Nat. Geol. Jour. India,* 9, (ii).

Rawat, J.S. 1987 : Modeling of water and sediment budget; concept and strategies. CATENA—A Cooper. Jour. of Interna. *Soci. of Soil Science,* W. Germany, 10, pp. 147-159.

Rawat, J.S. and Bisht, H.S. 1986 : Channel network capacity and geochemical properties of water of the Nana Kosi Basin, Kumaun Lesser Himalaya, Deptt. of Geog., Kumaun University, Almora, D.S.T. Project, 1st Annual Report, pp. 1-160.

Rawat, J.S. and Bisht, H.S. 1987 : Channel network capacity and geochemical properties of water of the Nana Kosi Watershed, Kumaun Lesser Himalaya, India, Deptt. of Geography, Kumaun Univ. Almora, D.S.T. Project, 2nd Annual Report, pp. 1-191.

Sharma, R.P. and Kashyap, S.R. 1971 : A note on the geology of Nathuakhan area, with special reference to its structure. *Himalayan Geology,* 1, pp. 302-311.

Valdiya, K. S. 1963 : The stratigraphy of the Lohaghat Subdivision, distt. Almora, U.P. *Quart. Jour. Geol. Min. Metal Soc. India,* 35, pp. 167-180.

Valdiya, K.S. 1980 : *Geology of Kumaun Lesser Himalaya.* Wadia Institute of Himalayan Geology, Dehradun, p. 102.

Valdiya, K.S. 1981 : The tectonics of the Central sector of the Himalaya. In : *Zagros-Hindukush Himalaya Geodynamic Evolution,* Gupta, H. K. and Delany (eds.) Amer. Geophys. Union, Washington, pp. 87-110.

Valdiya, K.S. 1988 : *Geology of Kumaun : An outline. In Kumaun Land and People,* Valdiya, K.S. (ed.), Gyanodaya Prakashan, Nainital, pp. 38-70.

3

Morphometric Personality

Morphometry is the precise measurement of landforms and measurement of the shape or geometry of any natural form be it plant, animal, relief feature, is termed morphometry (Strahler, 1969). In geomorphology the development of a landscape can be known by measuring morphometry of drainage and relief properties. In other words morphometry may be defined as the measurement and mathematical analysis of the configuration of the earth's surface and of the shape and dimensions of its landforms (Dury, 1970).

Drainage Morphometry

Channel networks occur within drainage basins which have clearcut boundaries known as waterdivides or watersheds. Within drainage basin the channels have their own systems for their development and have specific composition. Horton (1932 and 1945) is the pioneer worker who introduced the natural composition of channels which was further modified and developed by Strahler (1950), Schumm (1956), Chorley (1957), Melton (1959), Scheidegger (1965), Morisawa (1968), Shreve (1967), Woldenberg (1966), Lewin (1970), and numerous others. The drainage morphometry presented in this chapter includes stream ordering, drainage density, stream frequency, bifurcation ratio, stream length, stream length ratio, drainage texture, basin length, basin perimeter and basin circularity ratio.

Stream Ordering

A system of channel ordering was suggested by Gravelius (1914) but the works of Horton (1932 and 1945) marked the beginning of the widespread use of Channel ordering systems in geomorphology. According to this system, proceeding downwards from the headwater-tributaries which have no branches being designated as the first order, streams which receive only first order tributaries are second order, larger branches which receive only first and second order tributaries are designated the third order stream and so on (Horton, 1932). Horton's composition of stream ordering was found complicated in two stages (Gregory and Walling, 1973). Firstly, it involves an additional subjective decision in projecting the order of streams headward and secondly, all the smallest unbranched tributaries are not of the same order.

Horton's stream ordering system was further modified by Strahler (1952). He assumed that when two channel segments of order "N" join they form a channel of "N + 1". Thus all fingertip tributaries have been designated as first order, the two first order produce a second order segment, two second order produce a third order and so on.

To determine the stream ordering system of Nana Kosi Drainage Basin, the channel ordering system, as modified by Strahler from the originally proposed by Horton, has been used, because the advantage of this ordering is that it can be derived mathematically from concepts of elementary combinational analysis as Melton (1959) has suggested that it is a simple mathematical concept that can be derived from the notion of rooted tree without first postulation the existence of a single downstream direction on each channel segment. Strahler's system is broadly unique in this respect. Deriving this channel ordering, Melton (1959), testified it by using a linear graph and stated that it is an ideal channel hierarchy.

The drainage ordering map (Fig. 3.1 A) based after Strahler (1952), suggests that the Nana Kosi is a fifth order stream consisted of as many as 360 first, 80 second, 17 third and 5 fourth order streams (Table 3.1). The stream composition of the Nana Kosi Basin follows Horton's Law of Stream Number which reveals that stream order and number of streams have inverse geometric relationship (Horton, 1945). The strong negative correlation (i.e., r = -.75, Fig. 3.1 C A') between stream order and number of streams in the study area confirms Horton's Law of Stream Number.

Stream Length

The total stream length of the different order, measured from the topographic sheet is presented in Table 3.1. Table 3.1 reveals that the total stream length in the study area is 236.96 km. Out of the total stream length 66.04 per cent is constituted by the first order streams. The percentage of the second, third, fourth and fifth order streams stand at 16.51 per cent, 7.12 per cent, 6.75 per cent and 3.58 per cent respectively. The strong negative correlation (i.e. r = -.80) between stream order and total stream length (Fig. 3.1 C B') suggests inverse geometric relationship between these two parameters.

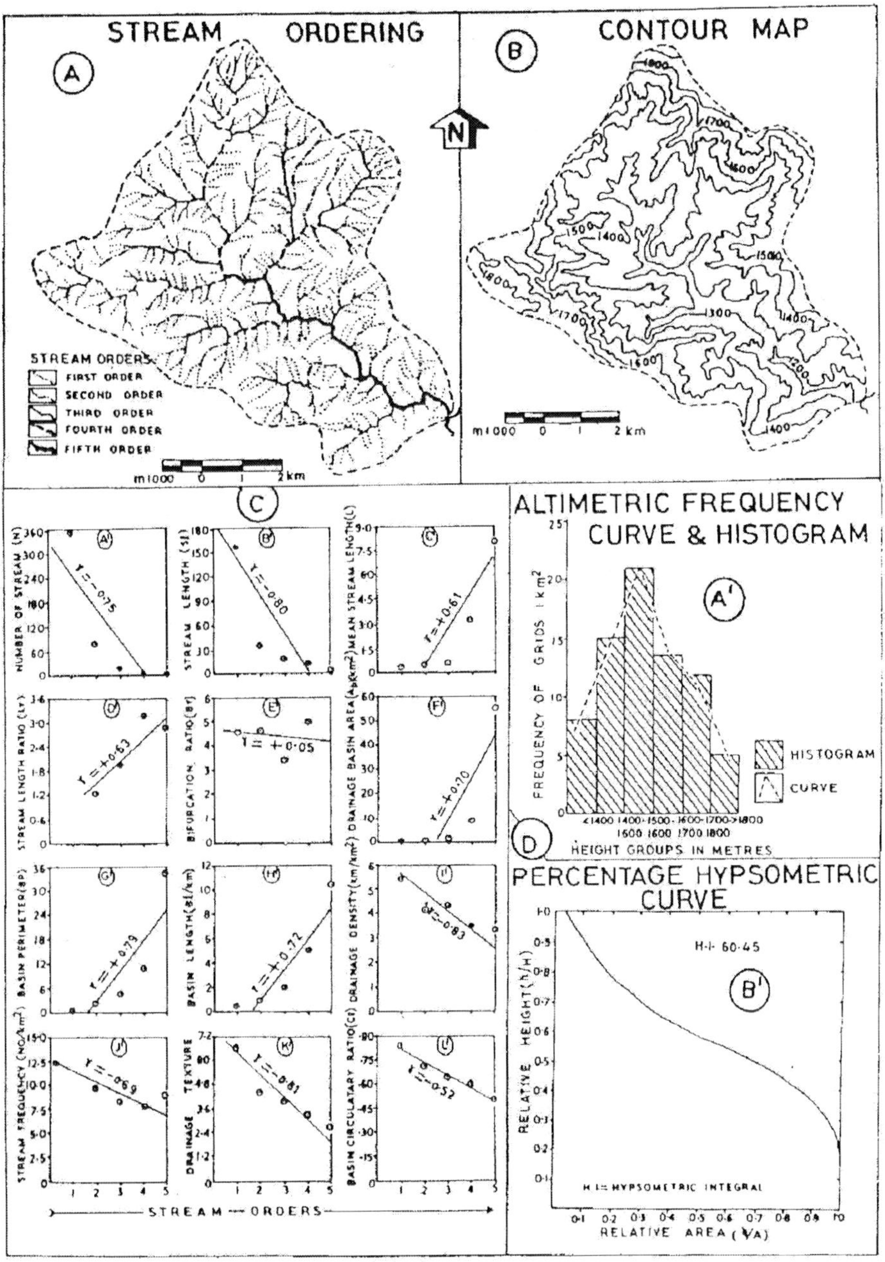

Fig. 3.1 : Showing the morphometric Characheristics of the Nana Kosi Watershed, Central Himalaya. (A) Stream ordering map (based on Strahler, 1952), (B) Contour map (based of S.O.I. Toposheet), (C) Statistical relationships between stream order and drainage morphometric parameters, (D) Altimetric frequency curve and histogram (A′) and percentage hypsometric curve (B′).

Mean Stream Length

The mean stream length of the different order streams of the Nana Kosi Watershed is presented in Table 3.1. The mean stream length of the first order stream in the study area is the smallest which stands at 0.43 km. The mean stream length of the second, third, fourth and fifth order streams stand at 0.49 km, 0.99 km., 3.20 km and 8.50 km respectively. The statistical relationship between stream order and mean stream length (Fig. 3.1 C C′) reveals that these two drainage basin parameters are strongly positively correlated (i.e., r = +.61). This strong positive correlation follows Horton's Law of Stream Length which expresses the length of stream of a given order in terms of stream order and takes the form of a direct geometric series (Horton, 1932).

Stream Length Ratio

The stream length ratio is obtained after dividing the mean stream length of the next higher order by the lower order as follows :

Table 3.1 : Stream Channel Networks and Morphometric parameters of the Nana Kosi Watershed, Central Himalaya

Morphometric Parameters	*Symbol used*	*Stream order (U)*				
		1st	*2nd*	*3rd*	*4th*	*5th*
Total Number of Streams	N	360.00	80.00	17.00	5.00	1.00
Total Stream Length (km)	L	156.47	39.12	16.87	16.00	8.50
Mean Stream Length (km)	L	0.43	0.49	0.99	3.20	8.50
Stream Length Ratio	Lr	—	1.13	2.03	3.23	2.66
Total Basin Area (km^2)	Ab	28.99	31.02	33.01	42.93	55.00
Mean Basin Area (km^2)	Ab	0.08	0.41	1.82	8.59	55.00
Bifurcation Ratio	Br	4.50	4.70	3.40	5.00	—
Drainage Density (km/km^2)	Dd	5.40	4.89	4.15	3.45	3.28
Basin Length (km)	B1	0.45	1.40	2.00	4.45	10.25
Basin Perimeter (km)	bp	0.85	2.40	4.70	11.00	35.00
Stream Frequency (no/km^2)	Sf	12.41	9.81	8.54	8.19	8.42
Drainage Texture	Dt	5.71	4.11	4.05	3.29	2.80
Basin Circularity Ratio	Cr	0.78	0.72	0.63	0.60	0.56

$$Lr = Lu+1/Lu$$

where, "Lr" is the stream length ratio, "Lu+1" is the length of higher order and "Lu" is the length of the lower order stream. Table 3.1 contains the stream length ratio of different orders of the Nana Kosi drainage basin. The stream length ratio in the study area ranges in between 1.13 and 3.23. Strong positive correlation between stream order and stream length ratio (r = +.63; Fig. 3.1 C D') reveals that stream length ratio increases as the order of the stream increases.

Bifurcation Ratio

The term bifurcation ratio was introduced by Horton (1945). The ratio of the number of segments of a given order to the number of segments of the higher order is termed as bifurcation ratio expressed as :

$$Br = Nu/Nu+1$$

where, "Br" is the bifurcation ratio, "Nu" is the number of streams of the lower order and "Nu+1" is the number of streams of the higher order. Table 3.1 contains the bifurcation ratio of the different order streams in the study area which shows that it has a constant nature and ranges in between 3.4 and 5.00 (Fig. 3.1 C E').

Drainage Basin Area

The drainage basin area drained by a particular order of stream, is the area of that particular order which is bounded by water divides on all sides with only one opening. These waterdivides separate the drainage basin area from the next higher or lower order drainage basins. The drainage basin area of different orders of the study area is summarized in Table 3.1. Table 3.1 reveals that the size of the first, second, third, fourth and fifth order drainage basin stand at 0.08 km^2, 0.41 km^2, 1.82 km^2, 8.59 km^2, and 55.00 km^2, respectively. The statistical relation between stream order and drainage basin area (Fig. 3.1 C F') suggests that the mean areal extent of the drainage basin increases as the order of the stream increases. It is evidenced by strong positive correlation (i.e., r = +.70) between these two parameters.

Basin Perimeter

Basin perimeter of all the drainage basins, i.e., the first, second, third, fourth and fifth orders was measured from the topographic sheet by using map measure. Table 3.1 contains the mean basin perimeter of different order drainage basin. It reveals that mean basin perimeter of the first, second, third, fourth and fifth order stand at 0.85 km, 2.40 km, 4.70 km, 11.00 km and 35.00 km, respectively. The strong positive correlation coefficient (r = +.79) between these parameters (Fig. 3.1 C G′) suggests that the mean basin perimeter in the lithologically homogeneous basin, i.e., Nana Kosi increases as the order of the basin increases.

Basin Length

Maximum length between drainage basin mouth and reach has been considered as basin length. The basin length was measured of all the drainage basin from the topographic sheet by using map measurer. Table 3.1 contains the summary of basin length. The mean basin length of the first, second, third, fourth and fifth order stand at 0.45 km. 1.04 km, 2.00 km, 4.45 km and 10.25 km respectively. Figure 3.1 C H′ depicts the statistical relationship between stream order and basin length which reveals that these parameters are strongly positively correlated (r = +.72).

Drainage Density

Drainage density is one of the most important parameters that indicates the landform in a stream eroded topography. The concept of drainage density was introduced by Horton (1932). He defined drainage density as the length of streams per unit of the drainage area or :

$$Dd = \Sigma L / Ab$$

where, "Dd" is the drainage density, "ΣL" is the total stream length and "Ab" is the area of the same basin. Table 3.1 contains the summary of drainage density of the Nana Kosi Basin. The mean drainage density of the first, second, third, fourth and fifth order drainage basin stand at 5.40 km/km^2, 4.89 km/km^2, 4.15 km/km^2, 3.45 km/km^2, and 3.80 km/km^2, respectively. Strong negative correlation (r = -.83) between stream order and drainage density in the Nana Kosi drainage basin reveals that the drainage density decreases as the order of the stream increases (Fig. 3.1 C I′).

Stream Frequency

In order to derive the stream frequency of a particular basin, the total number of streams of a basin is divided by the total basin area. Introduced by Horton (1945), the stream frequency is the total number of streams per unit area which may be computed as follows :

$$Sf = \Sigma N / Ab$$

where, "Sf" is the stream frequency, "ΣN is the total number of streams and "AB is the area of the same basin. Scheideggar (1961) has suggested that stream frequency is related to drainage density. The number of streams in a given unit or drainage basin is at once the most obvious of the facts in any analysis of landform features. In a region where streams are or have been the most important landform agents, their numbers is undoubtedly of very high significance. Further, their number is integrated with superficial material, amount of runoff, vegetation, topographic slope, all of which contribute in same measure or other, to geomorphic character of the area. Stream frequency of the Nana Kosi drainage basin was computed from the toposheet as defined by Horton (1945). Table 3.1 contains the summary of stream frequency. The mean stream frequency of the first, second, third, fourth and fifth order drainage basin stand at 12.41 no/km^2, 9.81 no/km^2, 8.54 no/km^2, 8.19 no/km^2 and 8.42 no/km^2 respectively. The correlation coefficient (r = -.69) between stream order and stream frequency (Fig. 3.1 C J') reveals that these parameters are inversely correlated.

Drainage Texture

Drainage texture defines the relative spacing of drainage lines (Thornbury, 1967). Horton (1945) suggests that drainage texture includes both drainage density and stream frequency (Mukherjee, 1963). Although the term drainage density, drainage texture and stream frequency refer to each other indirectly but fundamentally these are different where dealing with or defining the drainage network. Drainage density denotes the length of stream per unit area; stream frequency, the number of streams per unit area; while the drainage texture connotes the relative spacing of the drainage lines or closeness or proximity of one channel to another. Drainage texture was first introduced by Smith (1950) using the contour with most crenulations divided by the length of the perimeter of the basin :

$$Dt = \Sigma C/Bp^2$$

where, "Dt" is the drainage texture, "ΣC" is the total number of crenulations in the contour and "Bp" is the perimeter of the basin. The drainage texture for the drainage basin of the Nana Kosi was derived by using Smith's formula as given above. Table 3.1 contains the summary of drainage texture. The drainage texture of the first, second, third, fourth and fifth order drainage basins stand at 5.71, 4.11, 4.05, 3.29 and 2.80, respectively. The correlation coefficient (r = -.81) computed between stream order and drainage texture (Fig. 3.1 C K') reveals that these two parameters are negatively correlated to each other. In another words, the drainage texture decreases as the order of the basin increases.

Basin Circularity Ratio

The basin circularity ratio is a dimensionless parameter of the drainage basin. It was used by Miller (1953) to measure the shape or outline form of a drainage basin which is the ratio of the basin area of a circle with that of the basin perimeter. Basin circularity ratio is calculated with the help of the following formula :

$$Cr = 4\pi \, Ab/Bp^2$$

Where, "Cr" is the basin circularity ratio, "Ab" is the area of the basin and "Bp" is the perimeter of the same basin. Basin circularity ratio actually refers to the shape of the drainage basin and when it is equal to unity, it indicates a perfect circular basin. This ratio can be unity or less than that but never exceeds one. Obviously, any change in the ratio would certainly indicate the distortion of the basin. It is not an independent parameter of the drainage basin but is effected by a number of factors such as the underlying rock strata, slope, gradient, relief, basin elongation ratio (Schumm, 1956), stream discharge (Strahler, 1964), area of the drainage basin and irregularities in the ruggedness of the area. The basin circularity ratio for the lithologically homogeneous drainage basin, viz., the Nana Kosi was obtained by using Miller's formula as mentioned above. Table 3.1 contains the order-wise summary of circularity ratio. The first order drainage basins are least distorted as indicated by the highest value of circularity ratio (Cr = .78). As the order of the basin increases the magnitude of distortion increases. The circularity ratio of the fifth order, i.e., the Nana Kosi basin as a whole (Cr = 0.56) indicates that it is semi-circular basin. The mean basin circularity ratio of the second, third and forth order basin stand at 0.72, 0.63 and 0.60 respectively. Thus, the drainage basin circularity ratio and order of the streams are negatively correlated (Fig. 3.1 C L′) in this lithologically homogeneous basin. The correlation coefficient between these parameter stands at r = -.52.

Relief Morphometry

The relief morphometry of the Nana Kosi Basin includes the description of altitudinal zones, absolute relief, relative relief, altrimetric frequency analysis, hypsometric analysis, average slope and ruggedness number.

Altitudinal Zones

The visual impression of the general topography is depicted from the contour lines (Fig. 3.1 B) drawn at an interval of 100 m. With the help of these contour lines the Nana Kosi basin can be divided into eight altitudinal zones having an interval of 100 m. These altitudinal zones ranges in between less than 1200 m to more than 1800 m to more than 1800 m. Table 3.2 contains the aerial distribution of these altitudinal zones within the study area. The maximum area, i.e., 28.97 per cent of the total falls in between 1400-1500 m and the minimum area (i.e., 1.69%) falls in less than 1200 m. Approximately 3.64 per cent area of the total drainage basin falls in the highest altitudinal zone (1800-1900 m).

Absolute Relief

Absolute relief is the maximum height of a unit from the sea level. In the present study, the study area was divided into 74 grids of one square kilometer each and the absolute relief map (Fig. 3.2 A) was prepared by marking the maximum height of each grid, followed by drawing of isopleths at an interval of 100 m. In the study area the absolute relief ranges between below 1400 m to above 1800 m and it increases from south-east to north-west. Table 3.3 has been used to draw the frequency curve (Fig. 3.2 A′) which depicts the frequency of different absolute relief zones.

Table 3.2 : Showing the Areal Distribution of Altitudinal Zones of the Nana Kosi Watershed, Central Himalaya

Altitudinal zones (m)	*Area (km^2)*	*Area in (%)*
Less than 1200	0.93	1.69
1200-1300	5.88	10.69
1300-1400	9.88	17.96
1400-1500	15.93	28.97
1500-1600	10.00	18.18
1600-1700	5.75	10.45
1700-1800	4.63	8.42
1800-1900	2.00	3.64
Total	55.00	100.00

Table 3.4 contains the statistical measures of the absolute relief of Nana Kosi basin. It reveals that mean (u), median (m) and mode (z) values of the absolute relief in the Nana Kosi basin stand at 1578.37 m, 1566.66 m and 1542.85 m respectively. Small range (400 m) and low value of standard deviation (435.03 m) indicate that the distribution of absolute relief is normal. It is also evidenced by the bell shape frequency curve of absolute relief (Fig. 3.1 D A′).

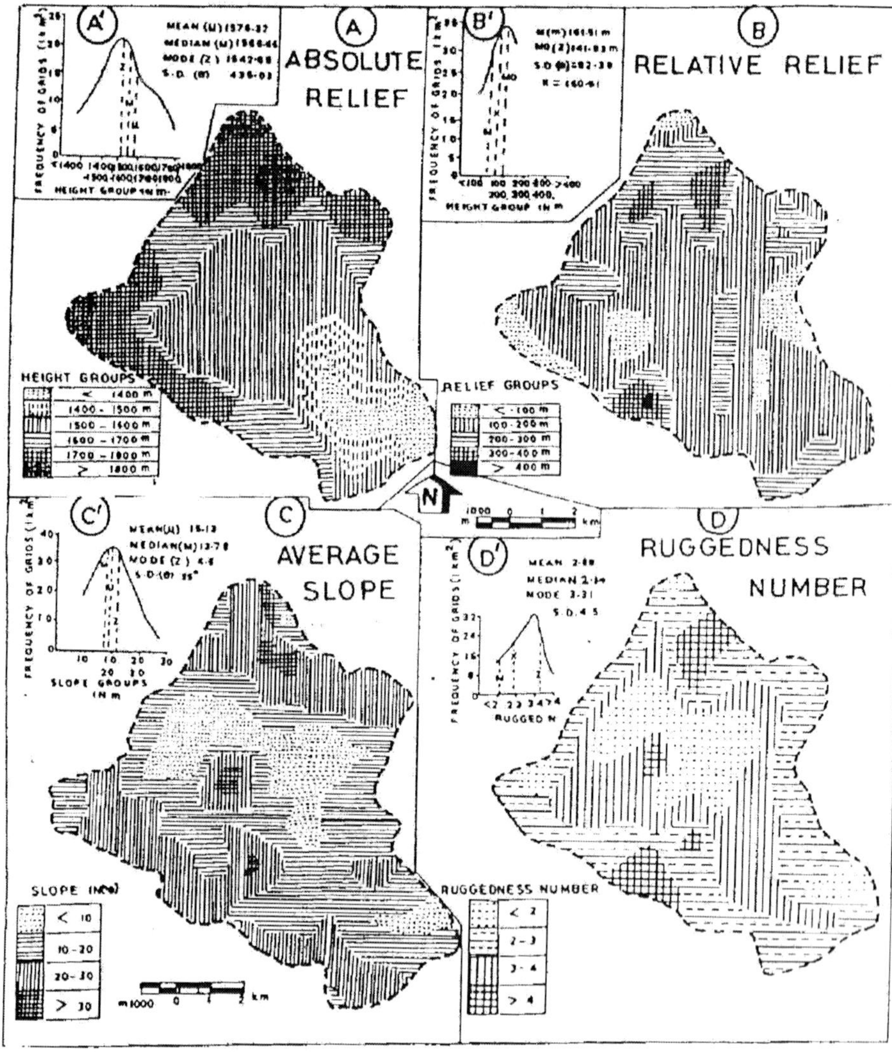

Fig.3.2 : Relief morphometric maps of the Nana Kosi Watershed, Central Himalaya. (A) Absolute relief map, (A′), Frequency distribution curve of the absolute relief, (B) Relative relief map, (B′) Frequency distribution curve of the relative relief, (C) Average slope map, (C′) Frequency distribution curve of the average slope, (D) Ruggedness number map, (D′) Frequencydistribution curve of ruggedness number.

Relative Relief

Relative relief is the result of the maximum relief minus minimum relief of a unit of one square kilometer. The relative relief map (Fig. 3.2 B) has been prepared by computing the relative relief of each unit and drawing the isopleths with an interval of 100 m. The relative relief in the study area ranges in between less that 100 m and more than 400 m. The lowest relative relief group (< 100 m) is mainly confined in the drainage basin divides because of summital flatness in the area. The frequency distribution of relative relief (Table 3.5) reveals that maximum area (i.e., 44.59%) falls in 100-120 m relative relief group and minimum area (i.e., 1.35%) falls in more than 400 m relief group. Table 3.6 contains the statistical measures of the relative relief. It reveals that mean (u), median (m) and mode (z) values of the relative relief in the Nana Kosi basin stand at 160.81 m, 161.51 m and 141.93 m, respectively. Small range (i.e., 300 m) and small value of standard deviation (32.38 m) indicate that the distribution of relative relief tends to be normally distributed (Fig. 3.2 B B′).

Table 3.3 : Altimetric Frequency of Absolute Relief of Nana Kosi Watershed, Central Himalaya

Height groups (m)	*Frequency of grids (1 km²)*	*Frequency in (%)*
Less than 1400	8	10.82
1400-1500	15	20.28
1500-1600	21	28.37
1600-1700	13	17.56
1700-1800	12	16.22
More than 1800	5	6.75
Total	74	100.00

Table 3.4 : Statistical Measures of the Absolute Relief of the Nana Kosi Watershed, Central Himalaya

Mean (u)	1578.37 m
Median (m)	1566.66 m
Mode (z)	1542.85 m
Standard Deviation (Q)	435.03 m
Range	400 m

Correlation Between Absolute and Relative Relief

The computation of the bi-variate frequency distribution of the absolute and relative relief (Table 3.7) reveals that the lower values of relative relief correspond to the lower values of absolute relief and vice-versa. Correlation coefficient has been conducted to get the exact degree of correlation between these two variables which stand at $r = +0.35$. It suggests that relative and absolute relief in the study area are positively correlated but this relationship is not strong. At this stage, the question may arise as to why the relationship is not strong between relative and absolute relief? This is explained by the fact that there exists an inverse relationship between relative and absolute relief at drainage basin divides such as in eastern, western and northern part of the basin. In these parts, the relative relief is less than 100 m but the absolute relief is more than 1800 m (see Fig. 3.2 A and 3.2 B)

Table 3.5 : Showing the Frequency of Relative Relief of Nana Kosi Watershed, Central Himalaya

Height groups (m)	*Frequency of grids (1 km²)*	*Frequency in (%)*
Less than 100	20	27.02
100-200	33	44.59
200-300	15	20.28
300-400	5	6.76
More than 400	1	1.35
Total	74	100.00

Table 3.6 : Statistical Measures of the Relative Relief of the Nana Kosi Watershed, Central Himalaya

Mean (u)	160.81 m
Median (m)	161.51 m
Mode (z)	141.93 m
Standard Deviation (Q)	92.38 m
Range	300 m

Altimetric Frequency Analysis

Another method of analyzing relief is to compute the frequency of height above sea level in the units of one square kilometer grid. The whole study area was divided into 74 grids each of one square kilometer; the highest point in each grid is noted either by spot height or by maximum value contour. The frequency of grids of different height groups at an interval of 100 m is counted. These data were used to construct altimetric frequency histogram and curve (Fig. 3.1 D A'). To recognize and correlate erosion surfaces, the altimetric frequency analysis has been used by several workers (Bauling, 1926: Hollingworth, 1938; Miller, 1953; Clark and Orrell, 1966; Thompson, 1941; Geyl, 1961; Singh, 1969; Shah, 1980). The altimetric frequency histogram for the study area (Fig. 3.1 D A') reveals that there are six summit levels in the Nana Kosi basin. These are between less than 1400 m, 1400-1500 m, 1500-1600 m, 1600-1700 m, 1700-1800 m and above 1800 m.

Table 3.7 : Bi-variate Frequency Distribution of Absolute and Relative Relief of the Nana Kosi Watershed, Central Himalaya

AR / RR	*1400*	*1400-1500*	*1500-1600*	*1600-1700*	*1700-1800*	*1800*	*Total*
Less than 100	5	6	2	1	4	2	20
100-200	3	9	7	7	6	1	33
200-300	—	—	4	3	6	2	15
300-400	—	—	1	—	3	1	5
More than 400	—	—	—	—	—	1	1
Total	8	15	14	11	19	7	74

AR—Absolute relief group in meters
RR—Relative relief group in meters

Hypsometric Analysis

Strahler (1952) rationalized the geometry of a drainage basin. He used the drainage basin for comparative purposes and to establish stage of denudation which can be applied to any basin. For this comparative analysis he used dimensionless units rather than an absolute unit which is necessary for a comparative analysis. The values that form the basis of the graph (Fig. 3.1 D B′) are the area above a certain contour as a ratio of the total height range between the lowest and highest point in the basin (Table 3.8). The 'y' axis of the graph is used to show the height ratio h/H, and the 'X' axis for the area ratio a/A. The curve obtained (Fig. 3.1 D B′) by using the ratio of height and area is called the percentage hypsometric curve which always runs from the top left hand corner of the graph to the bottom on the right hand corner. The hypsometric curve and hypsometric integral (H I = 60.45) obtained for the study area (Fig. 3.1 D A′, B′) indicate that about 39.65 per cent area of the Nana Kosi basin has eroded by various degradational processes and the drainage basin is passing through young stage of geomorphic development.

Table 3.8 : Data Related with percentage Hypsometric Curve of the Nana Kosi Watershed, Central Himalaya

Height group (m)	*Relative height (h/H)*	*Relative area (a/A)*
Less than 1200	0.125	1.00
1200-1300	0.250	0.98
1300-1400	0.375	0.88
1400-1500	0.500	0.70
1500-1600	0.625	0.41
1600-1700	0.750	0.23
1700-1800	0.875	0.12
More than 1800	1.000	0.04

Average Slope

The analysis of slope is an important aspect while in study of landforms of the region. Different form of slopes exhibit different type of landforms. The physical landscape is obviously no more than an assemblage of such slopes (King, 1975). The analysis of slope and its representation on the map has been of a special concern for landform geographers. The degree of slope controls the amount of runoff, mechanical breakdown as the angle of inclination of the ground surface on the horizontal plane, i.e., the plane parallel to the earth surface. All the landforms are controlled by their slope formation and their combination of many types of slopes—steep slopes, gentle slopes and slopes having intermediate steepness which are observed in the present study area.

A number of techniques for measuring the slope of a land area have been devised. In principal, the method for determining this value has been suggested by Finsterwalder (Monkhouse and Wilkinson, 1971). This involves measuring of the total length of all contours with an opismeter. The value obtained by this method approaches closely to the average inclination as far as the accuracy of the map and the character of the measurements will permit. The method is restricted in practice to map on which the contours are few and widely spaced. The method is subject to considerable inaccuracy also (Rich, 1951). Rich (1951) has used an alternative method essentially by counting the contour interactions along lines at right angles to the contours. This method is simpler as well as more readily applied than that of Finsterwalder (Wentworth, 1930) and is also applicable to more intricate maps. Wentworth (1930) developed and described a perfectly general and random method and introduced a simplified method of determining the average slope of land surface which can be applied to the most intricate topographic maps. In fact, the method is such that the more irregular, intricate and truly random the contours are, the more accurate the results are likely to be. Wentworth covered the contour map of the area with an east-west, north-south grid, and then finally determined the average number of contour crossing per grid. The procedure was repeated using an oblique grid over the same area and the two results were averaged. The average slope map (Fig. 3.2 C) for the study area is based on Wentworth technique of slope determination because entire the land surface of the study area is irregularly dissected and complex. For such a terrain, Wentworth has introduced this method (Wentworth, 1930). Table 3.9 contains the statistical measures of the average slope of the Nana Kosi basin. It reveals that mean (u), median (m), and mode (z) of the average slope stand at 13.13°, 13.78°, and 14.61° respectively. Small range (20°) and low value of standard deviation (15°) of the average slope indicate that it is normally distributed in this geologically homogeneous region. It is also evidenced by the bell shape curve of the frequency distribution of average slope (Fig. 3.2 C′).

Table 3.9 : Statistical Measures of the Average Slope of the Nana Kosi Watershed, Central Himalaya

Mean (u)	15.13°
Median (m)	13.78°
Mode (z)	14.61°
Standard Deviation (Q)	15°
Range	20°

Table 3.10 : Showing the Frequency Distribution of Average Slope of Nana Kosi Watershed, Central Himalaya

Slope group (°)	*Frequency of grid (1km²)*	*Frequency in (%)*
Less than 10	19	25.67
10-20	37	50.00
20-30	16	21.63
More than 30	2	2.70
Total	74	100.00

The frequency distribution of average slope of the study area is listed in Table 3.10. It reveals that the maximum area (i.e., 50%) falls in 10-20° slope group and minimum area (i.e., 2.70%) falls in more than 30° slope group (Fig. 3.2 C).

Correlation Between Slope and Absolute Relief and Relative Relief

The fundamental objective of the correlation here is to express the magnitude of association between slope, absolute and relative relief.

The correlation coefficient (r = +.21) computed from the bi-variate frequency table (Table 3.11) of average slope and absolute relief shows that these two variables are poorly positively correlated to each other. This suggests that in the study area the higher absolute zones are not always subject to higher slope inclination.

Table 3.11 : Bi-variate Frequency Distribution of Absolute Relief and Average Slope of the Nana Kosi Watershed, Central Himalaya

AR / *RR*	*1400*	*1400-1500*	*1500-1600*	*1600-1700*	*1700-1800*	*1800*	*Total*
Less than 10	—	—	—	1	—	—	1
10-20	2	2	4	5	4	2	19
20-30	4	5	6	3	9	3	30
More than 30	2	8	4	2	6	2	24
Total	8	15	14	11	19	7	74

AR—Absolute Relief-group in meters
RR—Relative Relief group in meters

The correlation coefficient (r = +.45) computed from the bi-variate frequency table (Table 3.12) of average slope and relative relief show that these variables are moderately positively correlated to each other. The higher magnitude or correlation coefficient between slope and relative relief (r = +.45) than that of slope and absolute relief (r = +.21) suggests that slope factor is more depended with relative relief rather than absolute relief.

Table 3.12 : Bi-variate Frequency Distribution of Average Slope and Relative Relief of the Nana Kosi Watershed, Central Himalaya

AS / *RR*	*10*	*10-20*	*20-30*	*30*	*Total*
Less than 100	1	8	7	4	20
100-200	—	7	14	12	33
200-300	—	2	7	6	15
300-400	—	1	2	2	5
More than 400	—	—	—	1	1
Total	1	18	30	25	74

AS—Average Slope group in degrees
RR—Relative Relief group in meters

Ruggedness Number

Ruggedness number, an important geomorphic attribute is the product of relative relief and drainage density :

$$Rg = \frac{Rh \times Dd}{Scale}$$

where, "Rg" is the ruggedness number, "Rh" is basin relief and "Dd" is the drainage density of the same basin. Strahler (1956) observed that ruggedness number increases directly with drainage density and relative relief of the area. High values of ruggedness number occur when the value of these variables is high. To combine the qualities of slope steepness and length, the dimensionless ruggedness number is the product of relief and drainage density where both terms are in the same unit, when drainage density increases the relative height remains constant, the average horizontal distance from divides to adjacent channels is reduced, with an accompanying increase in slope steepness. On the other hand of relative height increases while drainage density remains constant, the elevation difference between divides and adjacent channels will also increase and thus the slope steepness also increases.

The frequency distribution of ruggedness number (Table 3.13) reveals that the ruggedness number in the study area ranges in between less than

2 and more than 4. The maximum area (i.e., 43.26%) falls in more than 4 ruggedness number group and minimum area (i.e., 10.81%) falls in more than 4 ruggedness number group. The distribution of ruggedness number in the study area is shown in Figure 3.2 D. Table 3.14 contains the statistical measures of the ruggedness number of the Nana Kosi Watershed. It reveals that mean (u), median (m), and mode (z) of the ruggedness number stand at 2.88, 2.14 and 3.31 respectively. Small range (2) and low value of standard deviation (4.5) of the ruggedness number indicate that it is normally distributed in this geologically homogeneous region. It is also evidenced by (Fig. 3.2 D′) the bell shape curve of the frequency distribution of ruggedness number in the Nana Kosi Watershed.

Table 3.13 : Showing the Frequency Distribution of Ruggedness Number of the Nana Kosi Watershed, Central Himalaya

Ruggedness Number group	*Frequency of grids (1 km²)*	*Frequency in (%)*
Less than 2	13	17.56
2-3	21	28.37
3-4	32	43.26
More than 4	8	10.81
Total	74	100.00

Table 3.14 : Statistical Measures of the Ruggedness Number of the Nana Kosi Watershed, Central Himalaya

Mean (u)	2.88
Median (m)	2.14
Mode (z)	3.31
Standard Deviation (Q)	4.50
Range	2

REFERENCES

Bauling, H. 1926 : Sur Un methode altimetrique d' analysis a la *Bnelagne Perinerulorie Bulletin Francais,* Paris, p. 10.

Chorley, R.J. 1957 : Illustrating the laws of morphometry, *Geol. Magz.*, 94, pp. 140-150

Clarke, J.I. and Orrell 1966 : Morphometry from maps, *Essay in Geomorphology* (ed. G.H. Dury), London, pp. 235-274.

Geyl, W.F. 1961 : Morphometric analysis and worldwide occurrence of Steeped Erosion Surfaces, *J. of Geol.*, 69, pp. 388-416.

Gravelius, H. 1914 : Flusskunde : Goschensche Veriags-handlung Berlin, p. 176.

Gregory, K.G. and Walling, D. E. 1973 : *Drainage basin form and processes,* London, Edward Arnold, p. 456.

Hollingworth, S.E. 1938 : The recognition and correlation of high level Erosion surfaces in Britain : a statistical study, *Q. J. Geol. Soc.*, 94, pp. 55-84.

Horton, R.E. 1932 : Drainage basin characteristics, *Trans. Amer. Geo. Union*, 13, pp. 227-365.
Horton, R.E. 1945 : Erosional development of streams and their drainage basins : a hydrophysical approach, *Bull. Geol. Soc. Am.*, 56, pp. 175-370.
King, C.A.M. 1975 : *Techniques in geomorphology*, Great Britain, p. 244.
Lewin, J. 1970 : *A note on stream ordering*, Area 2, pp. 32-35.
Melton, M.A. 1959 : A derivation of Strahler's channel ordering system. *J. Geog.*, 67, pp. 345-346.
Miller, J.P. 1953 : Geomorphology in N. America, Polish, *Geof. Rev.*, 31, pp. 567-587.
Monkhouse, F.J. and Wilkinson, H.R. 1971 : *Maps and diagrams*, London, p. 118.
Morisawa, M.E. 1968 : *Streams : their dynamics and morphology*, New York, p. 215.
Mukherji, A.B. 1963 : Alluvial morphology of the Upper Ganga Yamuna doab, *Deccan Geographer*, 2, (1 and 2), pp. 1-36 and 100-126.
Rich, J.L. 1951 : Geomorphology as a tool for the interpretation of geology and earth history. *Trans, N.V. Acad. Sci. Ser.* 2, 13, pp. 188-192.
Scheidegger, A.E. 1965 : The algebra of stream order number, U.S. Geol. Survey, Prof. Paper No. 525 B.
Scheidegger, A.E. 1961 : *Geomorphology in the progress of Hydrology*, U.S. contribution to the International Hydrological Data, Univ. of Illinois, pp. 777-787.
Schumm, S.A. 1956 : The evolution of drainage systems and slopes in bad land, at Perth Amboy, New Jersey, *Bull. Geol. Soc. Am.*, 67, pp. 597-646.
Shah, M.P. 1980 : Landform and settlement analysis, eastern Ramganga tract, Unpublished Ph. D. thesis, Kumaun University, Nainital.
Shreve, R.L. 1967 : Infinite topologic random channel network. *J. Geol.*, 75 (2), pp. 178-186.
Singh, R.P. 1969 : Geomorphological evolution of Chota Nagpur Highlands, India, NGSI, Res. Pub., No. 5, Varanasi, pp. 46-48.
Smith, K.G. 1950 : Standard for granding texture of erosional Topography, *Amer. J.*, 248, pp. 655-668.
Strahler, A.N. 1950 : Equilibrium theory of erosional slopes, approached by frequency distribution analysis, *Am. J. Sci.*, 248, pp. 673-696.
Strahler, A.N. 1952 : Hypsometric (area-altitude) analysis of erosional topography. *Bull. Geol. Soc. Am.*, 66, pp.1117-1142.
Strahler, A.N. 1956 : Quantitative slope analysis. *Bull. Geol. Soc. Am.*, 67. p. 629.
Strahler, A.N. 1964 : Quantitative Geomorphology of drainage basins and channel networks, in a *Handbook of Applied Hydrology* (ed.) by Chow, V.T., McGraw Hill, U.S.A., pp. 40-73
Strahler, A.N. 1969 : *Physical Geography*, 3rd Edition John Wiley and Sons, Inc. New York, p. 482.
Thompson, H.D. 1941 : Topographic analysis of the Monteney section and Harrisonburg Quanrangle, *J. of Geol.*, 49, pp. 521-549.
Thornbury, W. D. 1967 : *Principles of Geomorphology*, New York.
Wentworth, C. K. 1930 : A simplified method of determining the average slope of land surfaces, *Am. J. Sci. Series* 5, 20, p. 186.
Woldenbergh, M. J. 1966 : Horton's Law justified in terms of allometric growth and steady state in open systems, *Bull. Goel. Soc. Am.* 77 pp. 431-435.

PART B

LANDSCAPES AND LANDFORMS

4

Indogenetic Processes and Geomorphic Environment

Indogenetic Processes

Environmental regions of the globe depend for their distribution on configuration of the earth's crust dictated by geologic and geomorphologic processes. These processes are powered by energy sources deep within the earth. The large scale relief features such as ocean basins, ocean ridges, ocean trenches, fold mountains and continents, and small scale features associated with faults and folds and volcano owe their origins to the processes which originate within the earth interior. These processes are known as indogenetic or hypo-gene (Thornbury, 1969) or constructional processes (Bloom, 1979). The processes acting below earth surface such as earthquake, volcanism, isostasy and plate tectonism owe their origin to certain physical aspects of earth interior.

Earthquake

An earthquake is a motion of the ground surface, ranging from a faint tremor to a wild motion capable of shaking buildings apart and caning gaping fissures to open up in the ground. The earthquake is a form of energy of wave motion transmitted through the surface layer of the earth in widening circles from a point of sudden energy release—the earthquake focus. Earthquake are produced by sudden movements along faults (Strahler and Strahler, 1983). Valdiya (1988) has presented a detailed account of seismicity in Kumaun (Fig. 4.1) which reveals that the north-eastern part of the Kumaun and adjoining north-eastern Nepal are frequently shocked by earthquakes of magnitude between 5 and 6. The earthquake of May 21, 1979 and July 29, 1980 were of scale 5 to 6, while the strongest so far recorded was 7.5 on October 28, 1916. The seismicity map of the Himalaya (Kalia and Narain, 1976) shows that this part of the Himalaya has the highest seismicity anywhere in the Himalayan arc with the value above 6.

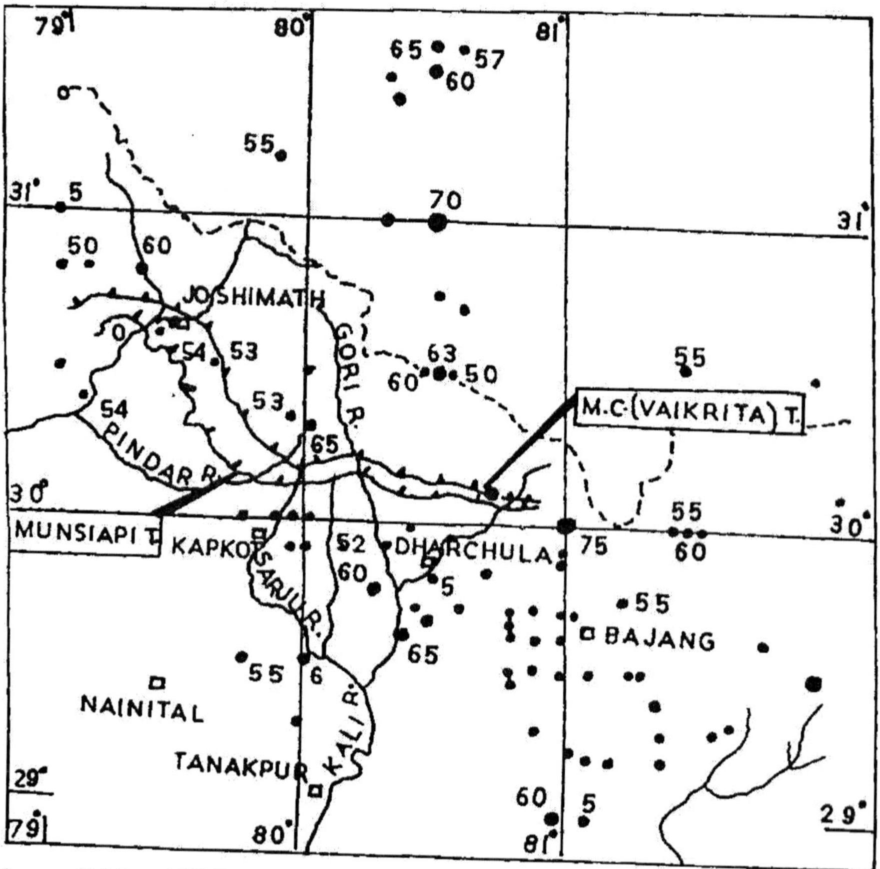

(*Source* : Valdiya, 1988 Fig. 24 A).

Fig. 4.1 : Spatial distribution of epicentres of shallow earthquakes in some parts of Kumaon Himalaya.

The occurrence of earthquakes is less frequent in the outer belt of the Himalaya but their magnitude is comparatively higher. Fault-Plane mechanism solutions of six earthquakes in the whole of outer Himalaya indicate that the movement is mainly dip-slip, the dip angle ranging from 30° to 70°C (Chaudhury and Srivastava, 1976). Valdiya (1988) believes that this movement may be associated with the Main Boundary Thrust which is already demonstrated, shows signs of recent tectonic activity. This corroborates the deductions that the movement of the plates has now largely shifted from the MCT to the MBT (Valdiya, 1988) of particular interest in connection with earthquakes as environmental hazards are their secondary effects. At Anchor-age, most of the damage was from secondary effects because buildings of wooden-frame-construction often experience little damage by shanking alone when built on solid rock areas. Damage was largely from earth movements in the weak clays underlying the settlements. The present study area is farthest from these northern (MCT) and southern (MBT) earthquake zones of the Himalaya and lies in the least affected zone of seismicity.

Plate Tectonics

The general theory of lithospheric plates with their relative motions and boundary interactions is plate tectonics. Tectonics is a noun meaning the study of tectonic activity. Tectonic activity, in turn refers to all forms of breaking and bending of the entire lithosphere, including the crust. Large scale tectonic landform—the Himalaya is a product of plate-tectonic mechanism, i.e., the collision between Indian and Asian plates in three different periods (Fig. 4.2 A). According to Valdiya (1988), the Indian plate collided the Asian plate about 50-55 million years ago. As the pressure of the converging continents grew, parts of Tethes ocean floor were squeezed up and out from the narrow Tsangpo Suture and transported as nappes (Fig. 4.2 A and B) 80 kilometers southward to Malla Johar (in Kumaun). Valdiya (1984) designated this upheaval as the Malla Johar phase. This upheaval marks the collision of the Indian and Asian continents leading to obduction of the oceanic material (Fig. 4.2 A) and riding up the crystalline basement in the northern belt, represented by exposures in the Gurla Mandhata and Rakshas Tal areas. The continuation of this collision was the bucking up and sinking deep into the mantle of oceanic crust in front of the Asian lithosphere, leading to the melting of the former and widespread granitic activity in the belt immediately to the north of the Sindhu-Tsangpo Suture. The plutonic bodies of the quartz-diorite-granodiorite granite association formed the magnetic arc of Kailas Range (Valdiya, 1988). Simultaneously, a narrow elongate fore-arc basin was formed in the Tsangpo belt in which locally approximately 200 m thick conglomerate and sandstone were deposited and in the south sedimentation in the Sirmur Basin came an end, and sediments were compressed, folded and overthrust by Lesser Himalayan rocks. A foreland basin was formed in front of the emergent Himalaya. This was the Siwalik Basin (Valdiya, 1988). In the middle Miocene period there was a violent renewal of tectonic activity in the north as the Indian continent once again pressed hard against the Asian landmass. The folds and faults in the Tsangpo suture became north-vergent (Fig. 4.2 A), the Kailas molasse deposits were deformed and thrust over by older flysch, and there were intense folding, spitting, uprooting and southward advance of the sedimentary pile, particularly in the Lesser Himalayan belt. The incipient high grade metamorphic basement ridge running through the middle of Himalayas was thrust up and southwards over the Lesser Himalayan rocks

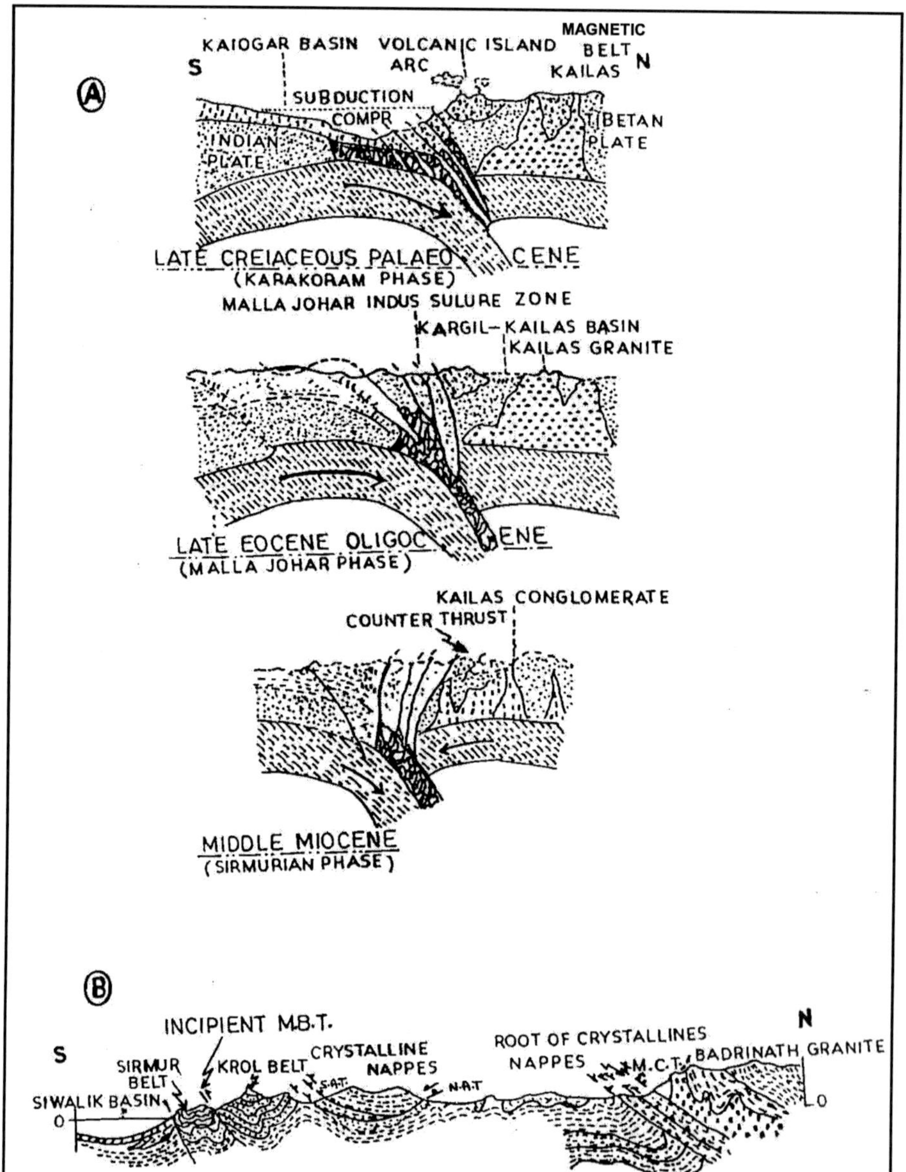

Fig. 4.2 : Showing the evolution of the Himalaya. (A) The Collision of the Indian and Asian plates and evolution of the Indus-Tsangpo-Suture zone (B) Structural framework of the Kumaun Himalaya (*Source* : Valdiya, 1984)

in the form of a huge tectonic slabs (Valdiya, 1988). The Nana Kosi drainage basin lies on one of these slabs, known as Almora Nappe (Fig. 4.2 B). Following the climatic phase of the Himalayan orogeny there was in the later Pliocen to middle pleistocene, yet another severe phase of deformation when the frontal part of the Lesser Himalaya adjoining the Siwalik Basin was cut by Main Boundary Thrust. The outer Himalayan sedimentary pile advanced southwards compressing, folding and faulting the Siwalik (Valdiya, 1988).

The tectonic activities related to the orogenic evolution have as yet not ceased (Valdiya, 1988). This is evident from neotectonic activities exhibited by almost the entire Himalayan province, but more conspicuous by the belts of intracrustal boundary thrust and tear faults (Middlemiss, 1890; Pande 1974; Sinvhal, *et al.*, 1973; Valdiya, 1969, 1981, 1988; Valdiya, *et al.*, 1984; Rupke, 1974; Nossin, 1971; Nakata, 1972; Krishnaswamy, *et al.*, 1970; Jalote and Mithal, 1971; Jalote, 1966; Hukku, *et al.*, 1974; Pascoe, 1963; Wadia and West, 1964; Gansser, 1964 and Gill, 1951).

Pascoe (1963) recapitulates the following conclusions regarding the morphogenesis and the morphotectonics of the Himalayas:

1. The line of the Himalayas may have been the locus of gentle initial uplift in Cretaceous times.
2. There are no signs of any intense compression, capable of building up a mountain chain, until well into the Tertiary era.
3. It had become a barrier of sufficient height and width to isolate the Tibetan Plateau by a date estimated to have been the middle Tertiary.
4. If this estimate is correct the slope of the southerly streams, many of which probably rose behind the line of what is now the Great Himalaya, was not steep enough for them to bring down to the plains any abundance of coarse detritus.
5. It was not until the Pleistocene period that the slope of the southerly drainage became steep enough to effect the transport of such coarse material, much of which may have travelled during the first stages of its downward journey on glaciers produced by high altitude.
6. The appearance of coarse gravels and boulders in the last Siwalik epoch may be due partly to an intensification of the compressional movement resulting in a rapid steepening of the southerly slopes.
7. The bulk of this late movement took the form of thrusting, large slices of the hills being raised to higher altitudes without suffering any marked additional implication or metamorphism.
8. This thrust movement has not yet ended and is the cause of the frequent and often severe earthquakes which afflict the Himalaya and its neighbourhood. It was only towards the commencement of the Pliocene that the Himalaya attained an elevation comparable to that it now possesses.

Geomorphic study of the foothills of the Himalaya conducted by Nakata (1972) has presented a detailed account of tectonic and neotectonic activities in the outer Himalaya which reveals (1) the evidences of general tendency of the crustal movements of the Himalayan ranges, (2) geomorphic structure of the Himalaya, and (3) regional characteristics of the neotectonics along the Himalayan Foot-Hills. A brief description of these conclusions is given below based on Nakata (1972).

1. General tendency of the crustal movements of the Himalayan range and the basements of the Indo-Gangetic plain. The distribution of the geomorphic surfaces are not ubiquitous through the foothill zone. Generally speaking, the multi-cyclic development of geomorphic surfaces are seen in the sub-Himalayan zone and mono-cyclic surface in the plains, indicating that upheaval movements have been taking place in the former area and subsidence in the latter. The multi-cyclic surfaces seem to have been formed by the super-imposition of aggradation by the climatic change and upheaval crustal movement of the areas. The boundary between the upheaval and subsidence area is clearly marked by the Himalaya Front Tectonic Line, both sides of which two structural units i.e. the Himalayan range and the basements of the Indo-Gangetic plain, have reversed crustal movement that are distinctly reflected to the Quaternary tectonic movements throughout the Himalayan Foothills except Central Bhutan Foothills. The Main Boundary Fault is the more distinct boundary both in geological and morphological sense. The Pre-Tertiary rocks constitute the lower Himalayas with considerably high altitude to the north of the Main Boundary Fault and the Tertiaries constitute the low-lying sub-Himalayas to the south, except in the North-Western Himalayan Foothills as seen in Pinjore Dun and Beas River Basin. The altitudes of the two units on both sides of the Main Boundary Fault differ as much as 2000 m. It is well known that the major earthquakes in India concentrate in or along the Foot-hills of the Himalayas i.e., probably on the thrust plane of the Main Boundary Fault (Guternberg and Richter, 1949). The depth of the hypocenters tends to increase north-ward in accordance with the depth of the Fault plane. The isoseismal lines of some major earthquakes along the Main Boundary Fault had longitudinal axes along the Fault. This indicates that the most active crustal movements have been happening along the Himalayan Foot-hills in the recent geological period.

2. The pattern of major straight valleys and ridges, and discontinuous zones of altitude in the neo-orogenic zone are considered to be attributed to the crustal movements. It is quite clear that the trends (NE-SW, NW-SE) discordant to the general Himalayan trend (E-W) are predominent in the Himalayan ranges to the north of the Main Boundary Fault, though the geological structures essentially attributed to the thrusts are more or less parallel to the general Himalayan trend. The discordant trends in the Himalayan ranges, however, agree with the dominant lineaments of the shears in the Pre-Cambrian basements of Peninsular India (Swaminath,

et al., 1964). The same trends of lineaments can be traced as discontinuous lines in the basement below the Ganges plain surveyed by the aeromagnetic method (Mathur, *et al.*, 1963). On the contrary, the trends of geomorphological as well as geological structure of the sub-Himalayan zone coincide with the general trend on the Himalayas. These trends are essentially related to the directions of the Main Boundary Fault and Himalaya Front Tectonic Line. These two major tectonic lines do not run parallel to each other where the sub-Himalayan zone is wide and therefore, the geomorphological and geological trends differ each other in such areas. The direction of the Pre-Cambrain shears can be recognized in the sub-Himalayas as transverse trends of the sides of the re-entrants in the Piedmont type Foot-hills, though the idea proposed by Swaminath, *et al.* (1964) that the present area and re-entrants along the Himalayan Foot-hills are due to the revived activities of the basement blocks along the Pre-Cambrian shears during Cenozoic diastrophism can not be supported in general. The above findings of Nakata (1972) suggest an idea that the morphogenic movements taking place in the Higher Himalayan Range and sub-Himalayas have been caused by different forces which are attributed to the crustal movement in the depth.

3. Regional characteristics of the neotectonics along the Himalayan Foothills : The type, scales, trends, ages and distubution of the crustal movements known by the deformation of geomorphic surface along the Himalayan Foot-hills are summarized by Nakata (1972) as follows :

(a) Tilted upheaval dipping toward the plain in front of the re-entrant in the sub-Himalayas as discernible in the Central Bhutan Foot-hills.
(b) Tilted upheaval dipping toward the Himalayan ranges in the re-entrant in the sub-Himalayas, as discernible in North Bengal Foot-hill and Kota Dun.
(c) Normal fault steps around the northern boundary of the sub-Himalayas with a zone of subsidence to the south, as discernible in the Western part of Dehra Dun and Pinjore Dun.
(d) Fault steps with small narrow rift around the northern boundary of the sub-Himalayas, as discernible in the Central part of Dehra Dun.
(e) Gentle undulatory upheaval with occasional fault movements along the major thrusts in the sub-Himalayas, as discernible along the Beas river in the Punjab Re-entrant.

The various types of deformations in the unconsolidated Quaternary deposits along the Himalayan Foot-hills seen essentially to be the surfacial expression of a vertical dislocation of subsurface blocks as these soft deposits could not have been subjected to the vertical deformation to a considerable extent in area by a horizontal stress. Therefore, the nature of the dislocations along the lines of abrupt surface deformations, is important in knowing the mode of tectonic movements in the sub-surface basements.

It is clear that there are two leading trends in their lineaments, i.e., the trends of the Main Boundary Fault and of the Himalaya Front Tectonic Line. Tectonic lines parallel to the Main Boundary Fault are generally seen marking the northern boundary of the sub-Himalayas. It may be, therefore, justified to group these tectonic lines as Main Boundary Fault system. This Fault system is more distinct in the Dun type of foot-hills and is composed of a group of thrusts, including thrusts confronting each other which form a narrow rift. On the other hand, tectonic lines which coincide with the Himalaya Front Tectonic Line trend are more prominent in front of re-entrants of the Piedmount type foot-hills. The echelon arrangement of the tectonic lines of the same trend were observed by Nakata (1972) where the Piedmont type of foot-hills turns into the Dun type to the south of Kota Dun. The Himalaya Front Tectonic Line as well as the Main Boundary Fault extends through the whole length of the Himalayas as noticed from the outline of the Himalayan front. However, the tectonic lines expressed on the geomorphic surfaces in the sub-Himalayan zone is generally about 20 km in length and the reason for their limited extent are not well understood but it may be attributed to certain characteristics of the Siwalik formation. It is significant to note here that along most tectonic lines, especially along the Himalaya Front Tectonic Line, the surfaces are displaced dipping toward the mountain.

Nakata has not encountered any morphological evidence of the horizontal movements along the tectonic lines. Offsets of some major stream courses in order of 20-100 km along the major thrusts may suggest the general dextral movements along the lines. The recent activities along the tectonic lines have occurred as the final phase of the Himalayan uplift and have been rather continuous on the whole. However, sometimes lags have been noticed in the activities of tectonic lines in the sub-Himalayas. In the northern part of Dehra Dun, central part of Pinjone Dun and Kota Dun the same type of movements which deformed the Siwalik formation, have been taking mainly along the boundary tectonic lines in the Siwaliks. On the other hand, in the re-entrant of North Bengal Foot-hill and in front of the re-entrant of Central Bhutan Foot-hill, the upheaval movements have been taking place where once the subsidence which resulted in accumulation of thick old gravel beds had occurred prior to this upheaval. In any case, since the highest geomorphic surfaces were constructed in each area, similar tendencies in the crustal movements have been continuing along the respective tectonic lines. Thus the mode of neotectonics recognized from the deformation of the geomorphic surfaces is related to the type of the foot-hills which may be attributed to the condition of the basements in the depth.

The sub-surface crustal structure around the Himalayan Foot-hills have been revealed by the recent geophysical and geological studies. Many workers estimated the thickness of the earth crust below the Ganges Plain and the Himalayan ranges, and found the thick crust beneath the Himalayas and northward dipping shallow crust beneath the Ganges Plain (Sen Gupta, 1964; Qureshy, 1969). The recent gravity studies proved that the major relief attained isostatic equilibrium over most parts of India, however, the young Himalayan ranges have not attained isostatic stability. The distribution of the isostatic anomaly, i.e., the gravity minima over the Ganges plain and maxima over the Himalayas is comparable to that over the pacific Types Arcs and Oceanic Trenches. Hence, the isostatic gravity anomaly reflects the local subsurface structure along the Himalayan Foot-hills. The relationship between the width of the sub-Himalayan zone and isostatic anomaly along the Himalayan front indicates the negative coefficiency in the relationship between them. The basement structure and depth below the Ganges plain shows the same tendency of crustal deepening below the plain. Therefore, the variation in the width of the Foot-hill zone may be attributed to the fluctuation in the depth of the crustal layer. The large area of gravity minima over the Ganges Plain may be explained by the crustal thickening caused by the down-warping of the crust extending from the Peninsular India below the Himalayas as explained in gravity distribution over the Oceanic Trench and Island Arcs, though it is still questionable whether the underthrusting of the crust continues northward below the Himalayas and Tibetian Plateau as explained by Holmes (1965). Thus three major types of the Foot-hills indicate the stages in the sequence of development of the Himalayan Foot-hills by the northward drift and down-warping of the Peninsular Indian Mass below the Himalayas.

The Himalayan Foot-hills are assumed to have originally been composed as the present Baluchistan mountains of Tertiary formations with wide and simple structures without predominant underthrusting of the old Continental Masses, before the beginning of the deformation caused by the northward drift of the Peninsular India. The Re-entrant type Foot-hills are wide and their geological structures are complicated with large scale folding and intraformation thrusts, and their basement is shallow and rather flat. At the early stage of the disturbance by the drift, the downwarping is no more than the up-buckling making the complicated structures. In response to the further northward drift of the Peninsular mass, stronger down-warping caused more severe block movements which brought the distinct break along the geological boundaries in the Siwaliks and the longitudinal tectonic depressions as Duns. In the Eastern

Himalayas, the Peninsular mass approached earlier and closer to the Himalayas and deformed the sub-Himalayan zone to a maximum extent, exhibiting the narrow and simple outline and structure of the Foot-hill zone. In some sections, the sub-Himalayan rocks have been lost by the continuous down-warping and underthrusting below the Lower Himalayan rocks. The recent activities along the Himalaya Front Tectonic line are more prominent where it lies closer to the Main Boundary Fault.

Geomorphic study along the MBT in the Balia Valley, District Nainital (Valdiya, *et al.*, 1984) suggests intermittent activities in the MBT zone from the line of formation of the oldest terrace. The study reveals the following conclusions regarding the tectonism along the MBT :

1. The Main Boundary Thrust marking the tectonic junction between Lesser Himalaya and Siwalik molasse represents a zone along which under-thrusting still occur.
2. Depositional terraces formed as a consequence of sub recent and historical landslides have been faulted and displaced vertically as well as horizontally in the Balia Valley, which follows the zone of the MBT.
3. Vertical scarps and triangular facets on the hillsides, uplift and dissection by faults of terraces and landslide fans, and presence of abandoned valleys across the MBT further bears testimony to recent movements.
4. The burden of evidence points to uplift of the Siwalik domain by 30 to 80 m relative to the Lesser Himalayan belt.
5. At places where the Balia Valley is strictly concordant to the trend of the MBT, there is a marked increase in the gradient of the thalweg and also in the relative heights of the exposed terrace surfaces. Furthermore, the gradients of the thalweg exhibits divergence with respect to the gradient of the terrace surfaces, the former being greater than latter.
6. The strongest evidence in favour of neotectonic activity is the occurrence of fan-remnants at a relative elevation of 60 m above its counterpart across the MBT.
7. The present distribution of fans and terraces at a higher elevation on the south-western flank relative to their counterparts of the north-eastern flank across the MBT indicates uplift of the south-western (Siwalik) block relative of the north-eastern (Lesser Himalayan block).
8. Development of landforms in this unique plate tectonic setting bears out a sequential history of development of terraces and fans. The landform at the Balia Valley also suggest intermittent activity in the MBT zone from the time of formation of the oldest terrace.

Tectonic Landforms

An assemblage of landforms, genetically tectonic are termed as tectonic landforms. According to Bloom (1979), during the recent times it has become the convention to describe the landforms that result from crustal movements are tectonic. Tectonic landforms suggest that crustal movement is rapid or young than the rate of denudation. It is believed that the rate of mountain building is eight times higher than the rate of maximum denudation (Schume, 1963) as the present rate of denudation of the earth surface stands at 3 cm/thousand years (Staddart, 1969). Under such a geomorphic condition of the earth surface the availability and survival of imprints of the tectonic movements or tectonic landforms is natural. The life of the tectonic landform is smaller than those of the other landforms because various denudational processes start to deform these landforms differentially from their incipient stage of formation. The differential denudation generates various kinds of environmental hazards such as landsliding, slumping, creeping, soil erosion and rockfall, etc.

Genetically as well as distributional point of view, tectonic landforms are localised phenomenon because the development of such landforms are confined on those areas which are tectonic or tectonically active zones. In the study area these landforms are confined along the fault zones. Directly or indirectly the faulting activities produces varieties of landforms. The direct results of the faulting activity such as fault scarp, triangular facit, waterfall and abandoned valley, etc. are termed here as tectonic landforms. Apart from the direct geomorphic consequences, there are some indirect product of the faulting activities. These are, the landforms evolved by tectonically controlled erosional processes and landforms modified by faulting activities. Landforms evolved by tectonically controlled erosional processes are termed here as tectonically controlled landforms.

Tectonic Landforms of the Nana Kosi Watershed

The Nana Kosi watershed has many characteristic morphological features which are genetically tectonic. This include scarps, abandoned valleys, polycyclic terrace scarps and diversing nature of terrace scarps, etc. All these tectonic landforms are associated with regional uplift, north-eastern tilting, and reverse and transverse faulting.

Regional Uplift and Landforms

Several episodes of erosion and deposition caused by successive uplift have produced multiple terraces at different levels in the study area. These terraces are mostly in the isolated patches. The downstream margins of these terraces are marked either by vertical scarps (in case of younger terraces (Fig. 6.8 A, B and C; Plate 15) or by convex slope in case of the older terraces (Fig. 6.8 A, B and C; Plate 2). Three major and eleven minor groups of terraces are recognized in the hillslopes of the Nana Kosi watershed (Table 6.9). A detailed account of these terraces has been presented in Chapter Six.

The multitier scarps of these terraces indicate that the Nana Kosi terraces are polygenetic and suggest regional uplift of the watershed since the formation of the oldest (T_{11}) terrace. From the configuration of terrace scarps (Table 6.9) total uplift in the order of 140-245 meters is concluded since the formation of the oldest terrace (T_{11}) i.e., high level terrace, 25-85 meters since the formation of the oldest middle level terrace (T_6) and 5-15 meters since the formation of the oldest terrace of the low level (i.e., T_3). These multitier terraces of the Nana Kosi watershed also suggest that the regional uplift is successive rather than continuous.

Vertical scarps on either side of the Nana Kosi stream from reach to mouth are also tectonic features which are caused by the regional uplift of the watershed. The Nana Kosi stream is deeply incised into the bedrock (Plate 17, 18 and 19) indicating rapid tectonic uplift of the area. Table 4.1 contains the height of some scarps along the Nana Kosi River from mouth to upstream. The elevation of these scarps is not more than the height of the oldest middle terrace (T_6) and suggest 10-85 meters of regional uplift of the Nana Kosi watershed since the formation of the oldest terrace of middle level terrace (T_6).

Tectonic Tilting and Landforms

The relative height of terrace scarps increases downstream (Table 6.8) which suggest the diverging tendency of terraces (Fig. 4.3 A, B and C). Nakata (1972) has advocated that the diverging tendency of terraces is caused by tectonic tilting. Judging from the mode of deformation of these terrace surfaces, the tilting has been continuing through the formation of oldest river terrace surface in the Nana Kosi watershed (Fig. 4.3 A, B and C). Figure 4.3 A shows that the height of the high level terraces is diverging downstream. The height of the T_{11} terrace stands at 245 m near mouth and 140 m near the reach. Similarly, the height of other terraces also decreases from mouth to reach. The middle (Fig. 4.3 B) and low level (Fig. 4.3 C) terraces indicate the same tendency. Thus, the diverging tendency of the terraces from reach to mouth in the Nana Kosi watershed suggest the North-eastern tilting of the area due to the compression caused by the converging tendency of the Indian and Asian plates. The same diverging tendency of high, middle and lower level terraces has been reported by Nakata (1972) along the Kosi river.

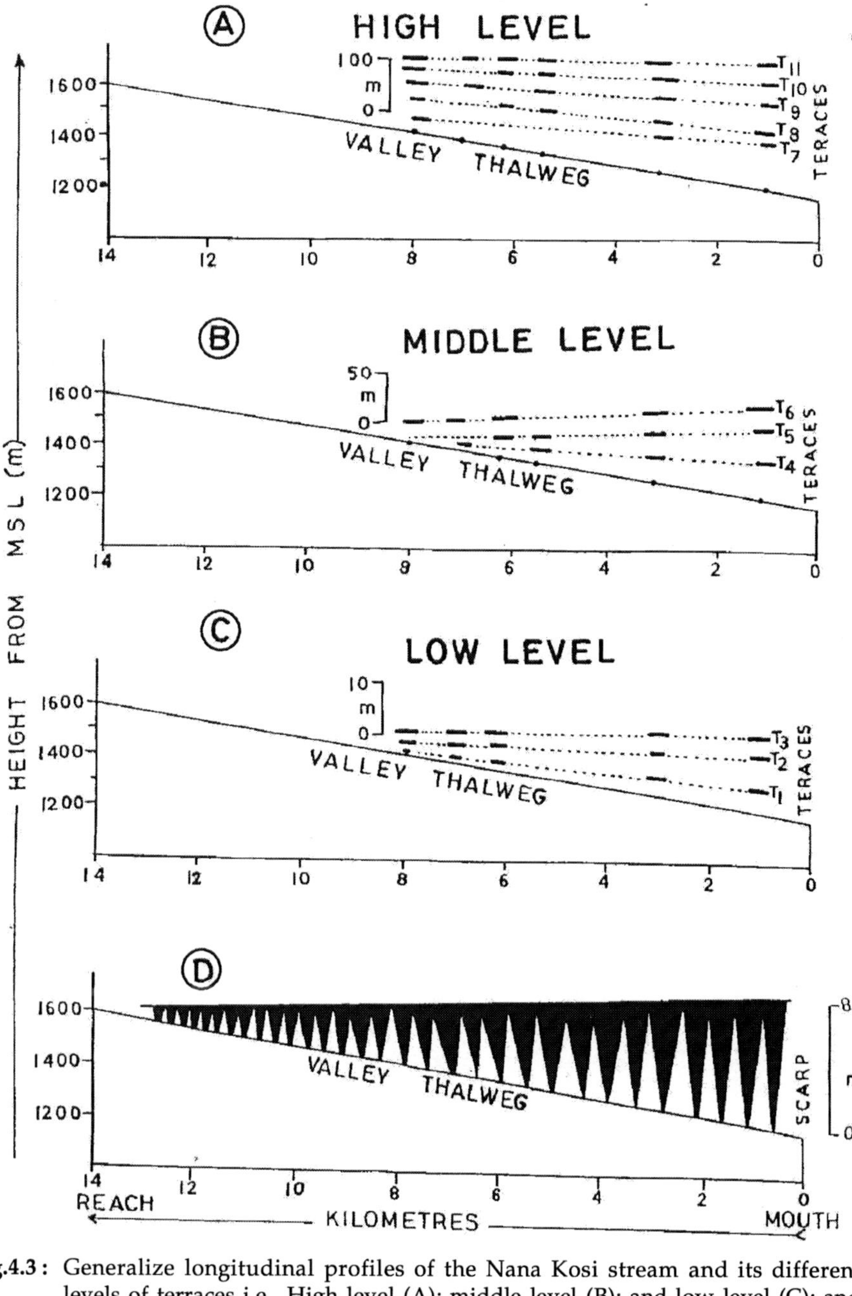

Fig.4.3 : Generalize longitudinal profiles of the Nana Kosi stream and its different levels of terraces i.e., High level (A); middle level (B); and low level (C); and valley scarps (D); *Note* : The diverging tendency of terrace levels and valley scarps from reach to mouth of the Nana Kosi Watershed, Central Himalaya, India.

Table 4.1 : Vertical scarps along the Nana Kosi River valley from its mouth to reach, Central Himalaya, India.

Scarp	*Distance upstream from outlet (km)*	*Altitude of the stream bed (m)*	*Altitude of the scarp head (m)*	*Scarp height (m)*
Pajgaon	0.4	1160	1245	85
Nana Kosi	0.8	1170	1235	65
Mairi	0.9	1175	1235	60
Syona	2.1	1185	1240	55
Dugardeo	3.1	1190	1240	50
Kakari	3.9	1200	1245	45
Burusia	5.4	1230	1270	40
Bhaudak	7.1	1270	1300	30
Benskhet	11.8	1400	1420	20
Gulli	12.8	1410	1420	10

Apart from the diverging tendency of terrace surfaces towards downstream, the increasing tendency of scarps height downstream along the Nana Kosi river (Table 4.1 and Fig. 4.3 D) is the second important evidence of tectonic tilting towards north-east. The height of scarps along the channel, ranges in between 10-85 m. It is minimum (10 m) near the reach and maximum near the mouth (85 m) of the Nana Kosi river.

Faults and Landforms

Due to the compressional forces, caused by the conversion of Indian and Asian plates, there are number of reverse and transverse faults in the Himalaya trending East-West/Northeast-Southwest and North-South, respectively (Valdiya, 1980). Within a small area like the Nana Kosi watershed which encompasses an area of only 55 km^2, there are three reverse (viz., Patharkot-Kayela Reverse Fault, Pajgaon-Jyoli Reverse Fault and Baburkhola-Burusia Reverse Fault) and three transverse faults (viz., Golchhina-Kathpuria Transverse Fault, Kwerali-Paikham Transverse Fault and Basyur-Chauna Transverse Fault). A brief description of these faults and associated landforms is given below.

1. Patharkot-Kayela Reverse Fault—Originating from the southeast of the village Manaun, this fault runs to village Patharkot and Kayela (Fig. 4.4). The trend of this fault is WWN-EES. The overriding block (i.e., northern of this fault (Fig. 4.4 A) is characterized by a series of tectonic scarps from Manaun to Kayela. Plate 4 and 7 (below), show some of the important scarps associated with this fault. The hillslopes along this faults are characterized by tectonic scarps and the stream bed is characterized by rapids (near Kausila where the Nana Kosi crosses the fault) and waterfall (near Bari where the Bari Gadhera crosses the fault, Plate 29 below). The Nana Kosi stream is deeply incised into the bedrock on this fault zone (Plate 17 and 18) due to the vertical uplift of the overriding block.

2. ***Pajgaon-Jyoli Reverse Fault***—As shown in the geological map (Fig. 2.4), this fault trends WWN-EES from Pajgaon to Jyoli. The northern block of this fault is overriding block. The tectonic landform originated directly by this reverse fault are vertical scarps, triangular facets and waterfalls, particularly discernible on the Pajgaon spur (Plate 8 and 22) and abandoned valley at north-east of Katarmal (Plate 20 above). The Nana Kosi stream makes a waterfall (of 3 m height) in this fault zone (Fig. 6.12).

3. ***Baburkhola-Burusia Reverse Fault***—This fault trends NEE-SWW direction from village Baburkhola-Basyur to Burusia. The marked evidence of this reverse fault are triangular facets at Baburkhola and at Burusia, and a series of NEE-SWW trending vertical scarps overlooking the fault, particularly discernible at village Bangsar, Chhanadariyan and Takoli.

4. ***Golchhina-Kathpuria Transverse Fault***—Valdiya (1985) has identified parallel sets of N-S extending faults in the Himalaya caused by horizontal movement. The Golchhina-Kathpuria and two other faults described below are of the same kind, trending N-S. The Golchhina-Kathpuria Fault starts from Kathpuria in the study area (Fig. 4.4 B) and extends to Gurna, west of Ramara, Bangsar, Gulli and Golchhina in N-S direction (Fig. 2.4). Tectonic landforms directly caused by this transverse fault are triangular facets on watershed divides at Golchhina (Plate 10 above) and Kathpuria (Fig.4.4 B) and a large triangular facets east of village Pathura overlooking the fault (Fig. 2.4). Apart from these triangular facets directly produced by transverse faulting there are number of other morphological features associated with this fault which have been described in tectonic controlled landforms.

5. ***Kwerali-Paikham Transverse Fault***—Parallel to the Golchhina-Kathpuria Transverse Fault, the Kwerali-Paikham fault enters in the study area from south of the village Kwerali and extends to north running through the east of village Kayela, west of village Patharkot, Burusia, Chauna, Kesta and Paikham (Fig. 2.4). The tectonic features caused directly by this fault are vertical escarpment near the water-divide at south of village Kwerali and near north of village Kesta (Fig. 2.4). These escarpments are trending N-S and overlooking the Kwerali-Paikham fault. North of village Patharkot this fault crosses the Kathpuria-Papoli spur. At this crossing, the spur is characterized by steep triangular facet which is the fault plane of this transverse fault.

6. ***Basyur-Chauna Transverse Fault***—The Basyur-Chauna Transverse Fault trends NNW-SSE from village Basyur, Udla, east of Bhagoti to north-east of Chauna. Vertical escarpment trending NNW-SSE at village Udla, east of Bhagoti and north-east of Chauna are the direct geomorphic imprints overlooking to this transverse fault.

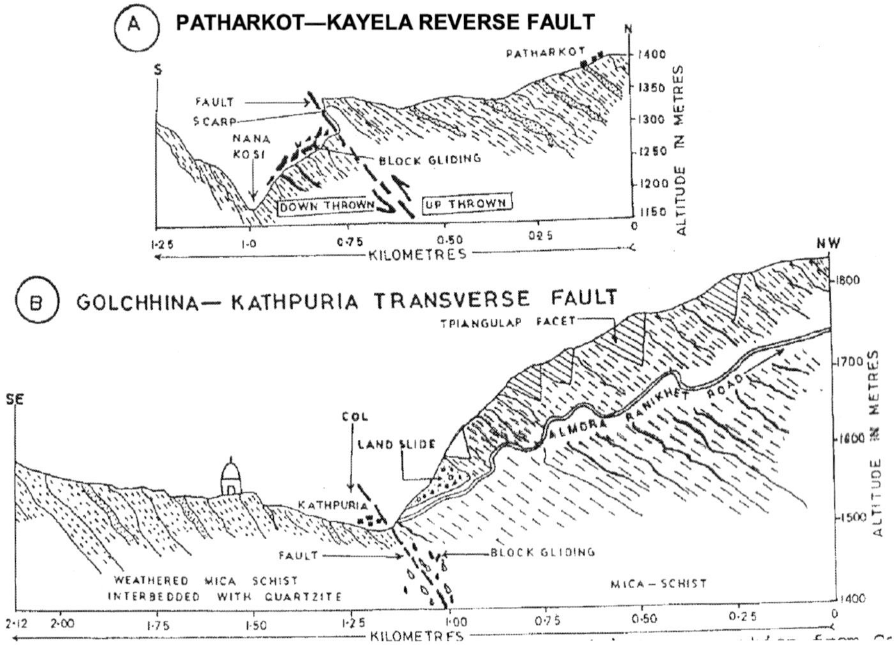

Fig.4.4 : Cross-section showing faults and associated landforms. (A) Cross-section from Gewapani to Patharkot, showing the Patharkot-Kayela Reverse Fault and associated features, i.e., block-gliding, fault scarp. (B) Cross-section from Papoli to Kathpuria, showing the Golchhina-Kathpuria Transeverse Fault and associated features, i.e., blockgliding, Col, landsliding and a series of triangular facets in the Nana Kosi Watershed, Central Himalaya, India.

Tectonically Controlled Landforms

Apart from the direct geomorphic consequences like scarps, triangular facets and waterfall etc., there are some indirect product of the faulting also. These are the landforms modified by faulting activities and are developed by tectonically controlled denudation processes in the fault zone. Landforms evolved by tectonically controlled denudational processes are the indirect product of tectonic activities termed here as tectonically controlled landforms rather than tectonic landforms. Such landforms are confined on the fault zones and are the characteristics of fault. Examples of such tectonically controlled landforms are bottlenecked valleys, subsequent streams and col, and various forms of fault aprons (Tricart, 1969) or mass wasting such as block gliding, rockfall, debris fall and debris flow, etc. A brief account of these landforms is presented below.

The extensive field study of the watershed have observed tectonically controlled landforms which are associated with reverse and transverse faults of the Nana Kosi watershed. The fault scarps are highly susceptible to erosion, due to being their deformed nature by crustal movements. The original fault scarp is deformed by the development of small rills on the fault scarp forming small valleys by headward erosion. Geometrically, these valleys are wider towards the reach and narrow towards the outlet. Such small valleys on the fault scarps are known as "bottlenecked valleys"(Bloom, 1979). Regarding the development of the bottlenecked valleys, Tricart (1968) advocated that when the fault scarp forms a water portring the evenness of the fault scarp slope is not conducive to the formation of stream. Therefore, rilling starts from place to place on the scarp and forms small drainage basins from which steep rills lead down the slope. The cross profile of these rills can not become smoother because of the continued downcutting due to the movement of the fault and their lower part forms a narrow gorge. Sometimes, indeed (as in case of the Nana Kosi watershed) rocks are difficult to erode, the gorges are suspended, and the stream cross the faultline in a waterfall (Plate 8 and 22). The area between two gorges is known as triangular facet. This state of affairs is usually called dissection in facets. Plate 8, 10 below and 22 show the examples of some bottlenecked valleys and triangular facets in the Nana Kosi watershed associated with different faults. Various weathering agents produces debris from the fault scarp which deposited at the foot of the fault plane. This weathering crag is known as fault apron (Bloom, 1979). The large fault apron are composed of coarse angular sediment and are confined on the downthrown block of the reverse faults such as discernible particularly near Jyoli along Pajgaon-Jyoli Reverse Fault (Plate 6). The small fault aprons are confined along the badly crushed fault plane and are composed of relatively finer sediment due to constant falls of debris from the crushed scarps. Such type of fault apron can be seen near Katarmal along Pajgaon-Jyoli Reverse Fault (Plate 5 below) and near Charpathar along Charpathar Transverse Fault (Plate 10 below).

Block glidings (Plate 4, 7) and rockfall (Plate 5 above) in the Nana Kosi watershed are also the examples of tectonically controlled landforms. These are associated with mainly reverse faults (Fig. 4.4 A) and with transverse faults at places (Fig. 2.4). The south-western downthrown block of the Patharkot-Kayela Reverse Fault is characterized by block glidings and rockfall (Fig. 2.4) along the fault-plane particularly discernible at Mauh (Plate 7 below), Patharkot (Plate 4 and Fig. 4.4 A) and east of Manaun (Plate 7 above). Similarly, the Golchhina-Kathpuria and Kwerali-Paikham transverse faults are characterized by rockfall and bolckgliding discernible particularly below Kathpuria, Kwerali and Kesta respectively.

When a fault passes along the valley and crosses ridges, forms fault controlled straight stream in the valley and col on the ridge. These are other forms of tectonically controlled landforms. A keen observation of drainage networks and geological maps (Fig. 3.1 A and 2.4) of the Nana Kosi watershed suggests that at number of places, where the fault passes through the valley, the stream course is controlled by fault plane. These are termed as subsequent streams/valleys. The longest subsequent channel in the Nana Kosi watershed is found along Kwerali-Paikham Transverse Fault. Near village Kesta, the Kesta stream closely follows the Kwerali-Paikham Fault up to a distance of about 2 km downstream from Kesta. Similarly, the Nana Kosi stream follows the fault plane of Golchhina-Kathpuria Transverse Fault from west of village Ramara to downstream up to a distance of 0.75 km. The Jyoli nala also closely follows the Pajgaon-Jyoli Fault from its reach to 1.16 km downstream.

When the reverse as well as transverse faults of the Nana Kosi watershed crosses the ridges, they form a depression on the crust due to differential denudation along the fault plane. These depression on the ridges are known as col. The Jyoli (Plate 6 above) and Pajgaon (Plate 9 above) cols are associated with the Pajgaon-Jyoli Reverse Fault. Similarly, the Golchhina-Kathpuria Transverse Fault has developed two major cols where it crosses the watershed boundary i.e., at Kathpuria (in southern part) and Golchhina (northern part, Plate 10 above) in south-western boundary of the watershed and at Golchhina in the north-eastern boundary of the watershed (Plate 10 above).

REFERENCES

Bloom, A.L. (1979) : *Geomorphology : A Systematic analysis of Late Cenozoic landforms.* Prentice Hall of India Pvt. Ltd., New Delhi, pp. 11-196.

Chaudhary, H.M. and Srivastava, H.N. (1976) : Seismicity and focal mechanism of some recent earthquakes in northeast India and neighbourhood, *Annalide Geofisica*, 29, pp. 41-57

Gansser, A. (1964) : *Geology of the Himalayas.* Inter-science, Wiley, London, pp. 1-289.

Gill, W.D. (1951) : The tectonics of the Sub-Himalayan fault zone in the northern Potwar region and in the Kangra district of the Punjab. *Quart. Jour. Geol. Soc.* London, 107 (4), pp. 95-421.

Gutenberg, B. and Richter, C.F. (1949) : *Seismicity of the earth and associated phenomena,* Princeton University Press, p. 273.

Holmes, A. (1965) : *Principles of Physical Geology.* Thomas Nelson, pp. 1-1288.

Hukku, B.M., Srivastava, A.K. and Jaitle, G.N. (1974) : Evolution of lakes around Nainital and the problems of hillside instability. *Him. Geol.*, 4, pp. 516-531.

Jalote, P. M. (1966) : Some observations on recent movements along the Krol Thrust, Rajpur, Dehra Dun district. *Third Symp. On Earthquake Engineering,* Roorkee, pp. 455-458.

Jalote, P.M. and Mithal, R.S. (1971) : Geological and tectonic evaluation of recent activity along Krol Thrust in the Dun Valley. *Jour. Engg. Geol.*, 6, pp. 421-428.

Kalia, K.L. and Narayan, H. (1976) : Evolution of the Himalayan based on seismotectonics and deep seismic soundings. *Proc. of the Seminar on Him. Geol.* (Sept.), Sp. Pub. of N.G.R.I. Hyderabad, p. 30.

Krishnaswamy, V.S., Jalote, S.P. and Shome, S.K. (1970) : Recent crustal movements in Northwest Himalaya and Gangetic foredeep, and related pattern of seismicity. *Proc. 4th Symp. Earthquake Engineering*, Roorkee University, Roorkee, pp. 419-439.

Mathur, L.P. and Kohli, G. (1963) : *Exploration and development for oil in India* Preprint, 6th Wld. Petrol. Congr. Sect.1, Paper 25.

Middlemiss, C.S. (1890) : Physical geology of the Sub-Himalaya of Garhwal and Kumaun. *Mem. Geol. Surv. India*, 24 (2), pp. 59-200.

Nakata, T. (1972) : *Geomorphic history and crustal movements of the Foot-hills of the Himalaya.* Inst. of Geog. Tohoku University, Sendia, pp. 1-177.

Nossin, J.J. (1971) : Outline of the geomorphology of the Doon valley, Northern U.P., India. *Z. Geomorph. N.F.*, 12, pp. 47-48.

Pande, I.C. (1974) : Tectonic interpretation of the geology of Nainital area. *Him. Geol.*, 4, pp. 532- 546.

Pascoe, E.H. (1963) : *A manual of the geology of India and Burma.* III, 3rd ed., Manager of Publications, Civil Lines, Delhi, pp. 2069-2070.

Qureshy, M.N. (1969) : Thickening of a basalt layer as a possible cause for the uplift of the Himalayas —A suggestion based on gravity data. *Tectonophysics*, 7 (2), pp. 137-157.

Rupke, J. (1974) : Stratigraphic and structural evolution of the Kumaun Lesser Himalaya. *Sedimentary Geol.*, 11, 1-232.

Schume, S.A. (1963) : The disparity between present rates of denudation and orogeny. U.S. Geol. Survey Prof. Paper 454 H, p.13.

Sen Gupta, S. (1964) : Possible sub-surface structures below the Himalayas and the Gangetic Plains. Internat. Geol. Congress Report, 22nd Session Part XI, pp. 260-276.

Sinvhal, H., Agrawal, P.N., King, G.C.P. and Gaur, V.K. (1973) : Interpretation of measured movement at an Himalayan (Nahan) Thrust. *Geophys. Jour.*, 34 (2), pp. 203-210.

Staddart, D.R. (1969) : World erosion and sedimentation. In *Water, Earth and Man* (ed) R.J. Chorley, London, pp. 43-64.

Swaminath, J., Venkatesh, V. and Sundarm, R.K. (1964) : Role of the Pre-Cambrian lineament in the evolution of Cenozoic Festoons of the Indian Sub-continent. Internat. Geol. Congress Report, 22nd Session, Part XI, pp. 316-333.

Thornbury, W.D. (1969) : *Principles of Geomorphology.* John Wiley and Sons, New York, p. 49.

Tricart, J. (1968) : *Structural geomorphology.* Societe d' Edition d' Enseignement Supereevr, Paris, pp. 210-234.

Valdiya, K.S. (1969) : A note on the tectonic history and the evolution of the Himalayas. Internat. Geol. Congress Report 22nd Session, Part XI, pp. 269-282.

Valdiya, K.S. (1980) : *Geology of Kumaun Lesser Himalaya.* Wadia Institute of Himalayan Geology, Dehra Dun, pp. 1-291.

Valdiya, K.S. (1981) : The tectonics of the Central Sector of the Himalaya. In Zagros-Hindukush-Himalaya (eds) H.K. Gupta and F.M. Delany. *Geodynamic Evolution,* Amer. Geophys. Union, Washington, pp. 87-110

Valdiya, K.S. (1988) : *Geology of Kumaun : An outline, In Kumaun Land and People* (ed) K.S. Valdiya. Gyanodaya Prakashan, Nainital, pp. 37-70.

Valdiya, K.S., Joshi, D.D., Sanwal, R. and Tandon, S.K. (1984) : Geomorphologic development across the active Main Boundary Thrust : An example from the Nainital hills in Kumaun Himalaya. *Jour. Geol. Soc. India,* 22 (12), pp. 761-773.

Wadia, D.N. and West, W.P. (1964) : Structure of the Himalayas. Internat. Geol. Congress, 22nd Session, India, pp. 132-140.

5

Petrovariance and Landscape

Introduction

The change in the exogenic forces due to climate predominates only on the broader scales. On more local scales it is outweighed by the more rapid structural change of different, chiefly aclimatic influences. Rawat (1988) has deduced that the two major aclimatic factors in geomorphology are geographical/geological. Thses are "epeirovariance", i.e., the variation in surface form caused by the operations of endogenic processes (Chapter four) and "petrovariance", i.e., the variation of rock types with different structural characteristic and to different capacities to resist erosion.

Petrovariance

It has long been a principle of geomorphology that the form of the landsurface reflects the structure of the underlying material, rocks resistance to the denudational processes support higher relief and steeper slopes than do these less resistant. Where variation in the resistance is slight, the topographic expression of structure may be quite subtle, but as the range of variations in resistance increases the expression of structural control becomes more and more obvious (Flint, 1963). In cross-section a relatively resistant rock may occupy low ground simply because it is a horizontal or gentle dipping stratigraphical sequence, but there are often reasons for inferring that higher areas owe their altitude to greater resistance of the rocks to weathering, particularly the areas of older or unstratified rocks. For instance (Flint, 1963) in pre-Triassic rocks of Connecticut quartz-rich rocks stand relatively high whereas carbonates rocks foliated rocks rich in mica and poor in quartz and plagioclase-rich rocks generally underlie lower areas. Flint has further suggested that to creating steps in the longitudinal profiles, resistant rocks may be related to valley constructions with the stream constructed in gorges or in incised meanders, compared with broader valley reaches in the less resistant rocks where lateral erosion is unimpeded. Similarly, in cross-section wave-cut benches in ingenuous and crystalline metamorphic rocks are narrow compared with the broader benches in less resistant sedimentary rocks (Flint, 1963).

Apart from the rock type, the character of rock is modified by folding. This produces lateral variation in the resistance of rocks to erosion and so controls the denudational processes. Thus, there are few aspects of the structural control of landforms i.e., variation in rocktype (lithology) and variation in rock structure. Petrovariance includes the both, i.e., the variation in the nature of rocks resistance due to rocktype and structure.

The effect of petrovariance can be grasped by examining control of rocktype and rock structure in the development of landforms. An attempt has been done to findout the same in the Nana Kosi watershed where the variation in the rocktype is considerably small.

The control of petrovariance in the development of landforms of the Nana Kosi watershed can be grasped in two ways :

1. By examining and comparing the landforms in the different rock types.
2. By examining the rock structure of the landforms.

These two ways have been discussed in the following paragraphs as lithologically controlled landforms and structurally controlled landforms, respectively.

Lithologically Controlled Landforms

Rock hardness is one of the major components of petrovariance. The hardness of the rock affects the work of the mechanical as well as chemical processes of erosion. Earlier geomorphic studies in the different parts of the Himalayas have shown profound effect of bedrock lithologies in the morphometric properties of drainage basins (Rawat, 1979; Joshi and Rawat, 1983).

Quantitative morphometric analysis of different rock formations in the lower Ramganga catchment, district Pauri and Almora have deduced the followings (Rawat, 1979) :

1. Bedrock lithologies have a profound effect on the different morphometric variables.
2. There is considerable difference between morphometric variables of the crystalline and the Krol rocks and between Krol and Siwalik rock.
3. The weak and less resistant permeable rocks of the Krol and Siwalik units are characterized by the high value of drainage density,

stream frequency, bifurcation ratio, drainage texture and relief ratio. While the relatively hard and more resistant rocks of crystalline unit show low values of the above variables.

4. The Krol unit may be differentiated from the Siwalik unit on the basis of drainage density and stream frequency. In the former the drainage density is high while in the later stream frequency is high.

Joshi and Rawat (1983) have concluded that the third order drainage basins draining to the hard and impermeable rocks of the Almora Crystalline Nappe are characterized by small value of drainage density (1.50 km/km^2), stream frequency (5.61 channels/km^2), ruggedness number (1.14) and drainage texture (2.00).

In order to examine the influence of bed rocks in the development of morphometric parameters such as stream length, drainage density, stream frequency and basin area, samples of the first order streams were selected from three major rock units of the Nana Kosi watershed i.e., weathered mica-schist, mica-schist and quartzites. Sample size was determined by the availability of sample from quartzites terrain as it has very small area within the watershed. Watershed stretching over more than one rock unit were avoided.

Table 5.1 : Mean values of some morphometric parameters of the first order streams draining to different rock types in the Nana Kosi watershed, Central Himalaya, India

Rock Types	*No. of Sample water-sheds*	*Stream length "L" (km)*	*Drainage Density "Dd" (km/km^2)*	*Stream frequency "Sf" (No./km^2)*	*Water-shed area "Ab"(km^2)*
Weathered Mica-schist	10	0.33	4.1	12.5	0.08
Mica-schist	12	0.41	3.2	7.7	0.13
Quartzites	8	0.49	2.4	5.0	0.20

The mean morphometric parameters of thirty micro watersheds of different rock units in the Nana Kosi watershed are listed in Table 5.1. It shows that there are considerable differences in the value of morphometric parameters from one rock unit to another. The morphometric personality of first order micro-watersheds of three rock units is broughtout in the following paragraphs.

Quartzites—The morphometric properties listed in Table 5.1 reveals that the hard and impermeable terrain of the Nana Kosi watershed composed of quartzites is characterized by the largest watersheds of the first order stream (Ab = 0.2 km^2, L= 0.49 km), and the lowest values of drainage density (2.4 km/km^2) and stream frequency (5.0 channel/km^2).

Mica-schist—The first order stream draining to the mica-schist (which is less resistant than quartzites) is characterized by moderate values of stream length (0.41 km), drainage density (3.2 km/km^2), stream frequency (7.7 channels/km^2) and watershed area (0.13 km^2).

Weathered Mica-schist—The permeable and weak rock i.e., weathered mica-schist which is frible at most places in the Nana Kosi watershed is characterized by the smallest drainage basins (Ab=0.08 km^2) of the first order streams (L = 0.33 km) and the highest value of drainage density (4.1 km/km^2) and stream frequency (12.5 channel/km^2).

Thus, with the help of this quantitative morphometric study it may be deduced that bedrock type effectively control the development of landforms.

Structurally Controlled Landforms

Tectonic movements such as due to plate movement (Fig. 4.2 A) after great horizontal pressure in the upper rock layers generate joints and folds. Joint density and fold pattern give rise to different types of landforms on the surface.

Joints and Landforms

Joints are of fundamental importance in weathering. They form, because of shearing under compression, because of tension or as a result of cooling on lithologies (Hills, 1963). Joints are the secondary structural features of rocks. The upper part of the earth crust is mainly jointed as the tensional processes are most active mainly up to the depth of 100 m from the earth's surfaces (Sitter, 1959). The density of joints, indicates the magnitudes and occurrence of tectonism and plays significant role in lateral changes of earth surface. These are closely spaced on the areas which have been the subject for high tectonic activities (Plate 5) and vice versa.

The hard rocks of quartzites are highly jointed than that of the mica-schist in the Nana Kosi watershed. Even within the quartzites, there is much variation in the joint patterns due to differential movements along the faults. Quartzites on the fault plane is largely jointed which is susceptible to continuous debris flow and produce small debris cones of finer sediment (Plate 5, below). Adjacent to the fault plane, i.e., fault zone, the quartzites is relatively less jointed which is not prone for continuous debris flow, but is subject for frequent rockfalls, when the closely spaced joint planes are saturated by water during monsoon rains. The closely spaced joint produces debris cones of coarse sediments (Plate 5, above). Widely space joints on the mica-schist along the fault plane produces blockglidings (Fig. 4.5 A and Plate 4, above) and sometimes rockfalls of very coarse materials.

Folds and Landforms

Much of the geomorphic diversity of landscape is due to folded layers of rocks (Bloom, 1979; Pritchard, 1979; Tricart, 1968). Folded landforms are due to entirely the crustal movements and are also, therefore, tectonic landforms (Pritchard, 1979 and Bloom, 1979). Warped landscape—domes and basin, monoclines and associated features, i.e., hogbacks, cuesta, flatinons, strike ridges and valleys, and asymmetric drainage works are some example of structural landforms caused by folding processes (Tricart, 1968).

When continuous lateral compression is applied to the earth's crust over a long period, the rocks react at first by gently warping. The uplifting and subsided part due to warping are known as upwarped and downwarped. It is very difficult to investigate such landscape because much of the warped surface is rapidly destroyed by denudational processes. Investigating such landscape in Africa, Pritchard (1979) has remarked that it is particularly true of west Africa where the ancient shield of Pre-Cambrian granaits, gneisses, schist and quartzites of the basement complex has generally resisted the great lateral pressure which elsewhere have folded and uplifted the earth's crust. This uplifting and gentle warping of the basement complex have formed broad plateau in Africa (Pritchard, 1979).

There are various landforms in the Nana Kosi watershed which are associated with overturned folding of the rocks (Fig. 5.1). These are linear and parallel to sub-parallel ridges and valleys or strike ridges or valleys, curved ridges and valleys, cuestas, homoclinal ridges and scarps, anticlinal valleys and synclinal ridges, etc.

Because of strains induced by folding the crest of the anticlines of the overturned folds of the Nana Kosi watershed tend to be weathered and wornaway. The structures are breached and the varied starta of the sedimentary sequence are exposed in the core of the anticlines. This is the principal significance of folding. Outcrops of the varied resistance to denudation are exposed at the surface and are differentially eroded to give ridge and valley topography (Fig. 5.1). The Linear and parallel to sub-parallel ridges along the straight fold limb, viz., "strike ridges" such as Tikhunkot-Pathura ridge, Sunoli-Gurna ridge, Chauna-Daulaghat ridge and Kwerala-Majkhali ridge (see geological map, Fig. 2.4) reflects the pattern of folding.

The accurate limbs of the fold have produced small curved ridges and valleys as discernible particularly on Nakuta and Pathura hills (Plate 12, below). In this section, the ridges (and hence intervening valleys) vary largely though not entirely avoiding to local dip of the starta and are arbitrarily accorded different names. Ridges formed of gently dipping

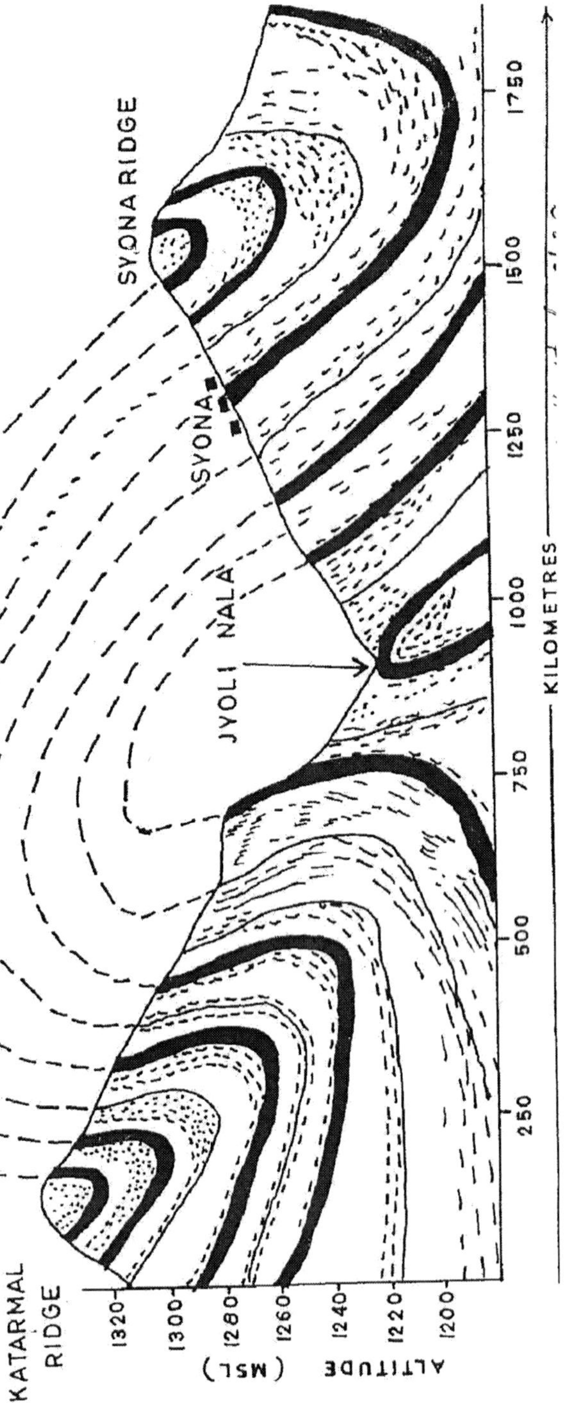

Fig.5.1 : Cross-section from Katarmal (south) to Syuna (north) showing topographic inversion on the overturned folded mica-schist and quartzites in the study area. Note the synclinal ridges which are parallel in pattern and anticlinal valley.

starta are distinctively asymmetrical in hill section are called "Cuestas" (Plate 16). The Kotuli cuesta in the study area was developed by steadily increased lateral pressure formed arches and through anticline and syncline.

Denudational processes of the limb of anticline produced a prominent erosion scarp named as Kotuli scarp. The inclination of the gentle dip slope of a cuesta closely corresponds to the dip of the starta, and in places consist of a single exposed bedding plane. The scarp associated with Kotuli cuesta (Plate 16) is "homoclinal scarp". The term homoclinal scarp was introduced by Powell (1875).

A loose terminology has evolved to differentiate structurally controlled ridges on tilted resistant layers (Bloom, 1979). If the more resistant unit is more or less horizontal—as found in case of the Nana Kosi watershed is synform, and caps a broad flat-topped hill. The hill is called "mesa". The remnant of such feature may seen near village Basur in the Nana Kosi Watershed where the diameter of the cap-rock (quartzites) is less than the height of the hill above the surrounding terrain. Geomorphologically such feature is known as "butte" (Plate 11).

Beyond the monoclinal scarp, the next degree of structural complexity in layered folded rocks is a series of parallel anticlines and synclines with horizontal fold axis. Tectonic hills are normally anticlines (Bloom, 1979), but in structurally controlled eroded landscapes such as in the Nana Kosi watershed the hills are commonly on synclinal and the valleys are anticlinal structures (Fig. 5.1). An early observation of this fact led to the concept of "topographic inversion". The strike ridges as shown in the geological map (Fig. 2.4) are all synclinal ridges in the Nana Kosi watershed.

REFERENCES

Bloom, A.L. (1979) : *Geomorphology : A systematic analysis of late Cenozoic landforms.* Prentice Hall of India Pvt. Ltd., New Delhi, pp. 253-276.

Flint, R.F. (1963) : Altitude lithology and the fall zone in Connecticut : *Jour. Geol.*, 71, pp. 683-697.

Joshi, S.C. and Rawat, J.S. (1983) : Metamorphism and development of morphometric parameters, an illustration from Bino basin—Almora Crystalline. *Jour. Geol. Soc. India,* 24 (5), pp. 248-253.

Hills, E.S. (1963) : *Elements of structural geology.* Methuen.

Powell, J.W. (1876) : Report on the geology of the eastern portion of the Uinta Mountains. U.S. Geol. and Geog. Survey Terr. (Powell), Washington, D.C., p. 218.

Pritchard, J.M. (1979) : *Landforms and landscape in Africa.* Edward Arnold, Pub. Ltd. London. pp. 80-85.

Rawat, J.S. (1979) : A quantitative morphometric analysis of the stratigraphical formations in the lower Ramganga catchment, distt. Pauri and Almora. *Him. Geol.*, 9, II, pp. 701-715.

Rawat, J.S. (1988) : Geomorphic outline of the Nainital watershed. *Geog. Rev. India.* 50 (1), pp. 53-62.

Sitter, L.U.DE (1959) : *Structural geology,* Mcgraw-Hill.

Tricart, J. (1968) : *Structural geomorphology,* Societe d' edition d' Eenseignement Superieur, Paris, pp. 1-277.

6

Exogenetic Processes and Geomorphic Environment

Introduction

Describing the controversies in the universe of exogenetic processes, Thornbury (1954) has remarked that there is a confusing variation in usage of the term that designate the common exogenetic processes. To a certain extent the confusion results from differences in opinion as to what is included under certain processes. Geomorphologists do not agree on what the seemingly simple process of erosion includes. Some includes weathering, although there has been an increasing tendency to recognize that weathering is not a part of erosion. There also may be a difference of opinion as to whether transportation is a part of erosion, but it is usually so considered. Certainly it is extending the meaning of erosion too far to consider aggradation as a part of it (Thornbury, 1954). Thornbury (1954) has used the term gradation to include all those processes which tend to bring the surface of the lithosphere to a common level. He recognised that gradational processes being to two categories—those which level down degradation, and those which level up aggradation. Geologists have used the term denudation as if it were synonymous with gradation, but as this term implies removal of material, it is hardly logical to include deposition under it. Planation has also been used in the sense in which gradation is being used but it also implies erosion and not deposition (Ruhe, 1975). In the present study the geomorphic processes originate outside the earth's crust are designated as exogenetic or distructive (Bloom, 1979) processes which include the gradational processes, including the man.

From the standpoint of the environment of man, the most significant zone of the solid earth is the thin outer most layer—the earth's crust. Weathering is the general term applied to the combined action of all processes causing rock to be disintegrated physically and decomposed chemically because of exposure at or near the earth's surface (Strahler and Strahler, 1983). The product of rock weathering tend to accumulate in a soft surface layer, called regolith. The regolith grades downward into solid, unaltered rock, known simply as bedrock. Regolith in turn, provides the source of sediment, consisting of detached mineral particles transported and deposited in a fluid medium, which may be water, air or glacial ice. Both regolith and sediment comprise parent materials for the formation of the true soil, a surface layer capable of supporting the growth of plants. Physical weathering, as well as the grinding and crushing processes to which mineral particles are subjected when transported by streams etc. continually reduce those particles to smaller and smaller diameters. Large particles, such as pebbles, are reduced in size by abrasion the grinding away of the surface. Abrasion thus produces myriads of very small particles. When a particle is reduced by abrasion to the size of a sand grain, it is quickly pulverized between much larger fragments. Chemical weathering, also known as mineral alteration, consists of a number of chemical reactions, all of which take place more or less simultaneously. Surface water—whether it be raindrops, water of streams and lakes, or water held in the soil—contains gases of the atmosphere. The presence of atmospheric gases dissolved in natural water is a matter of great environmental importance because of the inorganic reactions with mineral matter and because the presence of two gases is vital to life processes of plants and animals living in water (Strahler and Strahler, 1983).

In the Nana Kosi watershed, the exogenic processes are divisible into three main groups which have carved three different types of landscapes, i.e., pluvial landscape, riverine landscape or fluvial landscape and anthropogenic landscape. A brief account of pluvial and fluvial landscapes has been presented in this chapter. The anthropogenic landscape has been described in chapter seven.

Pluvial Landscape

Environmental geomorphology also deals largely with the action of fluid agents that erode, transport, and deposit mineral and organic matter. The rain and running waters in the surface and underground flow systems are the important agents. Invariably, man's attempts to control the action of running water produce unpredicted and undesirable side effects, some of which are physical, others ecological. An important reason to study the fluid agents is to predict the consequences of man-made changes and to plan wisely for management of the environment. Pluvial landscape is an assemblage of landforms genetically caused by the activities of rainwater on the hillslopes, viz., rainsplash and sheetwash (Chapter eight). The rainwater hits the ground and flows in unchannelled manner on hillslopes. This unchanneled waterflow on the hillslopes is known as surface flow or overland flow (Horton, 1945) and has been discussed in Chapter eight. Overland flow, by exerting a dragging force over the soil surface, picks up particles of soil ranging in size from fine clay to coarse sand or gravel, depending on the speed of the flow and the degree to which the particles are bound by plant rootlets or held down by a mat of leaves (Strahler, 1973). This section of the chapter examines the landforms developed by the works of rainwater on the hillslopes before reaching into the channels.

Hack and Goodlet (1960) and Hack (1965) introduced the examples of landforms on the earth surface caused by pluvial activities of rainwater on the hillslopes. These landforms are hollows and sheetwash flow cones and fans. The study area is not an exception. It is characterized by a series of hollows, and sheetwash flow cones and fans. A brief geomorphological account of these hollows and sheetwash flow cones and fans is given below.

Hollows

A hollow is "any area on the slope in which the contours are concave outward away from the ridge" and they "generally occur in the valley axis at the stream head as a short of extension of the channel" (Hack, 1965) (Fig. 6.1 A).

There is considerable variation between workers in different areas and with different backgrounds in the terminology used to describe hillslopes. For example Jacobson (1985) has started that the local usage of the term hollow in parts of the Applachians refers to the first and second order valleys. In forested areas of Oregon, hollows are reffered to as headwalls. In Japan, Tsukamoto (1973) introduced the term zero-order basin to refer to unchannelled basins. In the present study the terminology introduced by Hack (1965), i.e., Hollow, has been adopted. Recently, highlighting on the importance of hollows in geomorphic studies, Reneau and Dietrich (1987) has defined this term as follows. "Hollows are the concave out portions of hillslopes not occupied by channels". The observations during the extensive field study of such geomorphic phenomenon (hollows) in the Nana Kosi watershed shows that the hollows are confined on the upper crest of the ridges. The Kathpuria-Baburkhola and Korechhina-Golchhina ridges are characterized by several vegetated and deforested hollows near the crest (Plate 12, above). Similarly, Papoli-Patharkot ridge is characterized by a series of hollows (Plate 34). Apart from these, the hollows are discernible particularly on Kotuli homoclinal ridge (Plate 16, above) near Gazol (Plate 7, above) and near south of village Mairi (Plate 23, above). There are as many as about four hundred concave outportions of hillslopes not occupied by channels, viz., hollows in the study area. These hollows are 3 to 20 m apart along the hillslopes resulting in a frequency of 7 hollows axis per km^2. These hollows are erosional features of the pluvial (rainwater) activities. Due to rainsplash and sheetwash erosion on the hillslopes the sediment gradually flows with surface unchannel water and causes such concave depressions (Fig. 6.1 A).

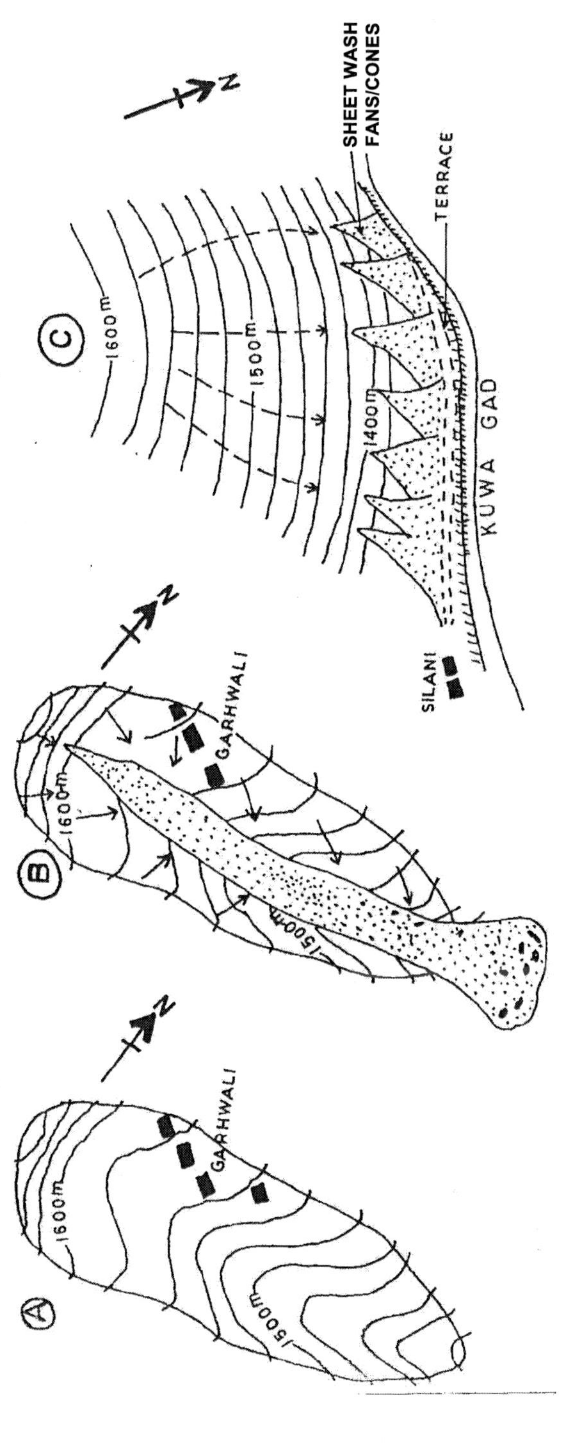

Fig. 6.1 : Topographic map of hollow, i.e., the concave outportion on the crest of Garhwali hillslope not occupied by channel (A); Long sheetwash cones/fan in the hollow caused by surface runoff during rainy season (B); and sheetwash fan/cones at the base of convex barren hillslope south of village Silani (C) in the Nana Kosi watershed, Central Himalaya, India.

Sheetwash Flow Cones and Fans

The debris flows are generally produced during high intensity rainstorms by rapid mobilization of soil particles on the hillslopes particularly in hollows (Plate 9, below) and on the convex hillslopes. Hollows and base of the convex hillslopes are the sites of long-term accumulation of colluvial debris of small and large size (Fig. 6.1 B and C). Various workers have done work on such mobilization of debris due to rainwater on the hillslopes. Some of the important works are of Hack and Goodlett (1960), Williams and Guy (1971, 1973), Woodruff (1971), Clark (1973), Bogucki (1976, 1977), Lessing, *et al.* (1976), Pomeroy (1984), Swanston (1967, 1969), O'Loughlin (1972), Pierson (1977), Dietrich and Dunne (1978), Reneau and Dietrich (1985, 1987), Swanson, *et al.* (1981), Swanson and Roach (1981), Kojan *et al.* (1972), Lehre (1981, 1982), Johnson (1984), Smith (1984), Johnson and Sitar (1986), Anderson, *et al.* (1985), Keaton *et al.* (1985), Pomeroy (1981, 1982), Hollingsworth and Kovacs (1981), Ellen *et al.* (1983) and numerous other.

There are as many as 140 sheetwash fans and cones in the study area and their average frequency stands at 1.2 per km^2. The large sheetwash fans are confined in the upper courses of the Nana Kosi river particularly near Golchhina (Plate 14, above), Bainskhet (Plate 14, below), Basyur (Plate 13, above), Chinuna (Plate 13, below), Galli ((Plate 12, above) and Nakuta (Plate 12, below). These large sheetwash fans are largely dissected by gully erosion and are underlain by thick mantle of regolith (Plate 26 and 27). These fans and cones are composed of fine material transported by surface runoff during monsoon rains. The rate of transportation of soil particles on the hillslopes of the study area, having different landuse pattern, is considerably different. A detailed account of the rate of hillwash erosion or sheetwash erosion of the Nana Kosi watershed has been presented in Chapter eight.

Fluvial Landscape

Fluvial landscape is an assemblage of landforms shaped by the fluvial processes of overland flow and stream flow. In other words, landforms shaped by running water are conveniently described as fluvial landforms to distinguish them from landforms made by the other fluid agents—glacial ice, wind and waves (Strahler and Strahler, 1983). Water on the land surface sometimes occurs as sheetflow over the whole of a slope (Chapter eight), but is commonly concentrated in stream channels (Fig. 6.2), and the processes arising from interaction of water with underlying surface act largely within these channels (Bradshaw et al., 1978). A watershed or drainage basin comprises the area drained by a trunk channel and its tributaries of different orders (Fig. 3.1 A). The channels which drains a single drainage basin can be seen as a system. Inputs of matter, i.e., water and sediment, and energy as provided by climate above the surface and endogenetic forces below the surface can be related to the outputs of water and sediment resulting from work carried out in the streams (Fig. 6.3). The interactions of the inputs of water and sediment with the characteristics of the drainage basin (i.e., morphometric personality—Chapter 3; geology and vegetation—Chapter 2) give rise to different patterns of waterflow, hydraulic geometry of channels and various types of landforms. A brief account of the pattern of waterflow and landform caused by the works of streams in the Nana Kosi watershed has been presented in this section which includes the study of water discharge flow characteristics, hydraulic geometry of the main stream, meanders, floodplains, point-bars, river terraces, fans, rapids and waterfalls. In terms of area, the fluvial landforms are dominant in the environment of terrestrial life and are the major source areas of man's food resources. Almost all lands in crop cultivation and almost grazing lands have been shaped by fluvial processes.

Stream Discharge and Velocity

Stream discharge may be defined as the volume of water passing through a given cross-section of the stream in a given unit of time. Information on daily discharge of streams is vital to a nation, not only as a measure of the surface water resource, but also for the design of flood-protection structures and for the prediction of stream floods as they progress down a river system.

The Nana Kosi is a shallow stream. The monitoring of stream discharge and stream velocity was done by using Pigmy Current Meter. The velocity of the cross-section is the rate of water passing through a particular cross-section at a given time. The velocity at a given point in a stream differs greatly according to whether it is being measured close to the banks and bed or out in the middle line, a single value, the mean velocity, is needed. Mean velocity is computed for the entire cross-section to express the activity of the stream as a whole. As the Nana Kosi river is shallow, therefore, one point method was employed to monitor the velocity of water. In one point method, velocity is measured at 0.6 depth (Ruhe, 1975). At places where the width of the cross-section was found more than 2 m, velocity was measured in each section of 2 m at 0.6 depth and than mean velocity was obtained (Table 6.1). The velocity area technique was employed to measure the amount of discharge as follows :

$$Q = (av)$$

where, "Q" is the total water discharge in m^3/sec, "a" is the cross-sectional area and "v" is the mean velocity of water in the cross-section.

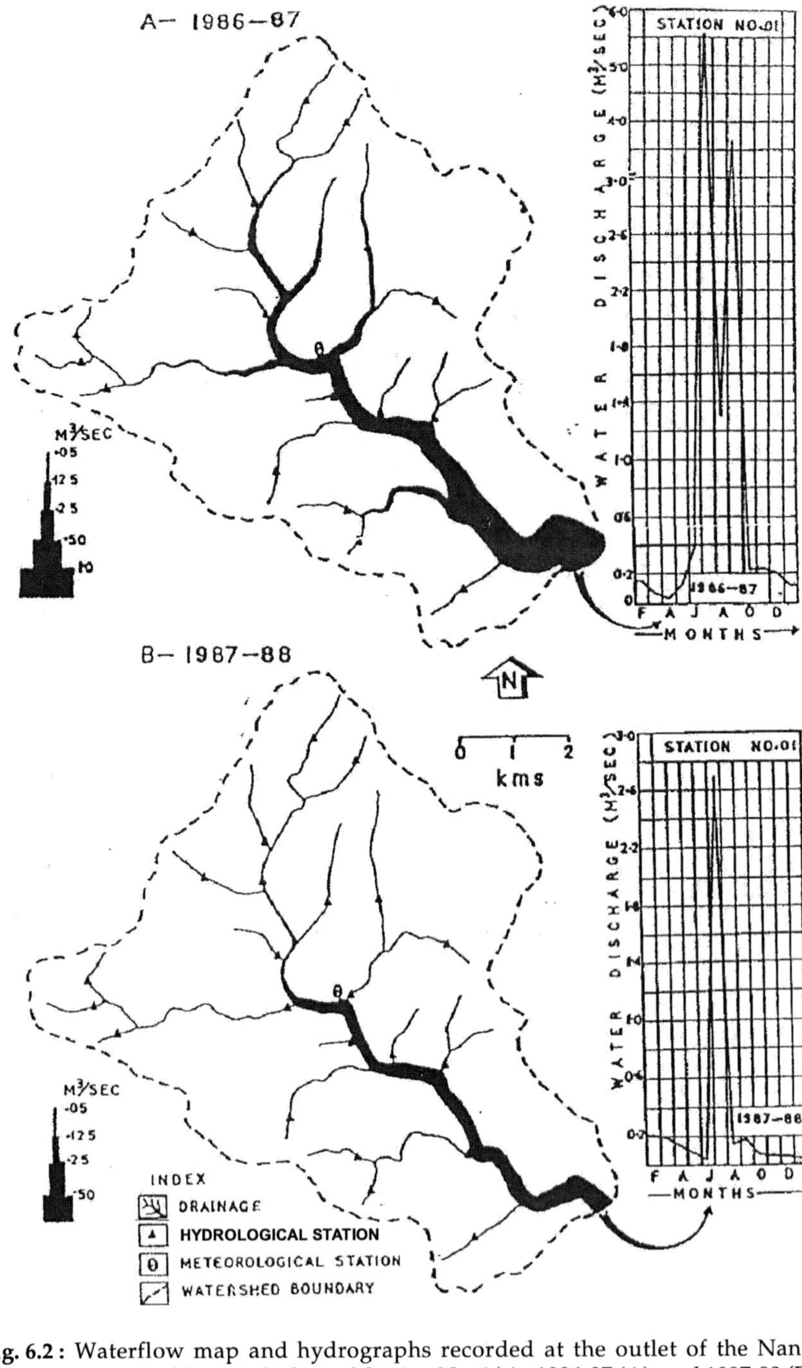

Fig. 6.2 : Waterflow map and hydrographs recorded at the outlet of the Nana Kosi watershed (i.e. Hydrological Station No. 1) in 1986-87 (A), and 1987-88 (B).

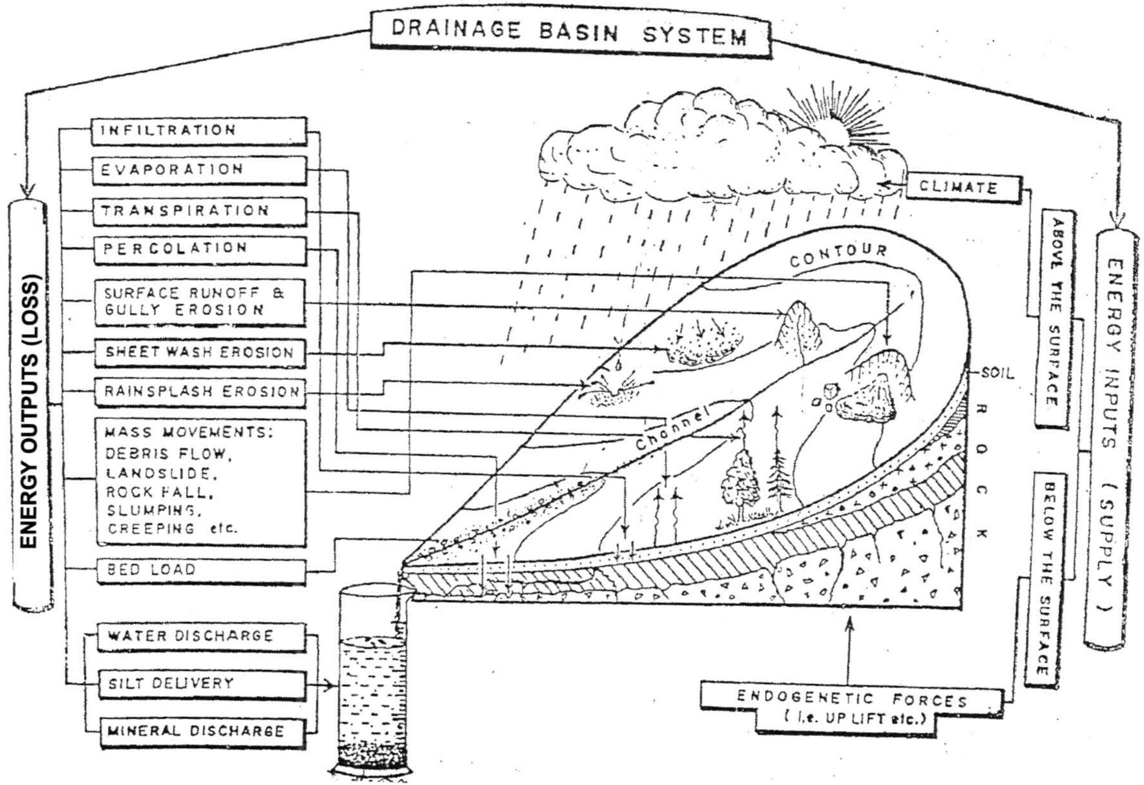

Fig.6.3 : The watershed system, its energy inputs and outputs. The Watershed is the most practical unit to monitor the parameters of hydrological cycle (After Rawat, 1987).

Figures 6.4, 6.5 and 6.6 depicts the hydrographs characteristics of the study period (1986-87) and (1987-88) at 24 different hydrological stations within the Nana Kosi watershed. Figure 6.2 depicts the hydrograph characteristics recorded at the mouth of the watershed in 1986-87 and 1987-88. Summaries of the channel runoff data as shown in hydrographs, have been presented in Table 6.1 (1986-77), Table 6.2 (1987-88) and Table 6.3 (average of two study years i.e., 1986-88. The hydrographs and runoff data tables reveal the following :

(1) In the study year (1986-87), the mean water discharge of the Nana Kosi stream was recorded 1.0321 m^3/sec (Table 6.1, hydrological station 1, Fig. 6.2 A).
(2) In 1987-88 due to the drought, it was drastically reduced more than three times. In this year the mean water discharge was found 0.2955 m^3/sec only (Table 6.2 hydrological station 1 and Fig. 6.2 B).
(3) The average water discharge of the Nana Kosi stream of the two study years, i.e., 1986-87 and 1987-88 stands at 0.6638 m^3/sec. (Table 6.3, hydrological station 1).
(4) The hydrographs (Fig.6.2) suggest that July is the month of maximum water discharge which contributed 45.59 per cent of the total annual discharge in 1986-87 and 64.1 per cent in 1987-88.
(5) The minimum waterflow (i.e., 0.44 per cent) of the total annual flow was found in the month of April in 1986-87 (Fig. 6.2 A) while in 1987-88 (i.e drought year) it was found minimum in the month of June which contributed only 1.8 per cent of the total annual flow (Fig. 6.2 B).
(6) The base flow of the Nana Kosi stream was 0.419 m^3/sec in 1986-87 (i.e., in the month of April, Fig. 6.2 A) and 0.356 m^3/sec in 1987-88 (i.e., in the month of June, Fig. 6.2 B).
(7) Although, geologically whole of the study area is homogenous but an observation of the hydrographs constructed for different hydrological stations of the study area (Figs. 6.4, 6.5 and 6.6) suggest that their shape and size is complex and are different from one hydrological station to another. This is mainly due to the different types of landuse patterns within the drainage basin. A detailed account of the effect of landuse pattern in these hydrographs has been discussed in Chapter nine.

Summaries of monthwise budget of the waterflow of different study years, i.e., 1986-87, 1987-88 and 1986-88 have been presented in Tables 6.4, 6.5 and 6.6. The tables reveal the followings regarding the monthly and seasonal waterflow characteristics of the Nana Kosi Watershed :

Table 6.1 : Mean water discharge data of 1986-87 of 25 hydrological stations (Fig. 1.1) of the Nana Kosi Watershed, Central Himalaya, India

Hydro-logical Station No.	*Water Velocity (m/sec.)*	*Water Dis-charge (m^3/sec.)*	*Water Discharge (m^3/day)*	*Water Discharge (m^3/year)*	*Water Discharge (m^3/km^2/ day)*	*Water Discharge (m^3/km^2/ year)*
1	0.742	1.03210	89176.06000	32549262.740	1621.374	591801.51
2	0.486	0.01061	915.04000	333988.687	949.878	346705.65
3	0.484	0.13366	4352.86400	1588795.360	948.598	346238.27
4	0.514	0.60439	52219.92500	19060272.625	1118.142	408121.83
5	0.479	0.01175	1015.41530	370626.584	1952.723	712743.89
6	0.534	0.01442	1246.03200	454801.680	2040.844	744908.11
7	0.433	0.01836	1323.61296	483118.438	796.822	290839.86
8	0.392	0.01788	1544.83225	563863.771	1968.505	718504.32
9	0.455	0.00765	660.96000	241250.400	1201.745	438636.92
10	0.440	0.00469	421.41400	153816.110	1404.719	512722.73
11	0.472	0.14179	12250.3320	4471371.180	1106.763	403968.49
12	0.414	0.00851	1129.04400	412101.060	1750.539	638946.84
13	0.508	0.05479	4734.29300	1728016.945	2705.312	987439.07
14	0.527	0.09166	2525.72400	921889.260	2328.034	849732.27
15	0.323	0.00806	695.75040	253948.896	1580.834	577004.38
16	0.465	0.10323	7701.75260	2811139.602	1404.480	512632.00
17	0.479	0.28250	24427.94300	8916199.195	1413.832	443048.83
18	0.449	0.00679	586.45440	214055.862	2022.256	738123.51
19	0.436	0.00453	494.48200	180485.796	566.150	206643.44
20	0.487	0.00890	769.06790	280709.783	1709.037	623798.54
21	0.498	0.01475	1274.26140	465105.411	1768.986	645679.89
22	0.341	0.01010	1700.70850	620758.602	1989.529	726178.30
23	0.485	0.01244	1074.52100	392200.092	933.535	340740.37
24	0.541	0.12416	11243.44900	4103858.733	1678.123	612515.07
25	0.381	0.00650	557.99000	203666.350	891.516	325403.43

Table 6.2 : Mean water discharge data of 1987-88 of 25 hydrological stations (Fig. 1.1) of the Nana Kosi Watershed, Central Himalaya, India

Hydro-logical Station No.	*Water Velocity (m/sec.)*	*Water Dis-charge (m^3/sec.)*	*Water Discharge (m^3/day)*	*Water Discharge (m^3/year)*	*Water Discharge (m^3/km^2/day)*	*Water Discharge (m^3/km^2/year)*
1	0.546	0.29550	25532.2836	9319283.514	464.223	169441.395
2	0.336	0.00264	227.9100	83186.568	252.729	92246.085
3	0.410	0.01189	1027.8590	375168.535	224.031	81770.980
4	0.467	0.14143	12220.0705	4460325.732	263.023	96003.486
5	0.269	0.00122	105.7620	38603.008	203.388	74236.559
6	0.380	0.00407	351.9721	128469.804	562.003	205131.247
7	0.409	0.00831	718.1994	262142.787	348.972	127374.673
8	0.456	0.00544	467.8157	170752.748	610.475	222823.375
9	0.351	0.00146	126.2952	46097.766	239.650	87472.432
10	0.352	0.00120	103.7016	37851.087	345.672	126170.310
11	0.491	0.04637	3941.6776	1438712.324	356.068	129964.728
12	0.395	0.00195	168.2662	61417.163	400.632	146230.680
13	0.431	0.00893	771.4080	281563.920	440.805	160893.737
14	0.363	0.00489	422.9224	154366.6821	355.396	129719.660
15	0.277	0.00169	149.2466	54475.003	332.326	121299.172
16	0.469	0.02509	3311.6251	1208743.155	535.459	195442.817
17	0.379	0.13077	15401.1917	5621434.988	298.979	109127.304
18	0.398	0.00133	114.5830	41822.804	395.119	144218.407
19	0.365	0.00114	98.7856	36022.689	129.856	47397.440
20	0.358	0.00186	160.7856	58686.744	357.296	130413.040
21	0.461	0.00434	369.0524	134704.126	505.551	184526.224
22	0.387	0.00452	390.8303	142653.060	868.528	317006.845
23	0.488	0.00507	437.9758	159861.167	371.166	135475.681
24	0.418	0.04127	3565.3900	1301367.350	563.261	205590.173
25	0.336	0.00191	164.8137	60157.000	261.609	95487.358

Table 6.3 : Average water discharge data of 1986-87 and 1987-88 (1986-88) of 25 hydrological stations of the Nana Kosi Watershed, Central Himalaya, India

Hydro-logical Station No.	*Water Velocity (m/sec.)*	*Water Dis-charge (m^3/sec.)*	*Water Discharge (m^3/day)*	*Water Discharge (m^3/year)*	*Water Discharge (m^3/km^2/day)*	*Water Discharge (m^3/km^2/year)*
1	0.644	0.66380	57354.1730	20934273.1270	1042.7985	380621.4525
2	0.411	0.00662	571.4737	208587.6275	601.3037	219475.8687
3	0.447	0.07280	2690.3615	981981.9475	586.3145	214004.6252
4	0.490	0.37291	32219.9977	11760299.1780	690.5825	252062.6580
5	0.374	0.00649	560.5880	204614.7960	1078.0550	393490.2270
6	0.401	0.00923	799.0020	291635.7420	1301.4240	475019.6809
7	0.421	0.01334	1020.9058	372630.6127	572.8960	209107.2605
8	0.424	0.01166	1006.3239	367308.2590	1289.4900	470663.8500
9	0.403	0.00455	393.6276	143674.0831	720.6970	263054.6787
10	0.396	0.00294	262.5578	95833.5988	875.1959	319446.5187
11	0.481	0.09407	8096.0048	2955041.7520	731.4150	266966.6119
12	0.405	0.00523	648.6551	236759.1115	1075.5850	392588.7600
13	0.469	0.03186	2752.8505	1004790.4325	1573.0586	574166.4051
14	0.445	0.04827	1474.3232	538127.9710	1341.7150	489725.9650
15	0.300	0.00488	422.4980	154211.9494	956.5802	349151.7757
16	0.467	0.06416	5506.6885	2009941.3785	969.9690	354037.4105
17	0.429	0.20664	19914.5673	7268817.0918	756.4056	276086.0652
18	0.423	0.00406	350.5187	127939.3331	1208.6870	441170.9603
19	0.400	0.00283	296.5871	108254.2430	348.0030	127020.4410
20	0.422	0.00538	464.9267	169698.2637	1033.1660	377105.7905
21	0.479	0.00950	821.6569	299904.7680	1137.2686	415103.0572
22	0.364	0.00731	1045.7694	381705.8310	1429.0207	521592.5735
23	0.486	0.00875	756.5087	276030.6295	652.3500	238108.0250
24	0.479	0.08271	7404.4195	2702613.0415	1120.0690	409052.6210
25	0.358	0.00420	361.4018	131911.6752	576.5627	210445.3940

Table 6.4 : Channel runoff flow in per cent of different months in the study year 1986-87 at 25 hydrological stations (Fig. 1.1) in the Nana Kosi Watershed, Central Himalaya, India

Hydrological Station No.	*FEB*	*MAR*	*APR*	*MAY*	*JUN*	*JUL*	*AUG*	*SEP*	*OCT*	*NOV*	*DEC*	*JAN*
1	1.3	0.7	0.4	1.3	3.9	45.6	10.6	29.3	2.0	2.0	1.8	1.1
2	5.6	3.8	2.6	3.5	4.6	33.2	14.8	13.1	6.2	5.0	4.5	2.9
3	1.2	1.4	0.8	1.0	8.6	68.2	2.4	9.2	2.4	1.9	1.6	1.3
4	3.4	4.4	2.5	3.0	4.4	30.5	12.8	28.3	3.2	3.4	2.5	1.6
5	3.6	1.4	1.0	2.0	6.8	34.8	19.8	23.3	3.3	1.9	1.0	1.1
6	5.9	3.8	2.6	4.6	5.4	35.4	10.5	17.8	2.9	3.4	3.9	3.8
7	3.3	1.1	0.9	1.8	5.2	35.4	21.8	14.8	4.4	4.4	3.6	3.2
8	1.3	1.3	1.0	1.0	6.3	42.4	11.3	19.6	5.6	4.0	3.1	3.1
9	3.9	3.0	1.1	2.0	8.6	34.7	6.6	20.5	8.3	3.3	3.8	4.2
10	3.5	0.4	0.3	0.7	4.9	58.8	7.8	4.7	1.8	6.6	5.9	4.6
11	3.2	2.4	2.0	0.9	3.8	43.6	13.3	13.1	4.8	5.2	4.0	3.7
12	2.8	1.9	0.8	1.8	7.1	55.8	13.3	1.7	4.2	4.2	3.5	2.9
13	1.6	1.5	1.2	1.6	5.3	68.8	7.8	5.0	2.2	1.6	1.6	1.8
14	10.1	4.2	1.9	0.7	4.3	35.0	23.4	9.2	3.0	3.0	2.4	2.8
15	3.9	3.3	4.9	0.3	2.7	32.6	12.9	21.9	5.8	4.4	3.4	3.9
16	5.9	5.4	6.1	6.9	1.4	11.8	22.5	21.9	4.5	4.4	6.9	2.3
17	2.3	1.9	2.4	2.4	3.6	36.5	14.8	18.9	3.8	7.0	3.0	3.4
18	5.3	2.6	1.9	2.3	6.0	24.8	12.5	32.8	4.4	2.5	2.6	2.3
19	16.2	2.4	2.2	2.4	6.8	27.8	15.5	5.3	6.6	4.6	4.9	5.3
20	7.9	2.7	1.4	2.1	3.4	39.0	6.9	6.0	11.3	8.3	6.0	5.0
21	2.0	1.7	2.2	2.9	5.5	40.9	6.8	11.6	6.5	5.9	7.4	6.6
22	7.0	1.8	1.3	3.2	5.6	40.5	9.5	5.9	10.0	8.2	4.4	2.6
23	4.3	2.2	1.7	2.0	5.2	5.6	22.4	24.5	8.0	7.3	10.2	6.2
24	2.1	0.8	1.2	1.4	4.9	57.3	10.4	8.3	5.4	4.6	1.8	1.8
25	3.8	2.2	2.2	1.3	2.8	28.5	28.4	19.8	4.4	2.8	2.1	1.7

Table 6.5 : Channel runoff flow in per cent of different months in the study year 1987-88 at 25 hydrological stations (Fig. 1.1) in the Nana Kosi Watershed, Central Himalaya, India

Hydrological Station No.	*FEB*	*MAR*	*APR*	*MAY*	*JUN*	*JUL*	*AUG*	*SEP*	*OCT*	*NOV*	*DEC*	*JAN*
1	6.0	5.3	4.1	2.6	1.8	64.1	4.5	4.8	2.0	1.7	1.8	1.3
2	10.2	13.8	8.9	4.3	3.6	11.8	14.8	7.3	6.3	5.9	7.5	6.4
3	15.5	11.2	8.8	5.5	2.9	19.7	6.2	6.0	7.0	6.0	6.1	5.1
4	10.7	10.5	9.7	5.0	1.8	23.2	7.9	9.0	7.0	6.0	4.8	4.4
5	11.3	11.7	9.0	3.4	4.1	5.2	8.9	11.1	10.3	7.6	8.2	9.2
6	13.8	11.5	8.1	5.4	7.5	9.1	9.8	10.2	5.6	7.2	6.0	5.8
7	6.4	5.3	23.6	2.3	3.7	24.6	4.6	3.5	6.3	6.0	5.7	8.0
8	11.0	6.4	5.4	2.8	1.8	19.6	5.2	9.7	10.5	9.8	8.5	9.2
9	17.2	7.0	5.4	4.2	1.8	13.9	16.2	5.0	7.0	5.7	7.8	8.8
10	9.9	1.2	0.5	0.2	0.0	14.5	7.6	13.4	14.0	13.8	12.0	12.9
11	14.6	12.8	10.2	11.5	2.8	17.0	6.6	3.4	4.9	5.8	5.9	4.5
12	16.1	7.5	7.2	6.9	8.1	11.5	10.4	13.4	3.6	5.4	5.8	4.1
13	8.2	5.4	5.3	6.9	3.3	9.6	12.9	13.6	9.4	7.7	9.9	7.8
14	12.5	5.2	5.2	4.6	2.6	6.5	3.9	4.8	13.3	12.4	15.2	13.8
15	13.4	13.7	5.0	5.6	3.4	17.8	7.3	8.8	6.1	4.8	7.8	6.3
16	9.5	7.2	6.8	5.4	9.2	9.2	11.2	11.9	7.4	7.2	6.8	8.2
17	12.6	5.1	4.9	41.6	2.8	12.3	3.8	5.5	2.8	2.5	2.8	3.3
18	11.0	9.7	7.0	5.5	4.4	23.2	11.3	6.0	6.4	4.1	5.0	6.4
19	15.9	11.8	8.9	3.6	3.5	18.5	7.5	6.9	5.4	6.2	6.4	5.4
20	19.1	9.4	7.9	2.9	1.8	13.2	6.6	7.2	8.8	7.3	6.5	9.3
21	15.9	14.7	12.1	8.3	5.4	5.4	5.6	5.8	6.0	6.3	6.9	7.8
22	9.3	9.3	6.6	4.0	7.6	15.5	8.3	10.6	7.6	7.9	7.7	5.6
23	9.6	7.6	6.0	6.2	3.7	11.6	7.4	7.9	8.8	9.4	10.9	10.4
24	5.7	11.5	10.4	2.5	2.5	7.5	11.2	10.4	10.2	9.9	8.4	9.8
25	9.8	8.2	7.3	3.5	0.8	10.2	9.3	10.9	10.4	9.2	11.0	9.4

Table 6.6 : Average channel runoff flow in per cent of different months in the study year 1986-87 and 1987-88 at 25 hydrological stations (Fig. 1.1) in the Nana Kosi watershed, Central Himalaya, India

Hydrological Station No.	*FEB*	*MAR*	*APR*	*MAY*	*JUN*	*JUL*	*AUG*	*SEP*	*OCT*	*NOV*	*DEC*	*JAN*
1	3.7	3.0	2.2	1.9	2.8	54.8	7.5	17.1	1.9	1.8	1.8	1.4
2	7.9	8.4	5.7	3.9	4.1	22.5	14.8	10.3	6.2	5.4	6.2	4.6
3	8.5	6.3	4.8	3.2	5.7	43.9	4.3	7.6	4.7	3.9	3.8	3.8
4	7.0	7.4	6.1	4.0	3.1	26.9	10.3	18.6	5.1	4.7	3.6	3.2
5	7.4	6.5	5.0	2.7	5.4	20.0	14.4	17.2	6.7	4.7	4.6	5.9
6	9.8	7.6	5.3	5.1	6.4	23.3	10.1	14.2	4.2	5.3	4.9	4.8
7	4.8	3.2	12.2	2.0	4.4	30.2	13.2	9.1	5.3	5.2	4.7	5.7
8	6.1	3.8	3.2	1.9	4.0	31.2	8.3	14.6	8.0	6.9	5.8	6.2
9	10.5	5.0	3.2	3.1	5.2	24.3	11.6	12.7	7.6	4.5	5.8	6.5
10	6.7	0.8	0.4	0.4	2.4	36.6	7.8	9.0	7.9	10.3	8.9	8.6
11	8.9	7.6	6.1	6.2	3.3	30.3	9.9	8.3	4.9	5.5	4.9	4.1
12	9.4	4.7	4.0	4.3	7.6	33.7	11.8	7.5	3.9	4.8	4.7	3.6
13	4.9	3.4	3.2	4.3	4.3	39.3	10.3	9.3	5.8	4.6	5.8	4.8
14	11.3	4.7	3.5	2.6	3.4	20.7	13.7	2.7	8.2	7.8	8.8	8.3
15	8.6	8.5	4.9	2.9	3.0	25.2	10.2	15.5	5.9	4.6	5.6	5.1
16	7.7	6.3	6.4	6.1	5.3	10.5	16.9	16.9	5.9	5.9	6.8	5.3
17	7.4	3.5	3.6	22.0	3.2	24.4	9.3	12.3	3.3	4.8	2.9	3.3
18	8.1	6.2	4.4	3.9	5.3	24.0	11.9	19.4	5.4	3.3	3.8	4.3
19	16.0	7.1	5.5	3.0	5.1	23.1	11.5	6.2	6.2	5.4	5.6	5.3
20	13.5	6.0	4.6	2.5	2.6	26.1	6.7	6.6	10.1	7.8	6.3	7.2
21	8.9	8.2	7.1	5.6	5.4	23.1	6.2	8.7	6.2	6.2	7.2	7.2
22	8.2	5.6	3.9	3.6	6.6	28.0	8.9	8.2	8.8	8.1	6.0	4.1
23	6.9	4.9	3.9	4.2	4.4	8.6	14.9	16.3	8.3	8.3	10.5	8.5
24	3.9	6.2	5.8	1.9	3.7	32.4	10.8	9.3	7.9	7.2	5.1	5.8
25	6.8	5.2	4.8	1.9	1.8	19.3	18.8	15.3	7.4	6.6	6.6	5.5

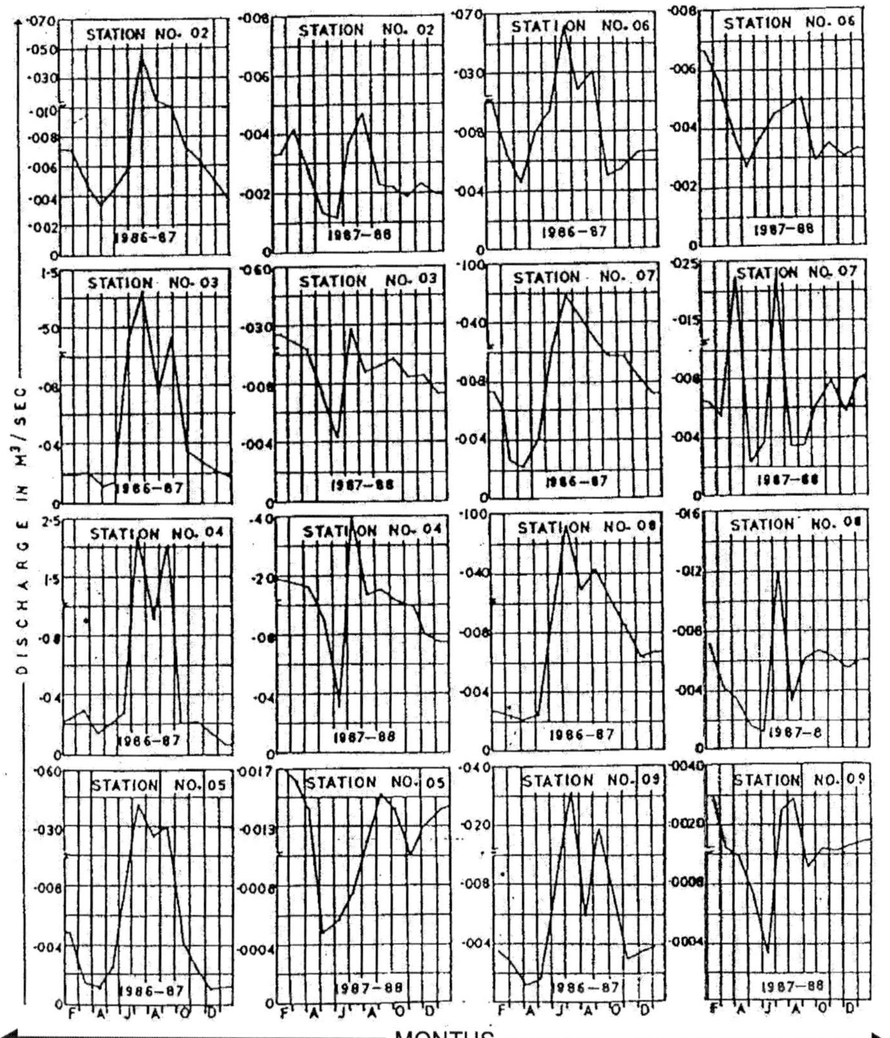

Fig.6.4: Hydrographs (1986-87 and 1987-88) of hydrological stations no. 2 to 9 of the Nana Kosi Watershed, Central Himalaya (See Fig. 1.1 for the location of hydrological stations).

(1) As discussed earlier in 1986-87 about 45.59 per cent of the total annual water budget flowed in the month of July. In this month the mean water flow capacity approaches maximum, i.e., 5.645 m^3/sec (Fig. 6.2 A). Water from entire basin flowed at the rate of 487728 m^3/day and the water generating capacity of the land of the Nana Kosi basin to channels was 8867.78 m^3/km^2/day.

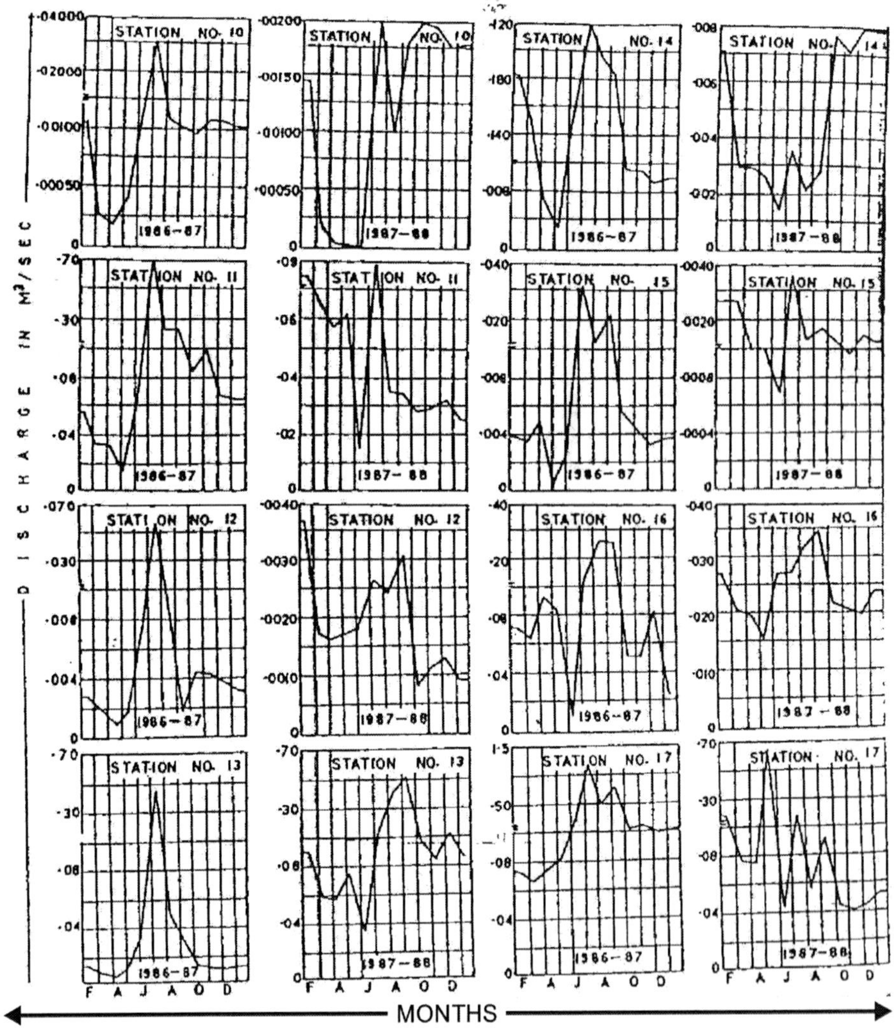

Fig.6.5 : Hydrographs (1986-87 and 1987-88) of hydrological stations no. 10 to 17 of the Nana Kosi watershed, Central Himalaya (See Fig. 1.1 for the location of hydrological stations).

(2) In 1986-87, April was the driest month which contributed 0.44 per cent water only in the total annual runoff. In this month the waterflow dropped up to 0.22 m^3/sec (Fig. 6.2 A). Water from the entire basin flowed at the rate of 4730 m^3/day and the water generating capacity of land to channels was reduced up to 86 m^3/day/km^2 (Table 6.1).

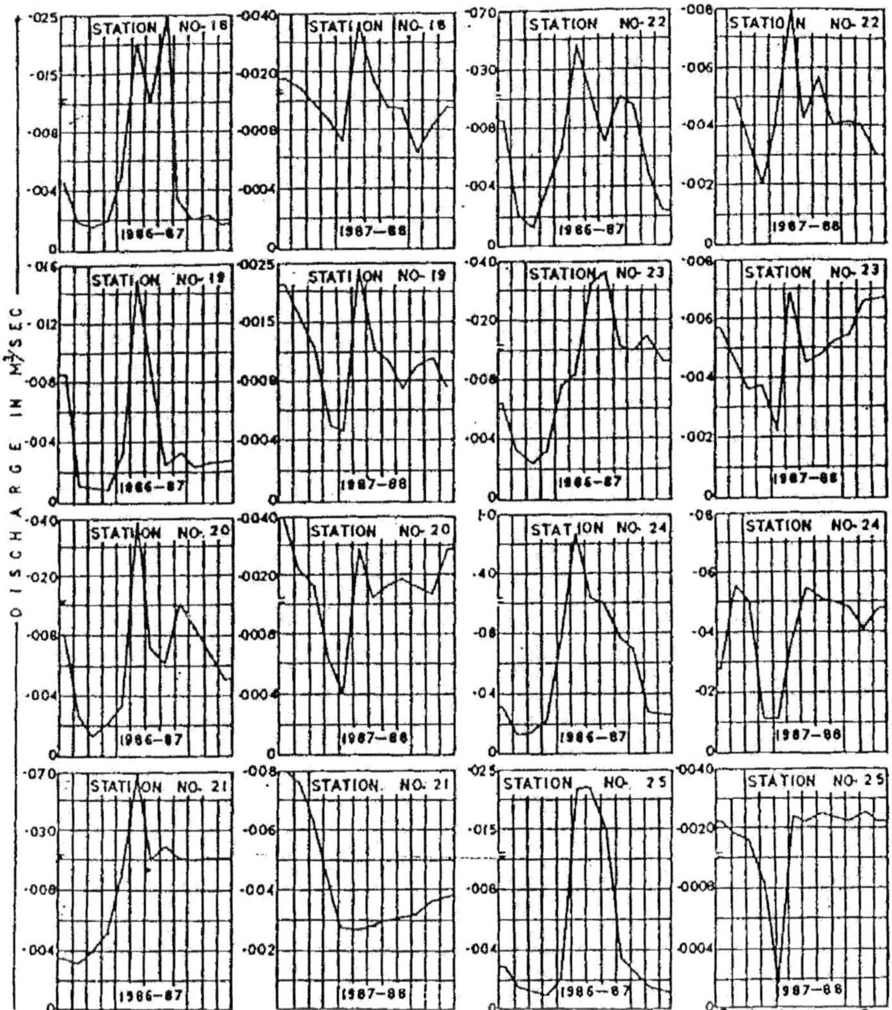

Fig. 6.6 : Hydrographs (1986-87 and 1987-88) of hydrological stations no. 18 to 25 of the Nana Kosi watershed, Central Himalaya (See Fig. 1.1 for the location of hydrological stations).

(3) In 1987-88 about 64.1 per cent of the total annual water budget of the basin flowed in the month of July. In this month waterflow capacity approaches up to 2.2725 m^3/sec (Fig. 6.2 B) water from the entire basin flowed at the rate of 19634.4 m^3/day and the water generating capacity of land to channels was increased up to 3569.9 m^3/km^2/day.

(4) In 1987-88, June was the driest month, which contribution to the total annual runoff was only 1.8 per cent. In this month waterflow concentration was 0.0661 m^3/sec (Fig. 6.2 B), water from the entire catchment flowed at the rate of 5711 m^3/day and the water generating capacity of the land to channels was reduced up to 103.84 $m^3/km^2/day$.

(5) The contribution of different seasons in the total annual water budget varies from 44 to 82.2 per cent in rainy season, 8.3 to 36.5 per cent in summer and 6.9 to 36 per cent in winter at different water-data stations (Table 6.7).

Table 6.7 : Average seasonal contribution of channel runoff flow in per cent, in the study years 1986-87 and 1987-88, at 25 hydrological stations (Fig. 1.1) in the Nana Kosi Basin, Central Himalaya, India

Hydrological Station No.	*Summer Season Feb to May*	*Rainy Season June to Sept*	*Winter Season Oct to Jan*
1	10.9	82.2	6.9
2	25.9	51.7	22.4
3	22.8	61.5	15.7
4	24.5	58.9	16.6
5	21.7	57.0	21.3
6	27.8	53.0	19.2
7	22.2	56.9	20.9
8	15.0	58.1	26.9
9	21.8	53.8	24.4
10	8.3	55.8	35.9
11	28.8	51.8	19.4
12	22.4	60.6	17.0
13	15.8	63.2	21.0
14	22.1	44.8	33.1
15	24.9	53.9	21.2
16	26.5	49.6	23.9
17	36.5	49.2	14.3
18	22.6	60.6	16.8
19	31.6	45.9	22.5
20	26.6	42.0	31.4
21	29.8	43.4	26.8
22	21.3	51.7	27.0
23	19.9	44.2	35.9
24	17.8	56.2	26.0
25	18.7	55.2	26.1

(6) On an average (1986-88), 82.2 per cent of the total annual waterflow, flowed in the rainy season (i.e., June to September). Summer (February to May) and winter (October to January) flows contributed 10.9 and 6.9 per cent, respectively. This is because of

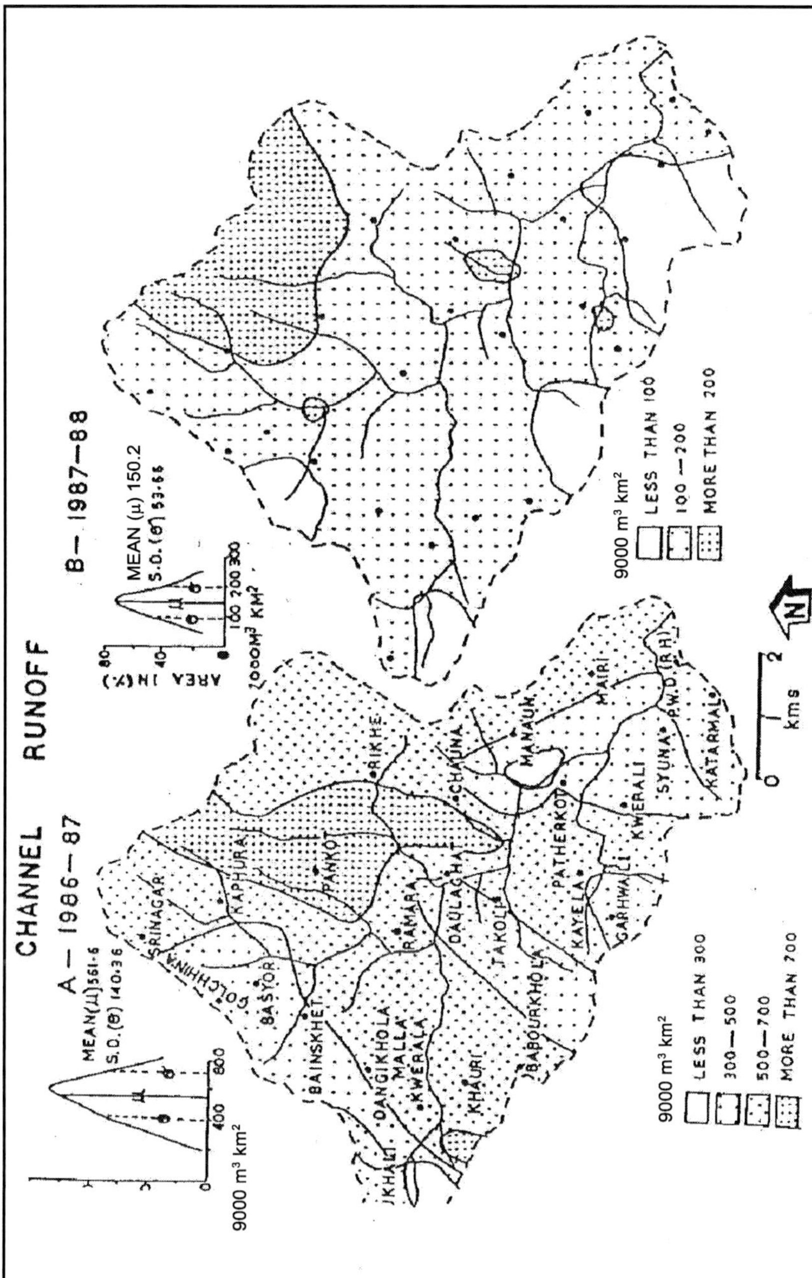

Fig.6.7 : Spatial distribution of water generating capacity of land (in thousand m^3/km^2) to channel runoff in 1986-87 (A) and 1987-88 (B), in the Nana Kosi watershed, Central Himalaya, India.

the higher proportion of overland flow during monsoon rains and low infiltration and small percolation due to the lack of significant vegetation cover in the entire catchment area.

Figure 6.7 shows the spatial distribution of water generating capacity of land to channels. It is based on the annual waterflow capacity of channels in terms of m^3/km^2 (Table 6.1 and 6.2) of 25 different hydrological stations. The map (Fig. 6.7) reveals the following.

(1) In 1986-87, the Nana Kosi catchment area generated water to channels at the mean rate of 561600 $m^3/km^2 \pm 140.36$ s.d. (Fig. 6.7 A) which was drastically reduced more than three times in the drought year (1987-88) when this capacity was only 150200 $m^3/km^2 \pm 53.665$ s. d. (Fig. 6.7 B). Thus drought played a significant role to reduce the water generating capacity of land to channels of the Nana Kosi drainage basin.

(2) In 1986-87, the entire study area was divisible into four groups of different water generating capacity of land, ranging from less than 300000 m^3/km^2 to more than 700000 m^3/km^2 (Fig. 6.7 A) while in 1987-88 it was divisible in three groups of relatively very low water generating capacity, ranging from less than 100000 m^3/km^2 to more than 200000 m^3/km^2.

(3) For two study years (1986-87 and 1987-88) the average rate of waterflow stands at 380621.45 $m^3/km^2/year$. For 1986-87 (normal year) it stands 591801.51 m^3/km^2 and for 1987-88 (drought year) it stands 169441.39 m^3/km^2 (i.e., more than three times lower).

(4) The major causes of the variations in the channels flow and water generating capacity of land to channels in the Nana Kosi watershed is the heterogeneity in landuse pattern within the basin rather than geological, climatic and geomorphic heterogeneities. A detailed account of the control of landuse pattern in channel flow and water generating capacity of land to channel has been presented in Chapter nine.

Hydraulic Geometry of Channels

A stream channel is a narrow trough, shaped by the forces of flowing water to be highly effective in moving the quantities of water and sediment supplies to the stream (Strahler and Strahler, 1983). Depth (D) is measured an any specified point in the stream as the vertical distance from surface to bed. Width (W) is the distance across the stream from one water's edge to the other. The cross-sectional area (A) is the area of a vertical slice across the stream. The wetted perimeter (P) is the length of line of contact between

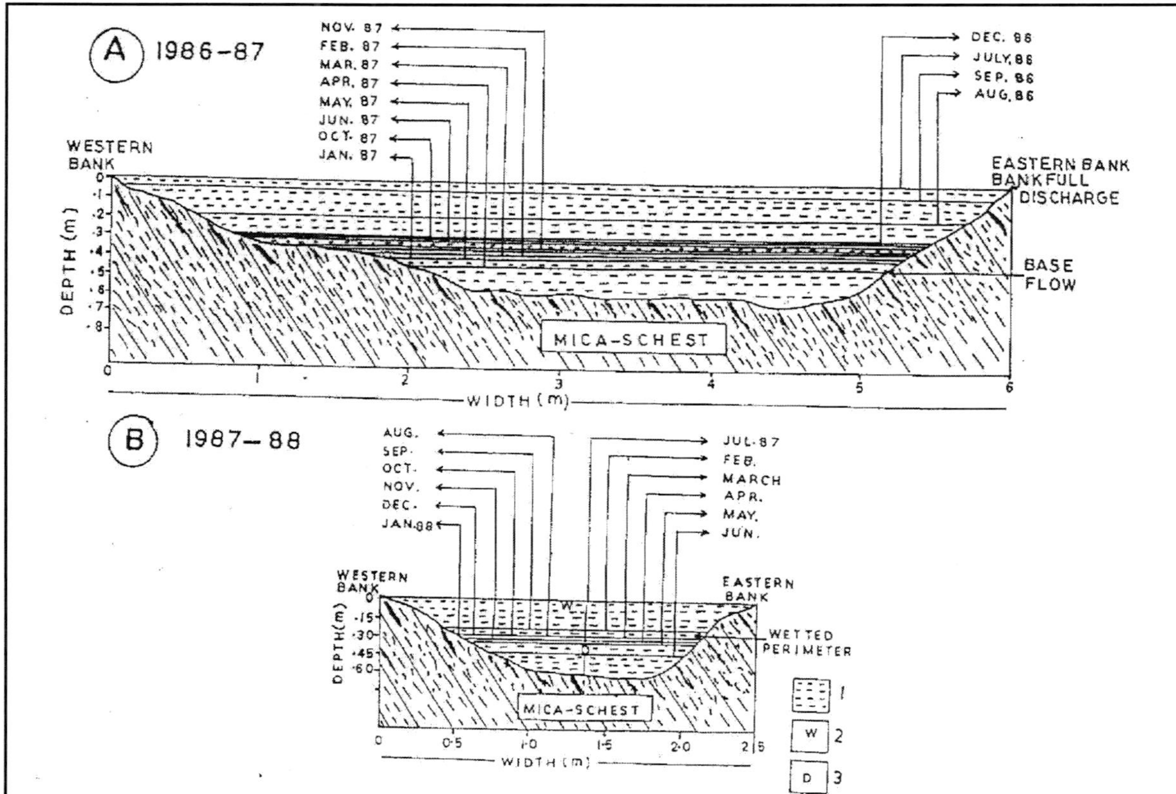

Fig.6.8 : Showing monthwise variations in the hydraulic geometry of cross-section at the outlet (i.e. Hydrological Station no. 1) of the Nana Kosi river. Note the variations in cross-section geometry of 1986-87 and 1987-88 (i.e. drought year). 1=cross-section area in m^2 2= width of cross-section in (m) and 3= depth of cross-section in m

the water and the channel as measured from the cross-section. The rate of fall in altitude of the stream surface in the down stream direction is the stream gradient.

The first step in analyzing the hydraulic geometry of stream channel is to study the changes in channel width, depth, velocity, cross-section area, hydraulic radius of the channel during conditions ranging from low to bankfull discharge (Leopoled and Maddock, 1953). The stream channel characteristics (depth, width, area, velocity and hydraulic radius) vary with discharge as simple power functions as follows (Ruhe, 1975):

$$w = a\,Q\,b$$
$$d = C\,Q\,b$$
$$v = K\,Q\,m$$

where, "w" is water surface width, "d" mean water depth, "v" mean velocity and Q is water discharge. The basic aim of the present section of this chapter is to define the hydraulic geometry of the Nana Kosi River, draining to the crystalline rocks of the Central Lesser Himalaya. The parameters related to the hydraulic geometry of the Nana Kosi stream, included in this study are cross-section width, depth, area, hydraulic radius and velocity of stream. Table 6.8 contains the values of the hydraulic geometry parameters (i.e., width, depth, area, velocity and hydraulic radius) of the Nana Kosi River recorded at the mouth i.e., the Hydrological Station No. 1 during between February 1986 and January 1988).

The hydraulic radius is the ratio of the cross-section area of the channel to its wetted perimeter (i.e., the length of the water channel contact at the cross-section) of the Nana Kosi River at mouth, is found in between 0.08 and 0.43 (Table 6.8) which is always less than the mean depth of the channel. It suggest the Nana Kosi is a very shallow stream.

The Maximum and minimum cross-section width of the Nana Kosi stream is 6.0 m and 0.51 m, respectively. The mean channel depth approaches maximum at 0.77 m and drops up to 0.13 m. The cross-section area of the channel varies in between 3.1 m^2 and 0.7 m^2. The maximum speed of waterflow of this stream stands at 1.83 m/sec and the minimum is 0.22 m/sec (Table 6.8).

The large fluctuations in the parameters of the hydraulic geometry of the Nana Kosi stream is due to the variation in rainfall input in different months and years. Figure 6.8 depicts the hydraulic geometry of two different study years i.e. 1986-87 (Fig. 6.8 A) and 1987-88 (Fig. 6.8 B). the drastic changes in the parameters of the hydraulic geometry (i.e., width, depth, area) in 1987-88 (Fig. 6.8 B) is due to the low rain-input in this year (Total 432 mm) due to drought. On an average the hydraulic geometry was reduced about two times lower in 1986-87 than that of 1986-87 when the total rain input of the year was 1000 mm.

Table 6.8 : Stream Channel Geometry of the Nana Kosi River recorded at its mouth (1986-88)

Date	*Channel Cross-section*				
	Width (m)	*Depth (m)*	*Area (m^2)*	*Velocity (m/sec.)*	*Hydraulic Radius*
28-2-86	1.70	0.32	0.444	0.40125	0.21
29-3-86	1.50	0.29	0.315	0.27600	0.19
30-4-86	1.45	0.20	0.248	0.22100	0.13
29-5-86	1.65	0.25	0.375	0.41900	0.17
30-6-86	3.80	0.36	0.838	0.57900	0.24
30-7-86	6.00	0.77	3.100	1.82100	0.51
29-8-86	5.30	0.55	1.921	0.68000	0.36
29-9-86	6.00	0.66	1.980	1.83300	0.43
30-10-86	1.50	0.38	0.380	0.63900	0.26
29-11-86	1.50	0.34	0.342	0.73300	0.22
30-12-86	1.35	0.39	0.351	0.62200	0.25
28-1-87	1.42	0.25	0.280	0.67700	0.16
28-2-87	1.40	0.31	0.309	0.69700	0.19
29-3-87	1.55	0.26	0.347	0.54800	0.17
30-4-87	1.30	0.23	0.259	0.50200	0.16
30-5-87	0.95	0.21	0.136	0.69700	0.14
28-6-87	0.51	0.13	0.186	0.35600	0.08
30-7-87	2.50	0.60	2.500	0.90900	0.33
30-8-87	1.15	0.27	0.199	0.71600	0.18
29-9-87	1.34	0.24	0.070	0.38900	0.15
28-10-87	1.20	0.21	0.168	0.43000	0.14
29-11-87	1.15	0.20	0.156	0.40700	0.13
30-12-87	1.20	0.22	0.184	0.35000	0.14
30-1-88	1.15	0.23	0.163	0.29300	0.15

Meanders

Winding of natural channels is known as meandering (Chow, 1964). When the stream flow becomes stronger and the load becomes heavier, it starts winding, first cutting at the one bank and than erode at the other. The loss of cutting power makes the stream avoid the obstruction created by its own silt load in its path if it cannot remove it easily. This cause a bend in the river when it goes around such an obstruction. The water current is always stronger and deeper on the outer side of the bend while sediments are deposited at its inner side where water is less deep and flow is slower. The eroded bends starts retreating making the bends shaper until loops are formed.

Regarding the mechanics of the meandering, Chow (1964) has suggested that although the mechanics of meandering is not completely understood at least from variables—valley slope, sediment load, discharge and the characteristics of the bed and bank material are known to control the process of meandering.

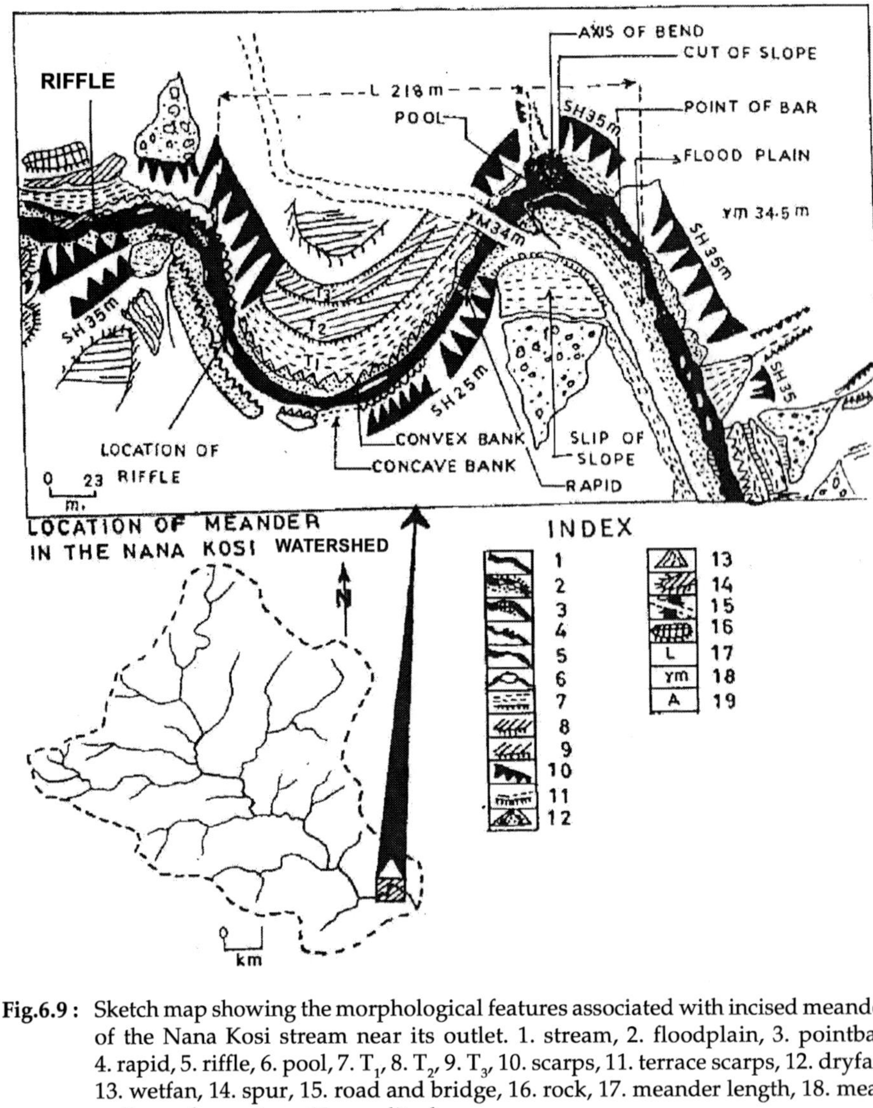

Fig.6.9 : Sketch map showing the morphological features associated with incised meander of the Nana Kosi stream near its outlet. 1. stream, 2. floodplain, 3. pointbar, 4. rapid, 5. riffle, 6. pool, 7. T_1, 8. T_2, 9. T_3, 10. scarps, 11. terrace scarps, 12. dryfan, 13. wetfan, 14. spur, 15. road and bridge, 16. rock, 17. meander length, 18. mean radious of curvature, 19. amplitude.

The master stream of the Nana Kosi drainage basin, viz., the Nana Kosi is flowing in sinuous pattern from village Kaphura and Bainskhet to its mouth. At places the streams makes small and large meanders particularly at Chaunmunia (Plate 15, below), Gewapani (Plate 16, below), south of village Mairi (Fig. 6.9) and near Burusia (Fig. 6.10). These meanders are deeply incised into the bed rocks, indicating the rapid vertical uplift of the area.

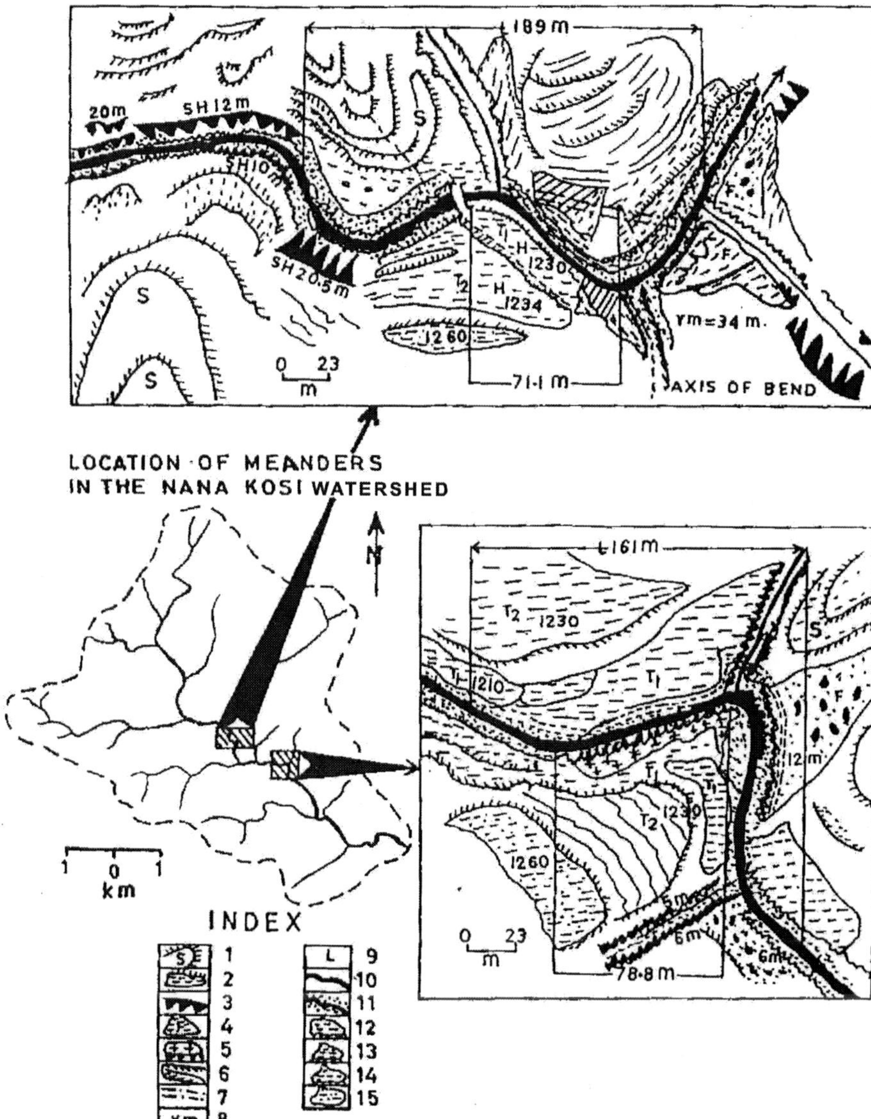

Fig. 6.10 : Sketch map showing the morphological features associated with incised meander in the middle courses of the Nana Kosi river. 1. spur, 2. terraces, 3. scarps, 4. alluvial fan, 5. rock, 6. gully, 7. abandoned valley, 8. mean radius of curvature, 9. meander length, 10. stream, 11. floodplain, 12. T_1, 13. T_2, 14. T_3, 15. T_4.

It has been suggested that the term meandering be restricted to channels exhibiting curves of considerable symmetry (Leopold, *et al.*, 1964). Figure 6.9 and 6.10 depict the shape, size and some geometrical parameters of the Nana Kosi stream's meander in its middle course (Fig. 6.9) and near the mouth (Fig. 6.10). Near the middle course, particularly at Chaunmania, the Nana Kosi stream makes large meander (189 m meander length or wave length) of high amplitude (71 m) and large mean radius (34 m) of curvature (Fig. 6.9). Near the mouth at south of village Mairi, lies the largest meander of the Nana Kosi stream where the meander length, amplitude and average radius of curvature stand at 218 m, 103 m and 50 m, respectively (Fig. 6.10).

Floodplains

Water discharge and sediment transportation in rivers varies greatly in space and time. Water discharge is normally confined below the banks of streams, but during the monsoon rains the channels are unable to contain the water discharge and water and sediment both spill on to and move across the adjacent surfaces. Adjacent to perennial streams these surfaces are "flood plains" which are created by fluvial system specifically to accommodate the larger, less frequent flows. Thus, a river floodplain results from the storage of sediment within and adjacent to the river channel. Two principal processes are involved (Cook and Doornkamp, 1978). The first is the accumulation of sediment, mainly coarse sediment within the river bed or shifting of river channel. Secondly, suspended sediment carried by over bank discharge across the valley floor may settle and provide a further increment of flood plain sediment either generally over the flooded surface or occasionally, locally along the channel margins. The Nana Kosi stream is characterized by narrow patches of floodplain along the channel bank from village Chinauna (near the reach) to mouth. The floodplain of the Nana Kosi stream is composed of coarser sediment by the shifting of stream channel (Plate 20, below, 23 above, 24 below, 22 above) near the mouth and finer sediment in the middle courses particularly at Chaunmunia (Plate 15, below). The width of floodplain along the Nana Kosi stream ranges in between 1 m and 7 m (Fig. 6.9 and 6.10).

Point Bars

Sediment deposited on the slip-off slopes on the inside of meander bends are known as point bars (Fig. 6.9 and 6.10, Plate 15, below). As the stream migrates in the direction of the outside of the bend, the point bars grows and the flood plain deposit is augmented much of the sediment is only temporarily stored in a point bar and it is moved further down stream from time to time by different rainstorms. Thus, the term point bar in geomorphology is applied the bar that develops on the inside of a meander bend (Thornbury, 1954). These point bars are also known as meander bar, meander scroll (Davis, 1913) or Scroll meander (Meltom, 1936). The point

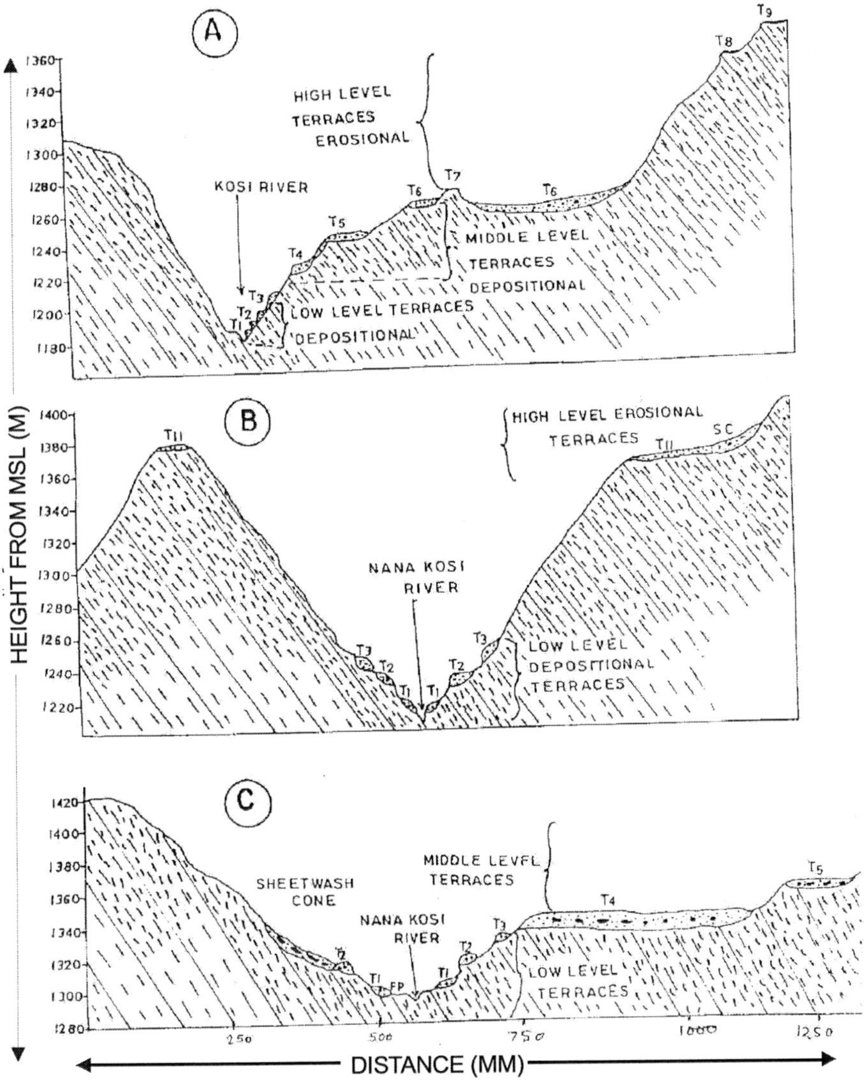

Fig. 6.11 : Cross profile of the Nana Kosi valley showing the associated morphological features. (A) across village Katarmal-Mairi, (B) across village Patharkot-Kotuli and (c) across Takoli-Chauna. T= terrace, SC= sheetwash cone.

bars of the Nana Kosi stream are caused by lateral migration of meanders during flooding. They are very small and composed of coarse sediment (Plate 23, above) and are not mappable even in the small scale. The sketch maps depicts the location of some of the major point bars of the Nana Kosi stream near its middle course (Fig. 6.10) and near the mouth (Fig. 6.9).

River Terraces

A terrace—a feature contained in a valley, is bordered on one side by a higher recognizable valley wall and on the other side by a scarp that desecends to some lower level. A terrace my be bounded on the valley wall side by a higher terrace so that a sequence of stepped surface from the floodplain to the valley wall. Each terrace is like a tread of a staircase and each intervening scarp is like a river (Ruhe, 1975). A terrace is usually a surface form of unconsolidated material carved from valley fill (Tator 1953). Terraces demonstrate episodic formation valley landscapes. They mark previous levels of valley fill and stream planation. Stream regimes changed and the causes of these changes are involved in the interpretation of terraces (Ruhe, 1975). Tectonic movement such as uplift, tilting (Fig. 4.4 A.B.C), faulting or warping regionally or locally cause an increase in stream gradient velocity increases and adjustments occur in the flow system of river an increase in slope causes an increase in width and depth of channel incision. If lateral planation during stream meandering follows channel incision, a surface is cut below the original level and a terrace forms. Several episodes of erosion and deposition caused by successive uplift have produced multiple terraces at different levels in the study area (Fig. 6.12). These terraces are mostly paired. The downstream margins of these terraces are marked either by vertical scarps in case of young depositional terraces or by convex slope—in case of old bedrock terraces (Fig. 6.11).

Following Nakata (1972), terraces (which record the fluvial process of geological past) of the study area may be classified as (i) depositional fluvial terraces and (ii) erosional fluvial terraces (Table 6.9). According to the height of the terraces, they are further divisible in three major (i.e. low, middle and high) and eleven minor levels (Fig. 6.12; Table 6.9). These levels indicate episodes of fluvial processes of the past and that are situated above the present river levels due to rejuvenation of landform. There are distinct differences and even contrasts in structure, origin and environmental conditions through which they were formed, between depositional (i.e., low level and middle level terraces) and erosional (i.e., high level) terraces.

Low Level Terraces—These are depositional terraces. Depositional fluvial terraces are topographic surfaces constructed by accumulation of loads transported by stream which aggravate to get an equilibrium of their course (Nakata, 1972). The low level terraces are covered by alluvium and are further divisible into three minor levels designated as T_1, T_2 and T_3 terraces.

T_1 Terrace : The height of this terrace ranges in between 1 m and 3 m in the study area (Table 6.9). These are in the form of small isolated patches

Table 6.9: Types, levels and height* of the Nana Kosi river terraces, Central Himalaya, India

Name of Place	*Distance from mouth (km)*	*Low Level Terraces*			*Middle Level Terraces*			*High Level Terraces*				
		T_1	T_2	T_3	T_4	T_5	T_6	T_7	T_8	T_9	T_{10}	T_{11}
Mairi	1.2	3	10	15	14	65	85	90	105	165	205	245
Patharkot	3.3	—	8	10	30	50	70	75	100	150	190	230
Kotuli	5.4	—	—	—	25	—	—	70	95	140	180	225
Chauna	6.2	2	6	8	25	45	65	—	90	140	170	220
Daulaghat	7.1	—	5	8	25	30	55	—	95	140	160	220
Bhagoti	8.0	1	2	5	—	—	25	—	60	100	120	140
Type		Depositional			Depositional			Erosional				

* Terrae height in meters from the river bed.

and are discernible particularly at Mairi (Plate 23, above), Patharkot, Chauna (Plate 15, below) Sunidhar (Plate 15, above) and Bagar. This terrace is composed of pebbles and cobbles of quartzites and mica-schist (Plate 26, below). This is the lowest topographic level of the terraces.

T_2 Terrace : The height of this terrace ranges in between 2 m and 10 m in the study area (Table 6.9). These terraces are also in the form of small isolated patches and are discernible particularly at Mairi (Plate 23, above), Chauna (Plate 15, below), Sunidhar (Plate 15, above) Daulaghat and Bagar. These terraces are composed of pebbles and cobbles of quartzites and mica-schist.

T_3 Terrace : The height of T_3 terrace ranges in between 5 m and 15 m in the study area (Table 6.9). This terrace is discernible particularly at basur (Plate 13, above), Chinuna (Plate 13, below), mairi (Plate 21, below), Patharkot, Chauna, Daulaghat and Bagar in the Nana Kosi basin. This is the highest topographic level of the low level terraces.

Middle Level Terraces—The middle level of terraces are covered by a thin layer of alluvium underlain by mica-schist rocks. The height of middle level terraces ranges in between 14 m and 85 m in the study area and are further divisible into three minor levels, i.e., T_4, T_5 and T_6.

T_4 Terrace : This is the lowest topographic level of the middle level terraces. The height of this terrace ranges in between 25 m and 45 m in the study area (Table 6.9). these are in the form of large patches (Fig. 6.11 C) and are discernible particularly at Gewapani (Plate 16, below) Chaunmunia (Plate 15, above), Mairi (Plate 20, above) Patharkot and Daulaghat. These terraces are composed of small pebbles and cobbles of quartzites and mica-schist (Plate 25, below and 26 above). At places the alluvium from this terrace have been completely washout by erosional processes (Plate 32).

T_5 Terrace : The height of T_5 terrace ranges in between 30 m and 65 m (Table 6.9). This terrace is discernible particularly at Gewapani (Plate 16, below), Chauna (Plate 15, above), Sunidhar and Daulaghat. This terrace is composed of a thin layer of pebbles and cobbles of quartzites (Plate 25, above).

T_6 Terrace : The height of this terrace ranges in between 25 m and 85 m in the study area (Table 6.9). T_6 terrace is covered by a thin layer of alluvium underlain by mica-schist rocks and discernible particularly at Mairi, Syona (Plate 3, below), Kotuli (Plate 16, below), Chauna, and Sunidhar (Plate 15, above) Daulaghat and Bagar.

High Level Terraces—The high level terraces of the Nana Kosi watershed are surfaces without alluvium. These are known as erosional terraces (Nakata, 1972). According to Bloom (1979) such type of flat surface caused by river erosion are known as bedrock terraces and are indicator of the rapid vertical uplift of the area (Leopold, et al. 1964). The height of high level terraces ranges in between 60 m and 245 m and are further divisible into five minor levels of terraces, i.e., $T_{7,}$ $T_{8,}$ $T_{9,}$ T_{10} and T_{11}.

T_7 Terrace : This is the lowest topographic level of the erosional or high level terraces. The height of this terrace ranges in between 70 m and 90 m in the study area (Table 6.9). This terrace is in the form of small flat surface of bed-rocks caused by river erosion and is locally known as "Dak". This bedrock terrace is discernible particularly at Mairi (Fig. 6.11 A), Panjgaon (Plate 9, above), Patharkot (Plate 6) and Kotuli (Plate 16, above).

T_8 Terrace : The height of this terrace ranges in between 60 m and 105 m (Table 6.9). This is the flat surface caused by river erosion. T_8 terrace is discernible particularly at Mairi (Fig. 6.11 A). Patharkot (Plate 2), Chauna, Daulaghat and Bagar.

T_9 Terrace : The height of T_9 terrace ranges in between 100 m and 165 m (Table 6.9). These are also in the form of flat surface of bedrocks caused by river erosion. T_9 terrace is discernible particularly at Mairi (Fig. 6.11 A) Patharkot (Plate 2), Chauna, Kotuli, Daulaghat and Bagar.

T_{10} Terrace : The height of this terrace ranges in between 120 m and 205 m (Table 6.9). This is also in the form of isolated flat surface and is discernible particularly at Mairi. Patharkot (Plate 2), Kotuli, Chauna, Daulaghat and Bagar.

T_{11} Terrace : This is the highest topographic level of terraces of the study area. The height of this terrace ranges in between 140 m and 245 m (Table 6.9). T_{11} terrace is discernible particularly ar Mairi, Patharkot (Plate 2), Kotuli (Fig. 6.11 B), Chauna Daulaghat and Bagar.

Alluvial Fans

Alluvial fans are not fairly common landforms in the Nana Kosi watershed because the tributary streams of the Nana Kosi are mainly ungraded. At places, at the mouth of few graded ephemeral rills, very small alluvial fans may be seen. For Example, rills draining to Kutuli-Manaun spur and rills draining to Pajgaon spur have small alluvial fans at their mouth. These fans are composed of fine gravel and sand and at most places they are wet—locally known as "Simar". The width and length of these fans in the Nana Kosi watershed ranges in between 20-80 m and 50-150 m, respectively.

Rapids and Waterfalls

Portion of a stream with accelerated current where it descends rapidly but without a break in the slope of bed sufficient to form a waterfall are known as rapids. Portion of a stream with accelerated current where it

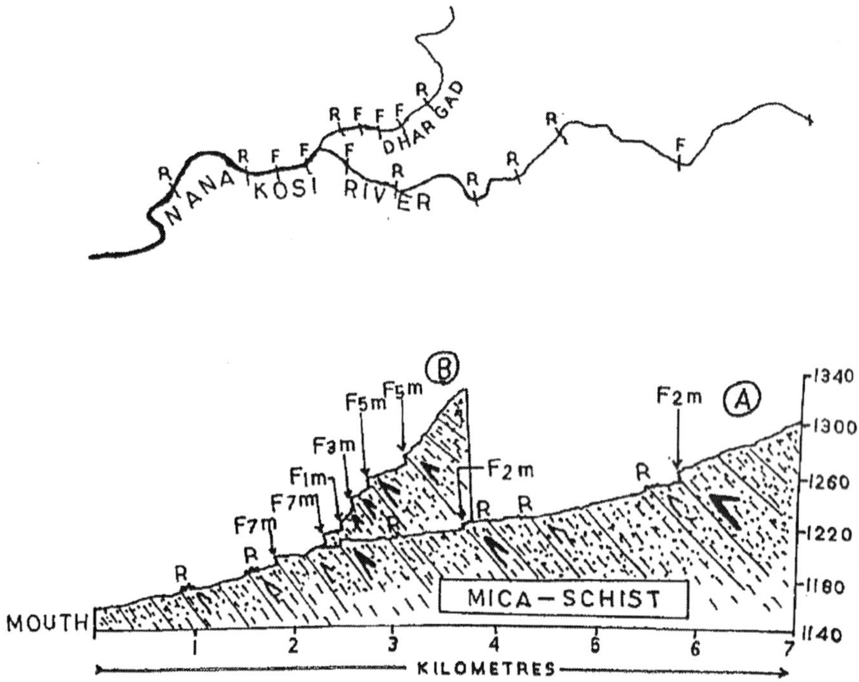

Fig. 6.12 : Interruption of the Nana Kosi stream and its tributary stream's long profile is frequently marked by rapids and waterfalls. *Note* : These interruptions at various places is without the presence of resistant rocks and are caused by vertical movements as indicated : (A) long profile of the Nana Kosi river, (B) long profile of the Dhar Gad.

falls abruptly with a vertical break in the slope of bed are known as waterfall (Fig. 6.12).

The interruption of the Nana Kosi and its tributary stream's long profile is frequently marked by rapids and waterfall (Fig. 6.12). The maximum height of the waterfall in the study area is found at the mouth of tributary stream (viz., Dhar Gad) i.e. at Goban (Plate 33, below). Upstream the confluence of the Dhar Gad and the Nana Kosi, there are as many as 6 waterfalls and number of rapids in the course of tributary stream, i.e., Dhar Gar, up to Bari of relatively lower height (Plate 33, 31, 30 above and 29, below). The height of waterfalls within the study area ranges in between 2 and 7 m.

The genetics of the rapids and waterfalls of the lithologically homogeneous area like the Nana Kosi watershed cannot be explained by the general principle that the interruption of river's long profile by a resistant bend of rock is frequently marked by waterfalls or rapids. The river is unable to erode the outcrops as easily as adjacent softer beds and the area immediately downstream from the interruption is worn to a lower level to cause a waterfall (Pritchard, 1979). The longitudinal profiles of the Nana Kosi and its major tributary, viz., Dhar Gad (Fig. 6.12) depict that these are interrupted at various places without the presence of any resistance bend. The interruptions, causing rapids and fall all along the courses of the Nana Kosi stream are genetically tectonic. Each interruption in the longitudinal profiles of the streams is associated with relative displacement of blocks (Fig. 6.12) due to faulting activities along the dip-plane (see Chapter four).

REFERENCES

Anderson, L.R., Keaton, J.R. and Brooks, R.K. 1985 : Swale formation, soil development and variation in hydraulic conductivity at a landslide in the Wasatch Range near Farmington, *Utah : EOS American Geophysical Union Transactions*, 66, p. 900.

Bloom, A.L. 1979 : *Geomorphology : A systematic analysis of Late Cenozoic landforms.* Prentice Hall of India, Pvt. Ltd., New Delhi, pp. 16-170.

Bogucki, D.J. 1976 : Debris slides in the Mt. LeConte area, Great Smoky Mountains National Park, USA. *Geografiska Annaler*, 58, pp. 179-191.

Bogucki, D.J. 1977 : Debris slide hazards in the Adirondack province of New York State. *Environmental Geology*, 1, pp, 317-328.

Bradshaw, M.J. Abbdt, A.J. and Gelsthorpe, A.P. 1978 : *The Earth's changing surface.* The English Language Book Society and Hodder and Stoughton, pp. 1-336.

Chow, V.T. 1964 : *Handbook of applied hydrology.* McGraw-Hill, New York, pp. 1424-1431.

Clark, G.M. 1973 : Appalachian debris slide-debris flow characteristics and distribution south of the glacial border : Actualization of knowledge in mapping high risk sites. *Geol. Soc. Amer. Abstracts with Programs*, 5, pp. 386-387.

Cook, R.V. and Doornkamp, J.C. 1978 : *Geomorphology in Environmental Management.* Clarendon Press, Oxford, pp. 1-105.

Davis, W.M. 1913 : Meandering valleys and underfit rivers. Assoc. Am. Geog. Anns., 3, pp. 3-28.

Dietrich, W.E. and Dunne, T. 1978 : Sediment budget for a small catchment in mountaneous terrain. *Zeitschrift fur Geomorphologic, suppl.* 29, pp. 191-206.

Ellen, S., Peterson, D.M. and Reid, G.O. 1983 : Map showing areas susceptible to different hazards from shallow landsliding; Marin Country and adjacent parts of Sonoma Country, California. U.S. Geological Survey Miscellaneous Field Studies Map, MF-1406.

Hack, J.T. 1965 : Geomorphology of the Shenandoah Valley, Virginia and West Virginia and origin of the residual ore deposits. *U.S. Geol. Surv. Proof. Paper-484*, p. 84.

Hack, J.T. and Goodlett, J.C. 1960 : Geomorphology and forest ecology of a mountain region in the Central Appalachians. *U.S. Geol. Surv. Prof. Paper-347*, p. 66.

Hollingsworth, R. and Kovacs, G.S. 1981 : Soil slumps and debris flows, Prediction and Protection. *Bull. Asso. Engin. Geol.*, 18, pp. 17-28.

Horton, R.E. 1945 : Erosional development of streams and their drainage basin, a hydro-physical approach. *Bull. Geol., Soc., Am.*, 56, pp. 48-95.

Jacobson, R.B. 1985 : *Spatial and Temporal Distribution of Slope Processes in the Upper Buffalo Creek drainage basin,* Marion Country, West Virginia (Ph. D. thesis). Baltimore, John Hopkins University, p. 484.

Johnson, A.M. 1984 : *Debris flow, in Brunsden, in slope instability,* Prior, D.B. (eds.), New York, John Wiley & Sons, pp. 257-361.

Johnson, K.A. and Sitar, N. 1986 : Techniques for identification of source areas for debris flows. Berkeley, Deptt. of Civil Engin. Uni. of California, Report No. UCB/GT/86-01, p. 38.

Keaton, J.R., Anderson, L.R. and Brooks, R.K. 1985 : Geomorphology, geometry and evidence for recurrence of slope failures in steep swales in metamorphic rock filled with colluvial and residual soil debris in the Wasatch Range near Farmington, *Utah. EOS Amer. Geoph. Union Trans.*, 16, p. 900.

Kojan, E., Foggin, T.G. III and Rice, R.M., 1972 : Prediction and analysis of debris avalanche incidence by photogrammetry, Santa Ynez Mountains, California. In *24th Intern. Geol. Cong,* section 13, pp. 124-131.

Lehre, A.K. 1981 : Sediment budget of a small California Coast Range drainage basin near San Francisco. In Davies, T.R.H. and Pearce, A.J. (eds.), *Erosion and sediment transport in Pacific Rim steep-land.* Intern. Assoc. of Hydro. Sci., Pub. No. 132, pp. 123-139.

Lehre, A.K. 1982 : *Sediment mobilization and production from a small mountain catchment : Loan Tree Creek,* Marin Country, California (Ph. D. thesis). Berkeley University of California at Berkeley, p. 320.

Leopoled, L.B., Wolman, M.G. and Miller, J.P. 1964 : *Fluvial processes in geomorphology.* Freeman, San Francisco, pp. 1-522.

Lessing, P., Kulander, B.R.,Wilson, B.D., Dean, S.L. and Woodring, S.M. 1976 : West Virginia landslides and slide prone areas. *West Virginia Geol. and Eco. Surv. Environ. Geol. Bulletin* 15, p. 64.

Melton 1936 : An empirical classification of flood plain streams, *Geog. Rev.*, 26, pp. 593-609.

Nakata, T. 1972 : *Geomorphic study and crustal movements of the foothills of the Himalayas.* Inst. of Tohoku University Sendai, pp. 1-177.

O' Laughlin, C.L. 1972 : A preliminary study of landslides in the coast Mountains of southwestern British Columbia, in Slaymaker, H.O., and McPherson, H.J. eds., *Mountain geomorphology: Geomorphological processes in the Canadian Cordillera.* Vancouver, Tantalus Research, pp. 101-111.

Pierson, T.C. 1977 : *Factors controlling debris-flow initiation on forested hillslopes in the Oregon Coast Range* (Ph.D. thesis). Seattle, Univ of Washington, p. 166.

Pomeroy, J.S. 1981 : Strom-induced debris avalanching and related phenomena in the Johnstown area, Pennsylvania with reference to other studies in the Appalachians. *U.S. Geol. Surv. Prof. paper-1191*, p. 22.

Pomeroy, J.S. 1982 : Geomorphic effects of the July 19-20, 1977, strom in a part of the Little Conemaugh River area, northeast of Johnstown, Pennsylvania. *North-eastern Geology*, 4, pp. 1-9.

Pomeroy, J.S. 1984 : Strom induced slope movements at East Brady, Pennsylvania. *U.S. Geol. Surv. Bulletin 1618*, p. 16.

Pritchard, J.M. 1979 : *Landforms and landscape in Africa.* Edward Arnold, Ltd. London, pp. 46-67.

Rawat, J.S. 1987 : Modeling of water and sediment budget; concepts and strategies. Geomorphological models, theoretical and empirical aspects, CATENE, *A Cooperating Jour. Intern. Soc. of Soil Sci., Supplement 10,* pp. 147-159.

Rawat, J.S. 1988 : Anthropogenic transformations of channel network capacity, an experimental study in Kumaun Himalaya. *Proc. of Indian Nat. Sci. Acad.*, 54 (4), pp. 605-615.

Reneau, S.L. and Dietrich, W.E. 1985 : Landslide recurrence intervals in colluvium mantled hollows, Marin Country, California. *EOS Amer. Geophy. Uni. Trans.*, 66, pp. 1-900.

Reneau, S.L. and Dietrich, W.E. 1987 : The Importance of Hollows in Debris Flow Studies, Examples from Marin Country. *California Geol. Soc. of Ame. Reves. Enginee. Geol.* 7, pp. 165-180.

Ruhe, R.V. 1975 : *Geomorphology, geomorphic processes and surfacial geology.* Houghton Mifflin Co., Boston, pp. 1-266.

Smith, T.C. 1984 : Delineating Areas Susceptible to Debris Avalanches and Debris Flows Near Pacifica. *California Geol. Soc. Ame. Abstracts with Programs*, 16, p. 661.

Strahler, A.N. 1973 : *Introduction to physical geography.* John Wiley & Sons, New York, pp. 300-317.

Swanson, F.J. and Roach, C.J. 1985 : Frequency of debris avalanches from clearcut hollows, Siuslaw River basin Oregon. *EOS Amer. Geophy. Uni. Trans.*, 66, pp. 1-900.

Swanson, F.J., Swanson, M.M. and Woods, C. 1981 : Analysis of debris-avalanche erosion in steep forest lands, an example from Mapleton, Oregon, USA. In Davies, T.R.H. and Pearce, A.J. (eds.) *Erosion and sediment transport in Pacific Rim steeplands.* Intern. Assoc. of Hydro. Sci., Pub., No. 132, pp. 67-75.

Swanston, D.N. 1967 : Soil-water peizometry in a southeast Alaska landslide area. U.S. Forest Service, Pacific Northwest Forest and Range Experiment Station Research Note, PNW-68, p. 17.

Swanston, D.N. 1969 : Mass-wasting in Coastal Alaska : U.S. Forest Service, Pacific Northwest Forest and Range Experiment Station Research Paper PNW-83, p. 15.

Talor, B.A. 1953 : Pediment characteristics and terminology. *Assoc. Am. Geog. Anus,* 42, pp. 293-317.

Thornbury, W.D. 1954 : *Principles of geomorphology.* John Wiley & Sons, New York, pp. 35-36.

Tsukamoto, Y. 1973 : Study on the growth of stream channel (1) Relation between stream channel growth and landslides occurring during heavy strom. *Shin-Sabo,* 25, pp. 4-13.

Williams, G.P. and Guy, H.P. 1971 : Debris avalanches—a geomorphic hazard. In Coates, D.R., ed., *Environmental geomorphology State* Uni. of New York Publications in Geomorphology, Binghamton, N. Y., pp. 25-46.

Williams, G.P. and Guy, H.P. 1973 : Erosional and depositional aspects of hurricane Camille in Virginia, 1969 : *U.S. Geol. Survey Prof. Paper-804,* p. 88.

Woodruff, J.F. 1971 : Debris avalanches as an erosional agent in the Appalachian Mountains. *Journ. of Geog.*, 70, pp. 399-406.

Plates

Plate 1 : There are 58.5 km long roads in the Nana Kosi Watershed. Every kilometer stretch of the road generated about 234x10^4 cubic meters of debris during construction and at present every kilometer is generating 64.87 cubic meters of debris due to landsliding each year. Photo near Gewapani (above) and Mairi (below in the Kosi-Daulaghat road. Note road induce debris downslope killing ground cover, scrubs and trees.

Plate 2 : The middle (T_6) and high level (T_7, T_8, T_9 and T_{10}) terraces at village Patharkot. Locally these terraces are known as "Dak" such as Sat Dak (T_7 Terrace). The middle level terrace (T_6) is capped by a thin layer of alluvium (see Plate-25 above). Note the deforested rocky hills (above) and settlements made of local material (below).

Plate 3 : The middle level terrace (T_6) at Mairi village capped by a thin layer of alluvium (above) and remnant of T_6 terraces at top of convex hill slope at Syuna village (below). *Note* the scattered pine forest (above) and linear settlement pattern (below).

Plate 4 : Block failures in the study area are confined at the downthrown block of the reverse faults along the dip plane trending NW-SE. Photo at patharkot along Patharkot-Kayala Reverse Fault (F = Fault, DW = down thrown block up = upthrown block).

Plate 5 : Active rockfall (above, photo near Golchhina) and debris fall (below, photo near Katarmal). The former is confined mainly at the foot of closely spaced jointed and fragmented quartzites while the second, at the foot of largely jointed, crushed and sheared fault scarps of quartzites (F = Fault, FA= Fault Apron—genetically such debris cones are known as fault apron

Plate 6 : Old debris fans (DF), degraded by slumping at Jyoli. These are largely dissected by gully erosion and modified by man for cultivation. Note wide col (C) on the crest at Jyoli (above).

Plate 7 : Geomorphic features associated with Patharkot-Kayela reverse fault. Vertical scarp overlooking to fault (F) at Bari (below); large zone of block failure (BF) on the anti-dip slope at Gazol (above). DC= Road induced debris cones. H= Hollows.

Plate 8 : Vertical scarps and waterfall in the tributary stream of the Nana Kosi at one kilometer upstream from the mouth of the Nana Kosi stream (above). Scarps, triangular facet over looking the Nana Kosi stream (below). Note the floodplain, T_1 - terrace and ungraded tributary stream of the Nana Kosi (Below).

Plate 9 : Col (C) at the northeastern water divide at the elevation of T_7 (high level) terrace at Pajgaon (above). Deeply incised gully on the sheetwash fan (SF) deposition near Korechhina (below). Note the upslope extension of agricultural terraces (below)

Plate 10 : The steep triangular facet (TF) overlooking the Golchhina-Kathpuria Fault (above). Strike-slip fault on the Paikham ridge (below). The dip-slope (DS) is subject for frequent rockfall and continuous debris flow (below).

Plate 11 : The triangular fault facet (TF) overlooking the Korichhina Fault (F) (above). Small butle capped by a remnant of the resistant quartzite bed in the gentle dipping mica-schist above village Gully (below). Note the abandoned agriculture fields on debris fan (below).

Plate 12 : A series of triangular fault facets on the upthrown block of the Gulli Fault (F) at village Gulli and sheetwash fan (SF) (above). Fold controlled small ridges (FR) and large sheetwash fans (SF) largely dissected by gully erosion, near village Nakuta (below).

Plate 13 : Largely dissected sheetwash fans and debris flow in the upper reaches of the Nana Kosi i.e. at Basyur (above) and Chinuna (below). These fans are underlain by thick mantle of regolith (see Plate 27).

Plate 14 : Late mature topography and large sheetwash fans in the upper reaches of the Nana Kosi stream largely dissected by gullies and modified by man, photo near Golchhina (above), and Bainskhet (below). Both the valleys are of third order streams.

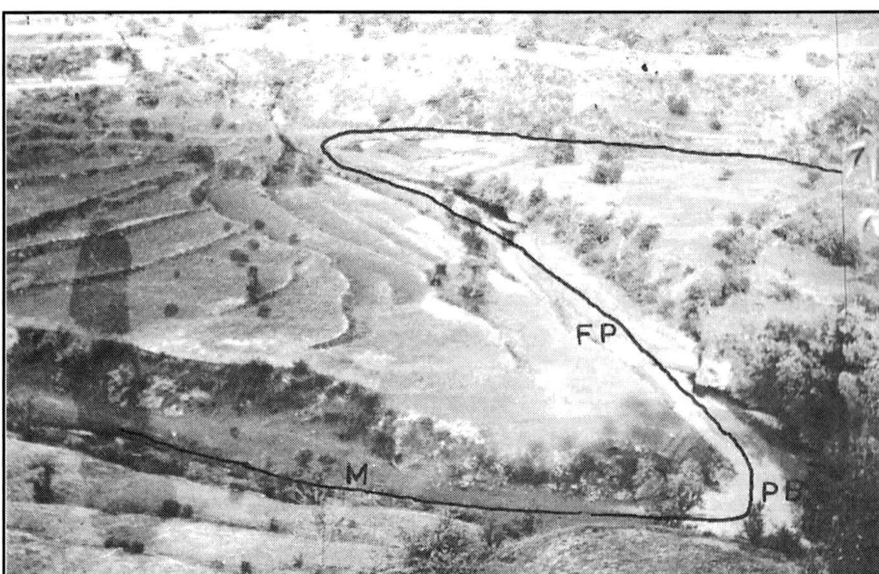

Plate 15 : The low level (T_1) and middle level terraces (T_4, T_5 and T_6) at Chaunmunia (above) and Sunia Dhar (below). *Note* the well developed meander (M) flood plain (FP) and point bar (PB) of the Nana Kosi stream (below).

Plate 16A : The middle level terrace (T_6) capped by alluvium and modified by man on both sides of the Nana Kosi stream at Patharkot and Kotuli villages. On back slope of this terrace at Kotuli is the Cuesta (cu) on the homoclinal ridge (HR) characterized by hollows (H).

Plate 16B : The T_4 and T_5 terraces at Gewapani are modified by man for cultivation; M = meander, SV = strike valley, DC = man induced cones.

Plate 17 : The middle course of the Nana Kosi stream-7 km down-stream from the reach, is deeply incised, the valley banks are characterized by large tension cracks due to gradual creeping caused by valley deeping (above) and the stream bed is filled by large blocks (below).

Plate 18 : Further downstream (Plate-17) deep incision of Nana Kosi stream (above) and large tension crack due to gradual creeping caused by valley deeping (below). *Note* hear the Nana Kosi stream is crossing the Patharkot Manaun reverse upthrown fault zone.

Plate 19 : Waterfall plung-pool, canyon and pot holes of the Nana Kosi stream near Churani (above), vertical scarp on the northern bank of Nana Kosi stream 3.5 km upstream the mouth (below).

Plate 20 : T_3 and T_4 terraces, abandoned valley (AV)- 1.5 km upstream the mouth of the Nana Kosi (above). Wide valley of Nana Kosi stream along the strike plane, viz. strike valley 1.25 km upstream the mouth (below).

Plate 21 : The Nana Kosi stream flowing on bedrock across the strike plane, 1.15 km upstream the mouth of Nana Kosi (above). Low level of terraces (T_1, T_2, T_3) of the Nana Kosi stream- 1.10 km upstream mouth. *Note* the road induced landslides (below).

Plate 22 : Triangular facets (TF) and floodplain (FP) along the Nana Kosi stream, 1 km upstream the mouth of the Nana Kosi. Note the ungraded tributary valleys. *Note* the widely spaced jointed quartzites without debris flow at base overlain by mica-schist rock (below).

Plate 23 : Floodplain (FP) and T_1 terrace, hollow (H) and point bar at the confluence of the Nana Kosi and its tributary viz. Mairi Gad (above). Three level of the low level terraces (T_1, T_2, T_3) overlain by debris cone (DC), 0.65 km upstream the mouth (below).

Plate 24: Water-data station No. 1 (W-D 1) at the mouth of the Nana Kosi (above) and the confluence of Nana Kosi and Kosi river (below). *Note* the graded confluence and flood plain (FP) (below).

Plate 25 : Vertical exposure of the middle level terrace (T_5) at Patharkot (above). Vertical exposure of the middle level terrace (T_4) at Gewapani (below).

Plate 26 : Vertical exposure of T_4 terrace at Mairi showing the thin layer of alluvium underlain by regolith (above). Vertical exposure of low level terrace (T_1) at Mairi showing the graded horizon of alluvium (below).

Plate 27 : Thick mantals of regolith in the upper courses of the Nana Kosi stream valley, photo near Galli village.

Plate 28 : Thick mantals of regolith in the upper courses of the Nana Kosi stream valley, photo near village Basyur.

Plate 29 : Dhar Gad, one of the major tributaries of the Nana Kosi originates from wide valley characterized by erosional environment (above). The valley becomes deeper and deeper downstream and stream forms waterfall and rapids when it crosses the reverse fault (below) waterfall at Bari.

Plate 30 : Waterfall further downstream, Plate-29 below (above). The channel (Dhar Gad) flows in graded pattern downstream (Plate-30 above) after crossing the fault plane (below).

Plate 31 : One km downstream from (Plate-30 above) viz, at Laterau, passes another reverse fault and the Dhar Gad stream again forms small waterfall (above), rapid and pool (below).

Plate 32 : Downstream from Plate-31, the channel forms meanders and valley banks are characterized by terrace (T_4), locally these terraces are known as "Dak". *Note* steep triangular facet along a transverse fault, viz. Syona Fault dissected by rills, Ghunphau "Dak" (T_4) and convex hill spur (below).

Plate 33 : Near the confluence of Dhar Gad and the Nana Kosi at Dugardeo passes, another reverse fault. Dhar Gad flows across the fault from overriding block and forms rapids and pool before reaching the fault plane (above) and 7 m high waterfall on the fault plane (below).

Plate 34 : Anti- dip slope of the Patherkot-Manaun homoclinal ridge dissected by rills (R) in the midcrest and hollows (H) at crest (below). Note one of the major reverse faults (F) passes from this ridge extending SE-NW. The overriding block of this fault, i.e., above the fault line is composed of mica- schist while the underlaying block is composed of highly weathered and friable mica-schist.

7

Anthropogenic Landscape

Introduction

Man in a modern technological society is an important geomorphic agent, producing many new landforms. Man's activities have been responsible for the production of highly distinctive landforms of both erosional (excavational) and depositional (constructional) origin (Bradshaw, *et al.*, 1978). Environmental geomorphology brings together and unifies several branches of natural science for the purpose of understanding the relationship of man to his natural environment. Man interacts with his environment with a shallow layer—the life layer, laying at the contact between the atmosphere and the landsurface. This contact zone known as "interfaces" (Strahler, 1973) experience intense activity in the form of exchanges of energy and matter. Man participates in the processes of the life layers. Energy and matter are stored in organic matters, later to be released to the physical environment. Environmental geomorphology is thus, a study of working an environment that not only nourishes and stimulates life processes, but also places constraints and limitation upon these processes.

Highlighting on man's role to interfere in the environment, Strahler (1973) has remarked that not only does man respond to the times of the environment but man in turns acts upon and modifies environmental processes and forms. He has further stated that man creates many forms of environmental degradation and pollution. With enormous quality of energy at his disposal, man is capable of severely damaging or destroying natural features of the environment and their ecosystems. The purpose of environmental geomorphology is to recognize man's impact upon the environment and particularly to investigate man's impacts on various environmental systems i.e., hydrological, geohydrological, geochemical and ecological, etc. Such knowledge can be put to use intelligently for landuse planning and various management and development of resources.

Man's Interference in Geomorphic System

Recent geomorphic studies (Cooke and Doornkamp, 1978; Singh, 1985; Rawat, 1985, 1987, 1988; Rawat and Rawat, 1994 a, 1994 b; Rawat *et al.*, 1992; Rawat, 1991, 1992, 1997 a, 1997 b, 1997 c, 1999; Rawat and Rawat, 1986; Rawat and Rawat, 1998; Rawat *et al.*, 1992, 1995; Rawat and Haigh, 1998; Rawat *et al.*, 1999; Haigh *et al.*, 1993 a, 1993 b, 1995; Gregory and Walling, 1973; Ives, 1985; Striffer, 1985; Singh and Singh, 1985; Misra, 1985; Gupta and Arora, 1985; Tewari *et al.*, 1985; Pande, 1985; Chaturvedi, 1985; Jalal, 1985; Bhandari and Gupta, 1985; Haigh *et al.*, 1987, 1989; Bichsel *et al.*, 1983; Collier, 1970; Doughlas, 1973; Glymph, and Holton, 1969; Haugen and Brown, 1971; Jacks and Whyle, 1939; Mellen, 1977, 1986; Shastry *et al.*, 1986; Wright, 1972) have shown the geomorphic systems are being transformed rapidly by various anthropogenic and technogenic activities on the earth surface. They reveal that any interference by man, whether it be deliberate or accidental, can set in motion a sequence of events that man extend throughout the whole system. Many of man's activities occurred within a drainage basin. When construction works, deforestation, cultivation, mining, etc., take place large scale changes are induced within the catchment both in terms of its hydrological characteristics and its sediment yield. When new ground is broken for road construction, agriculture and mining—vegetation is removed. Runoff and storm flow increase, land erosion is accelerated and the sediment load of the streams is often dramatically increased (Chapter nine). Valdiya (1985) has calculated that the construction of 44,000 km long roads in the Himalayan region has generated 2.650 x 10^6 m^3 of debris. One kilometer of road produces 550 m^3 of debris from landslides and rock falls annually. As a result about 24 x 10^6 m^3 of debris slides down the slopes each year removing vegetation, smothering springs and chocking mountain streams.

A large part of the Indian Himalaya has been deforested. Pathak (1983) suggested that in the catchment areas of the Central Himalaya 70 per cent of the total rainwater was used in denudation processes. In the deforested catchments excluding the evaporation loss the entire the rain input was available to the soil for denudational processes. Stripped off the protective vegetal cover, the Himalayan soils lose their capacity to absorb rainwater which instead runoff on the surface resulting in the damaging floods in the plains. Since little water percolates the hillsprings dry up. Deforestation resulting from overgrazing by an explosively large population of cattle and reckless exploitation of forest for fuel timber and fodder has reduced the protective vegetal cover to a mere 35 per cent of the surface area, thus exposing about 65 per cent of the ground to erosive forces (Valdiya, 1985). Similarly, experimental study of Rawat (1988) has shown that about

50 per cent changes in channel capacity are man induced in the Himalaya. He has also stated that geological, climate and topographic conditions being the same, the least disturbed forest land produce the minimum surface runoff (3.2% of the total annual flow). The greatly disturbed agricultural land produces the maximum surface runoff (20% of the total annual flow). It is evident from the above studies that the roles of human activities have very adverse impact on the channel capacity as manifest in increase of the floodwater and decrease of the baseflow water. The natural culmination of this phenomenon is acceleration of mass-movements and frequent floods. It is evident that a significant proportion of the rainfall goes waste as flood-water without replenishing the groundwater reserve, that is without recharging the springs. When the construction of houses and roads take place there is a decrease in the natural infiltration, groundwater level may be lowered.

A detailed account of the impacts of the anthropogenic processes in hydrological and erosion systems has been presented in Chapter nine. This Chapter describes the distribution of anthropogenic landforms within the Nana Kosi drainage basin (Fig. 7.1).

Anthropogenic Landforms of the Nana Kosi Watershed

Bradsaw, *et al.* (1978) have classified the landforms produced by man in two major groups. i.e., erosional and depositional. According to them all the features of the earth surface which are caused by excavational activities of man are erosional in origin. Similarly, the features caused by various constructional works of man are depositional in origin. Figure 7.1 contains the classification of anthropogenic landforms erosional and depositional origin of the Nana Kosi watershed.

Erosional Landforms

Roads

Figure 1.1 depicts the distribution of metalled and unmetalled (58.5 km long) road network of the Nana Kosi drainage basin. A brief description of these roads is presented below :

Metalled Road : The Almora-Ranikhet metalled road crosses the Nana Kosi watershed from the Mid-crest of the south-western water divide. The length of this road within the study area is 20.5 km from Kosi to Majkhali. The average width of this road stands at 7 m. This road encompasses an area of about 0.144 km^2 i.e. 0.26 per cent of the total study area. This is the oldest road of the area. The upslope and downslope of this road covered by grass/scrub or vegetation cover and are relatively stable than that of

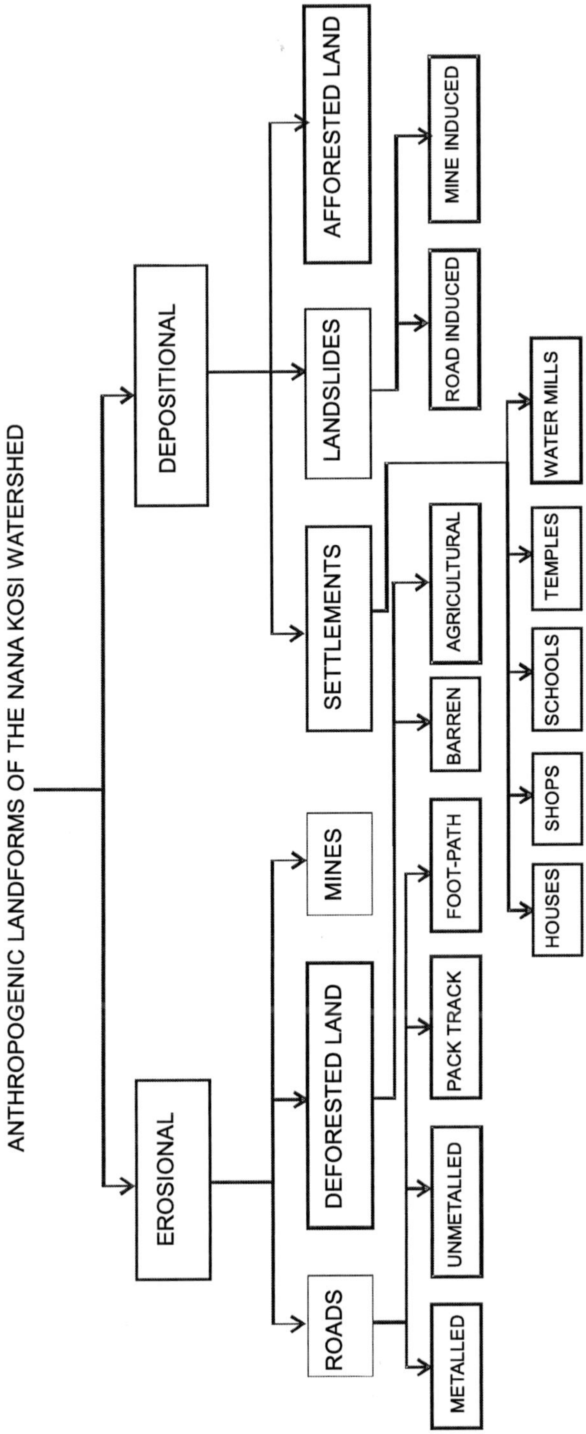

Fig.7.1 : Classification of anthropogenic landforms of the Nana Kosi watershed, Central Himalaya, India.

the unmetalled roads. This road is not suffering from the road induced landslide hazards and undermining of debris flow but at places when the road crosses fault zones such as particularly near Jyoli Fault (Plate 6, above) and Kathpuria Fault, the road is suffering from frequent outfalls of landslides which are of tectonic origin (Plate 5, below; Chapter four).'

Unmetalled Roads : There are three newly constructed unmetalled roads traversing from different parts of the Nana Kosi watershed (Fig. 1.1). These are :

Kathpuria-Daulaghat Road,
Majkhali-Someshwar Road, and
Kosi-Korechhina Road

Kathpuri-Daulaghat road originates from Almora-Ranikhet Road at Kathpuria and traverses from Papoli-Patharkot hillspur to Daulaghat. This 8 km long road (average width 6 m) constructed mainly along dip slope (Fig. 9.1 H). This road encompasses an area of 0.048 km^2 i.e., 0.09 per cent of the total study area. Majkhali-Someshwar road also originates from Almora-Ranikhet metalled road at Majkhali and runs through the northern water divide from Korechhina to Someshwar. This 11 km long road (average width 5 m) constructed mainly along anti-dip slope (Fig. 9.1 G) encompasses an area of 0.055 km^2 i.e., 0.1 per cent of the total study area. Kosi-Korechhina road orininates from Almora-Kausani road near mouth of the Nana Kosi river and traverses throughout along the Nana Kosi river (Fig. 1.1). This newly constructed (1987-88) 19 km long road has an average width of 5 m and encompasses an area of 0.095 km^2, i.e., 0.17% of the total study area.

Pack-Track and Foot-Path : The major pack track of the region, i.e., Almora-Dwarahat, was the only means of transport before road construction from Almora to Dwarahat. It enters into the basin from mouth and runs along the Nana Kosi river upstream up to Korechhina (i.e. reach of the stream). This is a narrow track, 2-3 m wide and 15 km long. Apart from above the villages are connected by the foot-paths. The networks of the footpaths of the study area is presented in Figure 1.1.

Deforested Land : Removal of protective vegetal cover for commercial, fodder and fuel purposes from the hill-slopes of the Nana Kosi watershed has caused new landforms, viz., barren and agricultural. About 68.76 per cent (37.81 km^2) area of the total basin is deforested.

Barren land : Out of the total basin area 35.23 per cent (19.38 km^2) falls under barren land. The barren land is mainly confined on the hillcrest and mid-crest and used for grazing. This deforested landscape has intensified all the denudational processes of land degradation.

Experimental study of erosion in the barren land has shown that barren land has reduced the water generating capacity of land to channels, and has increased the surface flow, sheetwash erosion and channel erosion many times higher than that of the adjacent undisturbed hill-slopes (see Chapter-nine).

Agricultural Land : Agriculture is the primary occupation of the inhabitants of the Nana Kosi drainage basin. About 33.53 per cent (18.44 km^2) area falls under agricultural land (Table 7.1 and Fig. 7.2). The distribution of agricultural land in different slope groups (Fig. 7.2) reveals that out of the total agricultural land about 5 per cent (i.e., 17 km^2) falls under level or gentle surface configuration (< 10°) in the low land areas where the agricultural terraces are relatively wider and larger (Plate 3, above, 14, 15 and 16), than that of the terraces of upland areas (Plate 14, 16, 15). Table 7.1 reveals that about 72 per cent of cultivated land area of the Nana Kosi lies in upland terrain, i.e., mid-crest and crest of the hill spur where the slope is always more than 10° (Plate 30, below, 34, 29 above; 1 above) and at places narrow and large patches of terraces have excavated in the steep slope (Plate 2, right) having more than 30° (Table 7.1 and Fig 7.2).

Table 7.1 : Distribution of agricultural land in different slopes in the Nana Kosi watershed, Central Himalaya, India

Slope groups	*Agricultural*		*Land site*
(in °)	*In km²*	*In %*	
Less than 10	5.01	27.17	Low land
10-20	7.11	38.56	Up land
20-30	5.51	29.88	
More than 30	0.81	4.39	
Total	18.44	100.00	

The agricultural land of the Nana Kosi watershed is suffering from gully and rill erosion, and field experimentation has shown that erosion in this agricultural landscape has accelerated 3.5 times higher than that of the adjacent undisturbed forested hill-slopes (see Chapter nine).

Mines

Slate has been used since times immemorial as a roofing material for houses. The Nana Kosi drainage basin consists of slates of brown and grey colour and slaty quartzites at places (Fig. 2.1). At two places in the Nana Kosi Watershed contain high quality of slates and paving stone (Pant, 1985). The deposits of village Chauna in the eastern water divide of the basin are

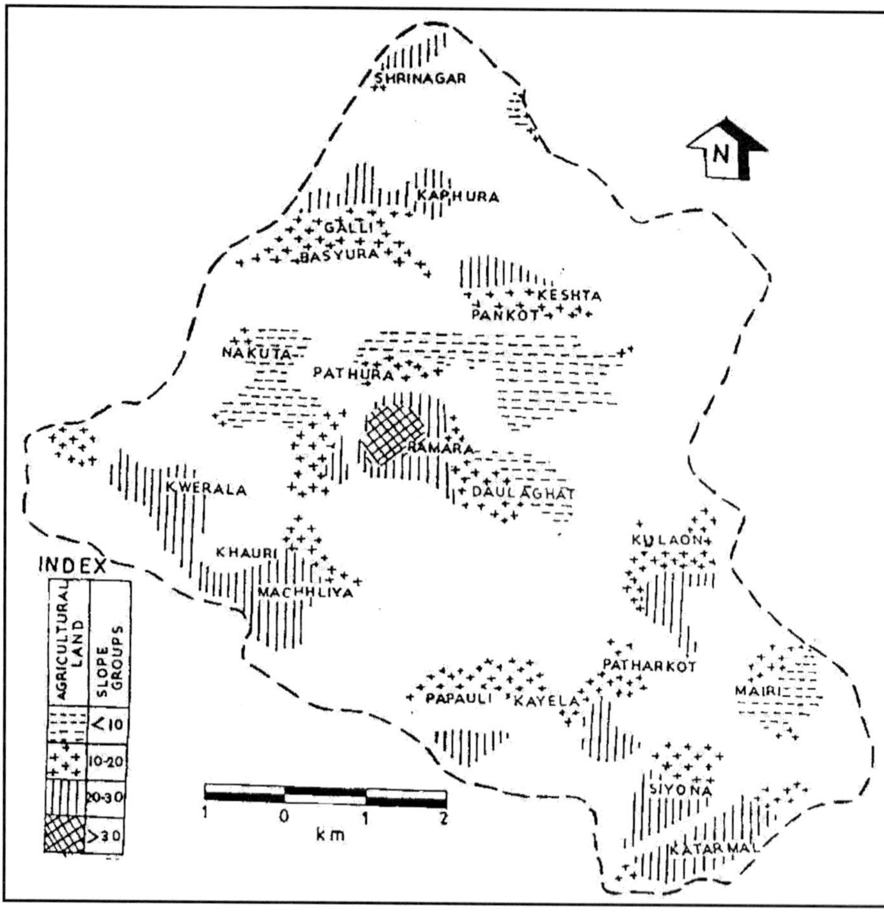

Fig. 7.2 : Distribution of agricultural land in different slope groups in the Nana Kosi watershed, Central Himalaya, India

of good quality slates and traditionally mined since olden times. The Dugardeo (near the confluence of Nana Kosi and Dhar Gad streams) deposit contains slaty quartzites relatively of inferior quality.

Depositional Landforms

Settlements

In the following paragraph a brief description of settlements, their types and distribution in the Nana Kosi watershed has been presented.

Types: The wide range of topographical characteristics right from the basin mouth to its reaches, result into the emergence of a variety in the types of settlements which can be broadly grouped under the following types :

(1) Isolated dwelling
(2) Linear pattern
(3) Partially agglomerated

The dissemination of settlements in the Nana Kosi watershed is largely a result of varying terrain conditions where the slope and the different elevations are usually the principal determinants of site for settlements. The condition of slope always determines the availability of agricultural land. Availability of water is the next important factor, which, through an uneven distribution and limited supply, greatly restricts tendencies of settlement agglomeration. The predominance of slopes over level in hills has largely conditioned the fertility, depth, extent of surface and the moisture retaining capacity of the soil. Consequently, areas of fertile soil are limited and scattered in different parts (Joshi, *et al.*, 1984). Thus, the paucity of agricultural land, combined with the difficulties of inaccessibility, often causes settlements to scatter as evidenced by the distribution of the villages within the Nana Kosi watershed.

In village Gulli, Chinuna and Kaphura the settlements have common water supply but the houses are mainly scattered throughout the length and width of the village and each settlement has its holdings near the house. Most of the cultivators have occupancy rights in the soil hence, they are free to build their settlements anywhere on their holdings. This gives rise to isolated settlement types (Plate 12, above; 10 : 2 right). In numbers of villages, specifically Syona, Kayala, Gurna and Ujgal, settlements represent a linear arrangement of house in a row consistings 5 to 10 houses almost at the same elevation. The houses face the same direction and in few of the cases, one of walls in the adjoining is common. This type of linear arrangement of houses is locally known as "Bhakhli" (Plate 3, below). The emergence of this type has its roots in the social background of the inhabitants and the dominating influence of the environment. Under such conditions, life in this area has been full of back-breaking tasks, dreary, monotony and unforeseen accidents. To lessen the influences of the hostile forces of nature, close community ties have developed among the dwellers, giving place to mutual aid and exchange of labour and cattle in various difficult and tedious processes of agriculture as well as matual co-operation in social and religious activities.

Generally, the construction of settlements results from the limited amount of cultivable land or shortage of water. This factor has given rise another picture of settlement types on the hillspurs, viz., partially

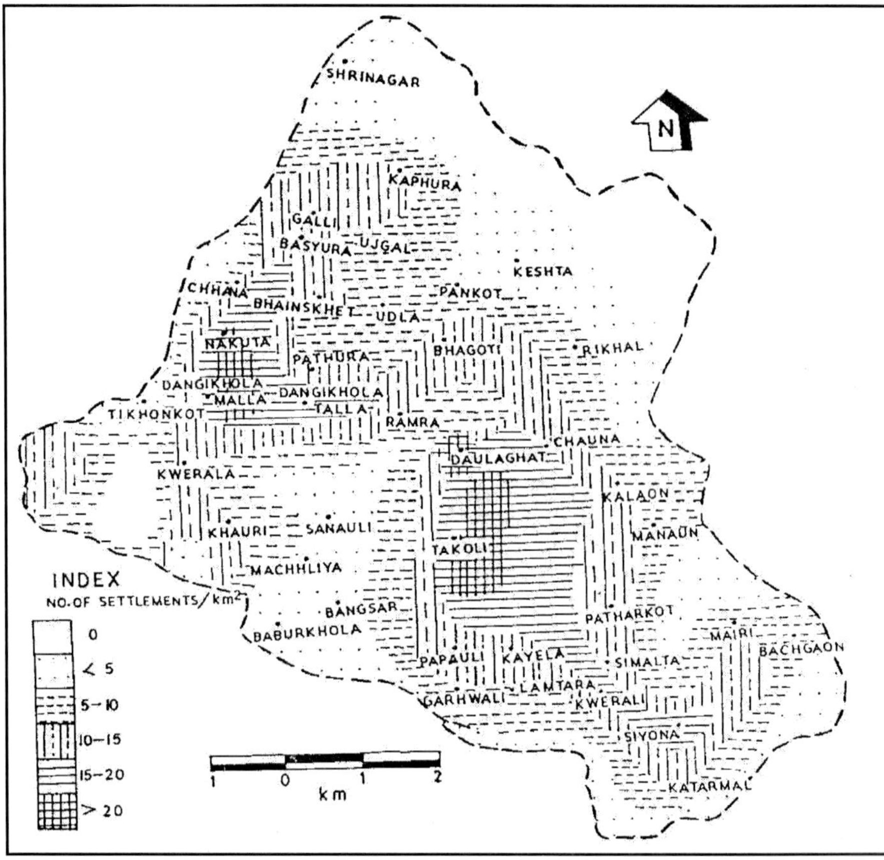

Fig. 7.3 : Settlement density map of the Nana Kosi watershed, Central Himalaya, India (based on S.O.I. toposheet)

agglomerated (Plate 34). This type of settlement in the Nana Kosi watershed is frequently available and is confined strictly to the hillspurs.

Settlement Density—Figure 7.3 depicts the spatial distribution of settlement density of the Nana Kosi watershed which suggests that the watershed is divisible into six groups of different settlement density :

(1) Areas of very high settlement density
(2) Areas of high settlement density
(3) Areas of moderate settlement density
(4) Areas of low settlement density
(5) Areas of very low settlement density
(6) Areas of devoid of settlements

Two small patches encompassing an area of 1.67 km^2 (i.e., 3.03% of the total basin; Table 7.2) in the areas of alluvial soils and bedrock terraces specifically in village Malla Dangikhola, Daulaghat and Takoli are the areas of very high settlement density, where the settlement density is more than 20 settlements/km^2. Adjacent to the areas of high settlement density, lies relatively larger area (5.09 km^2) of high settlement density (i.e., 15-20 settlements/km^2) in village Talla Dangikhola, Bainskhet and Nakuta. These villages are mainly situated in the low land areas of large colluvial fans. From the low land areas to upland, the settlement density gradually decreases. On the mid-crests of the basin, the settlement density is moderate (10-15 settlements/km^2) to low (5-10 settlements/km^2). The maximum area (31.48% of the total basin) of the basin falls under areas of low settlement density.

About one-fifth area of the basin falls under areas of very low settlement density (1-5 settlements/km^2) on the crest in southern water divide and near the crest in northern water divide (Fig. 7.3).

A large part of the dense pine forest area on the crest of northern water divide and a small patch of mixed forest in west of village Kwerala is devoid of settlement. These two areas of devoid of settlements constitute about 11.81% area of the total basin (Table 7.2).

Table 7.2: Distribution of area under different settlement density groups in the Nana Kosi watershed, Central Himalaya, India

Settlement density (no. of settle-ment/km^2)	*Area*		*Settlement density group*
	In km^2	*In %*	
0	6.50	11.81	Very low
1-5	10.68	19.42	Very low
5-10	17.31	31.48	Low
10-15	13.75	25.01	Moderate
15-20	5.09	9.25	High
More than 20	1.67	3.03	Very high
Total	55.00	100.00	

Landslides

Road Induced Landslides and Hazards—Field surveys conducted along Kathpuria-Daulaghat and Majkhali—Someshwar roads (Chapter-nine) reveal that these roads are suffering from man induced landslides from the unstable upslope and undermining downslope. During the monsoon rains the roads of the Nana Kosi watershed are producing 5.6 to 11 landslides per kilometer having 32.55 to 5 cubic meters volume. These landslides develop small fans and cones along the roads at the base of road-cut which are removed by Public Works Department each year. During the construction of 58.5 km long roads in the basin, about 13689 x 10^4 cubic meters of debris (Chapter-nine) was excavated which was allowed to slide down the slopes into valley (Plate 1 and 16, below). Moreover, the sliding of the debris destroys the ground cover scrubs and sometimes trees and the sediment charged river waters become very powerful agent of erosion. The debris is thus, carried away by stream water towards downstream, where it covers the fertile fields during floods.

Mine Induced Hazards—Open-cast mining of slates and slaty quartzite at Chauna and Dugardeo, respectively involves the removal of the overburden by use of manual operation starting from the outcrop and proceeding along the hillside has carved ugly disfigurement and ugly face of the natural landscape. Picking only the high grade slate and discarding the rest to slide the steep (30°-40°) slopes is causing great damage to ground cover (grasses and scrubs) and trees, and to springs and streams. When saturated with heavy rainwater, the loose waste material becomes debris flow in rills which descend in down slope clogg the rill and spread over agricultural terraces.

Afforested land

Only a negligible part of the basin (i.e., less than 1 km^2) falls under afforested land which lies in small patches near village Gurna and near Majkhali. This indicates that there is no marked awareness neither among the local inhabitants nor the concerning development authorities regarding the environmental regeneration of this highly disturbed basin.

REFERENCES

Bhandari, R.K. and Gupta, C. 1985 : Problems of landslides in the Himalaya and future directions. In : *Environmental Regeneration in the Himalaya,* Singh, J.S. (ed.), Cent. Him. Environ. Associ. & Gyanodaya Prakashan, Nainital, pp. 39-56.

Bichsel, M., Grounder, M., Kienholz, H. and Mool, P. 1983 : *Mountain hazard and slope stability, Kathmandu Kakani area.* U.N. University, Mountain hazard mapping project Map No. 4, Printed by Hallwag, A.G. Berne, Switzerland.

Bradsaw, M.J., Abbott, A.J. and Gelsthorpe, A.P. 1978 : *The earth's changing surface.* Edinberg, pp. 1-336.

Chaturvedi, A.N. 1985 : Fuel and fodder trees for man made forests in hills. In : *Environmental Regeneration in the Himalaya.* Singh, J.S. (ed.), Cent. Him. Environ. Associ. & Gyanodaya Prakashan, Nainital, pp. 309-312.

Collier, C.R. 1970 : *Erosion and sedimentation, influence of strip mining on the hydrologic environment of Beaver Greek basin,* Kentucky, 1955-59, B 48-B.

Cooke, R.U. and Doornkamp, J.C. 1974 : *Geomorphology in environmental management.* Oxford Clarendon Press, pp. 14-20.

Douglas, I. 1973 : Water resources. In : *Evaluating the human environment, essays in applied geography.* Arnold, London, pp. 57-87.

Glymph, L.M. and Holton, H.N. 1969: Land treatment in agricultural watershed hydrology research. In : *Effects of Watershed Changes on Stream Flow.* Moore, W.L. and Morgan, C.W. (eds.). Texas U.P. Austin, pp. 44-68.

Gregory, K.J. and Walling, D.E. 1973 : *Drainage basin form and processes.* London, Edward Arnold, pp. 1-270.

Gupta, R.K. and Arora, Y.K. 1985 : Technology for the rejuvenation of degraded lands in the Himalaya. In : *Environmental Regeneration in Himalaya,* Singh, J.S. (ed.). Cent. Him. Environ. Associ. Gyanodaya Prakashan, Nainital, pp. 169-195.

Haugen, R.K. and Brown, J. 1971 : Natural and man induced disturbances of permafrost terrane. In : *Environmental geomorphology,* Coates, D.R. (ed.). Publi. in Geom., State Univ., New York, pp. 139-49.

Haigh, M.J., Rawat, J.S. and Bartarya, S.K. 1987 : Impact of hillroads on dwonslope forest cover. Himalaya : *Man and Nature,* 11 (4) : pp. 2-3.

Haigh, M.J., Rawat, J.S. and Bartarya, S.K. 1989 : Environmental indicators of landslide activity along the Kilbury Road, Nainital, Kumaun Lesser Himalaya. *Mountain Research and Development,* 9 (1), pp. 25-33.

Ives, J.D. 1985 : Himalayan environmental regeneration : an overview—what are the problems and how can they be tackled? In : *Environmental Regeneration in Himalaya.* Singh, J.S. (ed.). Cent. Him. Environ. Associ. Gyanodaya Prakashan, Nainital, pp. 1-10.

Jackes, G.V. and Whyte, R.O. 1939 : *The rape of the earth—a world survey of soil erosion.* Faber, London, p. 313.

Jalal, D.S. 1985 : Environmental degradation in Kotadun, Uttar Pradesh Himalaya. In : *Environmental Regeneration in Himalaya.* Singh, J.S. (ed.). Centr. Him. Environ. Assoc., Gyanodaya Prakashan, Nainital, pp. 419-226.

Joshi, S.C., Joshi, D.R. and Dani, D.D. 1983 : *Kumaun Himalaya : A geographic perspective on resource development.* Gyanodaya Prakashan, Nainital, pp. 1-160.

Mellen, N.H. 1977 : Strip mines and fluvial systems; geomorphic effects and environmental impact in Northeastern Oklahome. Worcester, Clark University, doctoral dissertation, pp. 1-250.

Mellen, N.H. 1986 : *Fluvial sediment problems from strip-mining in northeastern Oklahoma;* Geomorphologicl Perspectives on Land Disturbance and Reclamation, Oxford, pp. 3-5.

Misra, R.C. 1985 : Environmental Problems created by exploration of mineral resources in Himalaya. In : *Environmental Regeneration in Himalaya.* Singh, J.S. (ed.), Centr. Him. Envir. Associ. Gyanodaya Prakashan, Nainital, pp. 155-184.

Pande, D.C. 1985 : Concept and strategy for forest management for the Himalaya. In : *Environmental Regeneration in Himalaya.* Singh, J.S. (ed.), Centr. Him. Envir. Associ. Gyanodaya Prakashan, Nainital, pp. 286-293.

Pant, C.C. 1988 : *Mineral Wealth of Kumaun, prospects and problems.* In : *Kumaun Land and People.* Valdiya, K.S. (ed.), Gyanodaya Prakashan, Nainital, pp. 213-221.

Pathak, P.C. 1983 : Vegetation hydrology and its impact on nutrient cycling in selected forest ecosystems of Kumaun Himalaya, Unpublished Ph. D. thesis, Kumaun University, Nainital, pp. 1-250.

Rawat, J.S. 1985 : The drainage basin as a unit for physical environmental studies. In : *Environmental Regeneration in Himalaya,* Singh, J.S. (ed.), Centr. Him. Envir. Assoc., Gyanodaya Prakashan, Nainital, pp. 734-743.

Rawat, J.S. 1987 : Modelling of water and sediment budget; Concepts and Strategies. Geomorphological models; theoretical and empirical aspects, CATENA—A Cooper. *Jour. of Intern. Soci. of Soil Science,* 10, pp. 147-159.

Rawat, J.S. 1988 : Anthropogenic transformation channel network capacity, an experimental study in Kumaun Himalaya. *Proc. Ind. Nat. Sci. Acad.,* 54 (4), pp. 605-615.

Shastry, G. 1986 : Lessons from a landslide reclamation project in the Himalayan foothills; *Geomorphological perspectives on Land Disturbance and Reclamation,* pp. 56-74.

Singh, J.S. 1985 : *Environmental Regeneration in Himalaya : Concepts and Strategies.* Cent. Him. Envir. Associ., Gyanodaya Prakashan, Nainital, pp. 1-468.

Singh, S.P. and Singh, J.S. 1985 : Structure and function of the forest ecosystems of Central Himalaya; Implications for Management. In : *Environmental Regeneration in Himalaya.* Singh, J.S. (ed.). Cent. Him. Envir. Associ., Gyanodaya Prakashan, Nainital, pp. 85-110.

Strahler, A.N. 1973 : *Introduction to physical geography.* John Wiley & Sons, New York, pp. 18-155.

Striffer, W.D. 1985 : Watershed management in the Himalaya. In : *Environmental Regeneration in Himalaya,* Singh J.S. (ed.), Cent. Him. Envir. Associ., Gyanodaya Prakashan, Nainital, pp. 58-67.

Tewari, A.K., Saxena, A.K. and Singh, J.S. 1985 : Inventory of forest biomass for Indian Central Himalaya. In : *Environmental Regeneration in Himalaya,* Singh, J. S. (ed.), Cent. Him. Envir. Assoc., Gyanodaya Prakashan, Nainital, pp. 336-247.

Valdiya, K.S. 1985 : Acclerated Erosion and Landslide Prone Zones in the Central Himalayan region. In : *Environmental Regeneration in Himalaya,* Singh, J.S. (ed.), Cent. Him. Envir. Associ., Gyanodaya Prakashan, Nainital, pp. 12-37.

Wright, R.L. 1972a : Some perspectives on environmental research for agricultural landuse planning in developing countries, *Geoforum;* 10, pp. 15-33.

PART C

DEGRADATIONAL PROCESSES AND THEIR MEASUREMENT

8

Pluvial Processes and Degradation

Introduction

The documentation of sediment and dissolved dynamics within a drainage basin is important to the geomorphologist in providing an index of the effects of water on the landscape and the rates of operation of pluvial and fluvial processes which include particular emphasis on those geomorphic processes concerned with the erosive action of water on the slopes and the supply of material to the channel at the foot of the slope (Gregory and Walling, 1973).

Erosion is the process by which soil particles are detached from the soil surface. Transportation is the process of moving detached soil particles to another location. Erosion and transportation are natural processes which have sculptured many of the topographic features of the present landscape. Erosion on the hillslope is of two general types : sheet erosion and channel erosion. The later includes rill and gully erosion as well as stream channel erosion (Chow, 1964).

The measurements are important to an understanding of these processes and there are also certain techniques available specifically towards the assessment of the processes of erosion, transportation and deposition within a catchment. The description of these processes and techniques is best achieved by subdivision into studies of, firstly, sediment transportation on the land or hillslope phase, the channel phase and secondly, dissolved sediment production, transport, and the overall fields; and thirdly, the associated rates of erosion or degradation.

Rainsplash and Sheetwash Processes

Rainsplash Erosion

The detachment or splash of soil particles under the impact of raindrops is known as rainsplash process (Chow, 1964). The force of falling drops causes a geyser like splashing in which soil particles are lifted and then dropped into new position, a process termed splash erosion (Strahler and Strahler, 1977). Sheet erosion is the removal of soil more or less uniformly

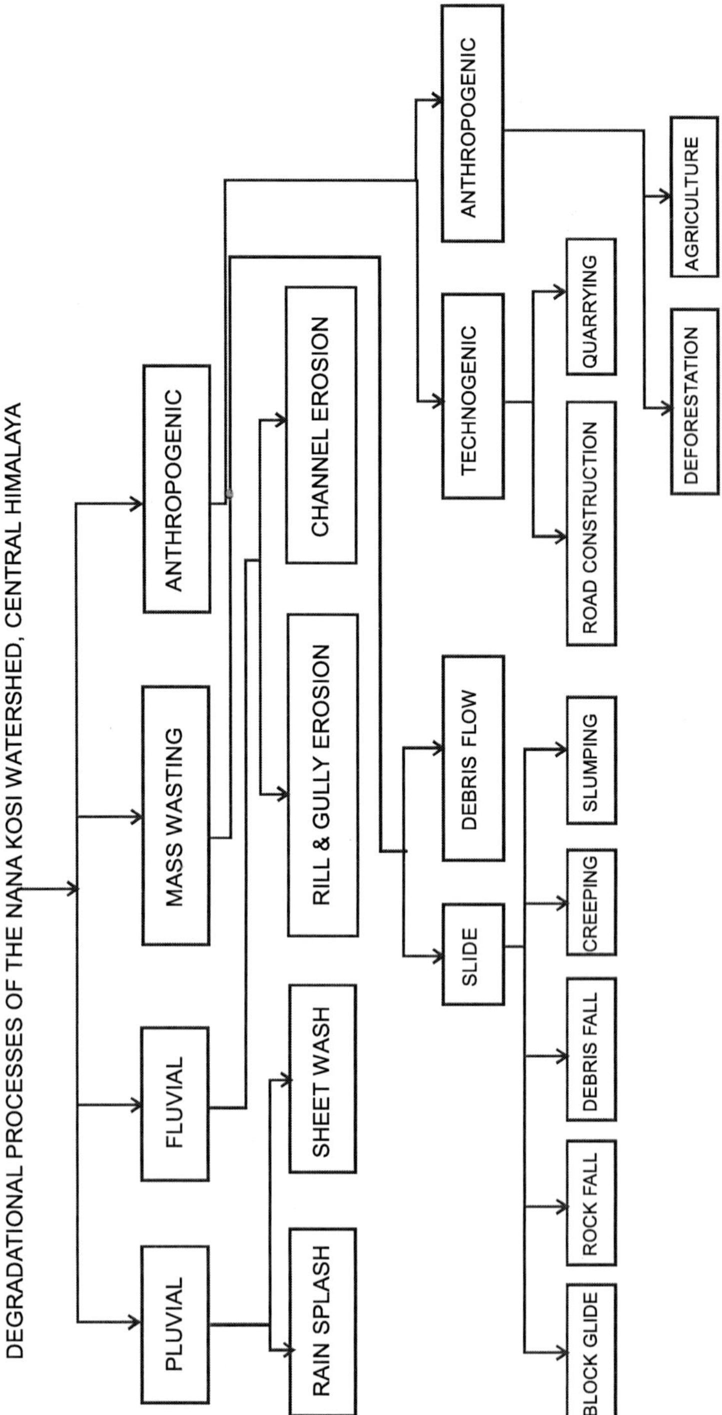

Fig. 8.1 : The classification of degradational processes of the Nana Kosi Watershed, Central Himalaya, India

over the entire soil surface. This type of erosion is not as spectacular as channel erosion and is caused by pluvial activities (rainwater) known as rainsplash and sheetwash processes.

When the land surface is first cleared of forest and ploughed for cultivation, little erosion will occur until the action of rainsplash has broken down the soil aggregates and sealed the larger opening. A simple gravimetric approach to the direct measurement of soil splash involves the use of trays of soil or small field plots surrounded by metal frames or troughs to catch splashed material. Osborne (1953) has developed this technique further to include the use of a rainfall simulator. High speed photography may be used to demonstrate the explosive effects of raindrop impact (Ellison, 1950), but more quantitative measurements are usually required.

Sheet Erosion

Following the rainsplash process, overland flow begins to remove the soil in rather uniform thin layers, a process termed sheet erosion (Strahler, 1973). Thus, sheet erosion is the removal of soil more or less uniformily over the entire soil surface. This type of erosion is not as spectacular as channel erosion and is not readily apparent to the casual observer. Overland flow or sheet flood give rise to the process of sheetwash. It occurs, where the rock or soil surface is smooth as a continuous film of water, or on slightly rougher terrain as a series of tiny rivulets connecting one water filled hollow with another (Selby, 1980). Sheetflow is usually very shallow towards the crest of a hill but the flow depth increases downslope.

Several workers have attempted to measure the erosion on hillslopes by pluvial processes, i.e., rainsplash and sheetwash. Gregory and Walling (1973) have reviewed all these works which include the works of Ellision (1950), Osborne (1953), Mcqueen (1963), Coutts, *et al.* (1968), Wooldridge (1965), Kazoo and Kilmes-Szmik (1962), Van Doren, *et al.* (1950), Geib (1933), De Poley (1967), Schick (1967) and Emmett (1965) and others. Various methods have been suggested by these workers to monitor hillslope erosion by pluvial process. Reviewing all these methods Gregory and Walling (1973) have concluded that soil splash is a component of sheet erosion, and in many instances it will be sufficient to measure the overall effects of sheet erosion. Appratus, Gerlach Trough, collecting sheetflow and the associated entertained sediment may be used (Gregory and Willing, 1973). An alternative approach to the assessment of sheet erosion involves measurement of the rate of lowering of the ground surface and calculation of volumes removed. Erosion pins can consists of a 25 cm nail with a washer below the head, driven into the ground so that the washer is flush with the soil surface (Emmett, 1965). A large number of pins will be required to provide a representative result for an area.

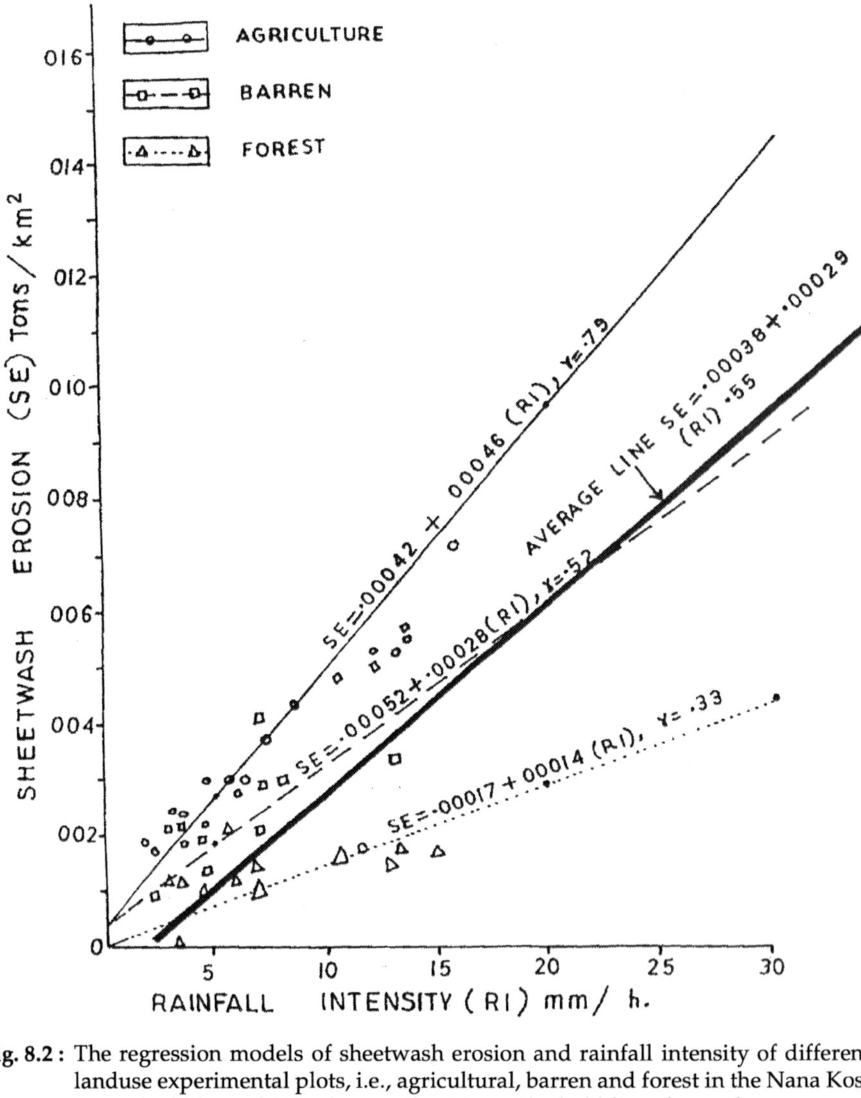

Fig. 8.2 : The regression models of sheetwash erosion and rainfall intensity of different landuse experimental plots, i.e., agricultural, barren and forest in the Nana Kosi watershed, Central Himalaya, India. *Note* : The bold line shows the average of three plots.

Data Collection

Following Gregory and Walling (1973), three plots (Table 8.1) were used to monitor erosion by pluvial processes on the hillslope of the Nana Kosi watershed near Daulaghat. Gerlech Troughs (20 x 10 x 10 cm) were used to monitor erosion from hillslopes. Twenty-six storms of rains of different intensities during the rainy season in 1986-87, were monitored in the field.

Results

Table 8.1 contains the field measurement data of different storms which includes total rainfall and total erosion of each storm in the experimental plots. Table 8.2 is the summary of the raw data (Table 8.1) which reveals the followings :

(1) During the experimental period the total rainfall (140.2 mm, average intensity 8.03 mm/hour) generated sheetwash sediment at the rate of 0.00266 tonn/km^2. With the help of this rate it can be extrapolated that in 1986-87, the sheetwash sediment was generated at the rate of 0.0191 tonn/km^2 at 999.9 mm total rain input. Similarly, in 1987-88 which was drought year, generated sheetwash sediment at the rate of 0.0082 tonn/km^2 at 431.7 mm rain input.

Table 8.1 : Sheetwash erosion data of 26 rainstorms in three different landuse plots, i.e., Agricultural (11 m^2), Barren (8.5 m^2) and Forest (15.5 m^2) under identical slope (13°) and geological (mica-schist) character in the Nana Kosi watershed, Central Himalaya, India

Event	*Date*	*Time*	*Rainfall*	*Total sheetwash erosion (g)*		
		From To	*(mm)*	*Agriculture*	*Barren*	*Forest*
1	9-7-86	11.00-12.00	3.5	25.9	16.2	0
2	9-7-86	13.00-14.00	2.0	19.8	8.9	0
3	26-7-86	11.00-11.45	5.0	33.0	17.2	13.8
4	26-7-86	14.00-15.00	4.0	23.4	10.9	7.8
5	26-7-86	16.45-18.00	2.5	19.9	8.9	0
6	31-7-86	11.30-12.00	3.5	45.1	25.1	23.3
7	12-8-86	10.45-12.00	8.0	26.5	17.2	19.4
8	12-8-86	13.00-13.30	15.0	176.8	87.1	73.6
9	12-8-86	14.00-14.10	2.0	58.4	32.0	26.4
10	12-8-86	17.45-18.00	1.5	32.8	17.0	17.8
11	12-8-86	15.00-15.30	3.5	41.3	19.7	15.5
12	29-8-86	16.00-16.15	1.5	31.4	18.3	19.4
13	29-8-86	13.00-14.00	12.0	55.0	26.8	27.9
14	8-6-87	10.00-12.00	5.5	16.0	10.2	0
15	9-6-87	14.30-15.00	5.2	52.8	25.5	26.5
16	6-7-87	17.00-17.45	10.0	62.2	32.7	28.7
17	6-7-87	15.00-16.00	4.5	25.3	17.4	18.4
18	11-7-87	14.30-14.45	2.0	47.5	26.2	24.8
19	12-7-87	12.00-14.00	6.0	27.5	17.9	20.2
20	18-7-87	11.15-12.00	5.0	42.4	25.5	18.9
21	12-8-87	15.15-16.00	3.0	33.6	17.9	16.3
22	12-8-87	10.00-12.00	9.0	27.6	15.7	20.2
23	28-8-87	13.00-14.00	4.0	25.3	16.2	20.0
24	4-9-87	16.30-17.00	8.0	85.8	42.5	39.2
25	20-9-87	9.45-10.15	7.5	59.9	27.6	27.3
26	20-9-87	10.30-11.00	6.5	58.9	28.3	24.6

(2) Thus, multiplying the average rates of sheetwash erosion of different years with area of the Nana Kosi watershed, it can be deduced that about 1.05 tonnes sediments (0.0191 tonn/km^2 x 55 km^2) in 1986-87 and 0.45 ton sediment in 1987-88 was transported by sheetwash process in the entire drainage basin.

(3) The variations in the sheetwash erosion is considerably high from one plot to another. It is due to different landuse pattern in the experimental plots. A detailed analysis of the influence of landuse change in the sheetwash erosion has been presented in Chapter nine.

Table 8.2 : Summary of sheetwash erosion data of 26 rainstorms in three different landuse plots, i.e., Agricultural (11 m^2), Barren (8.5 m^2) and Forest (15.5 m^2) under identical slope (13°) and geological (mica-schist) character in the Nana Kosi watershed, Central Himalaya, India

Event	*Rainfall Intensity (mm/h)*	*Sheet wash erosion tonnes/km^2*			
		Agriculture	*Barren*	*Forest*	*Average*
1	3.5	0.00235	0.00190	0	0.00142
2	2.0	0.00180	0.00105	0	0.00095
3	6.6	0.00300	0.00202	0.00085	0.00196
4	4.0	0.00213	0.00128	0.00050	0.00130
5	2.1	0.00181	0.00105	0	0.00095
6	7.0	0.00410	0.00295	0.00150	0.00285
7	3.7	0.00241	0.00202	0.00125	0.00189
8	30.0	0.01625	0.01025	0.00475	0.01042
9	12.0	0.00531	0.00376	0.00170	0.00359
10	6.0	0.00298	0.00200	0.00115	0.00204
11	7.0	0.00375	0.00231	0.00100	0.00235
12	6.0	0.00285	0.00215	0.00125	0.00625
13	12.0	0.00500	0.00315	0.00180	0.00332
14	2.8	0.00195	0.00120	0	0.00105
15	10.4	0.00480	0.00300	0.00171	0.00317
16	13.3	0.00565	0.00385	0.00185	0.00378
17	4.5	0.00230	0.00205	0.00119	0.00185
18	8.0	0.00432	0.00308	0.00160	0.00300
19	3.0	0.00250	0.00211	0.00130	0.00197
20	6.6	0.00385	0.00300	0.00122	0.00269
21	4.0	0.00305	0.00210	0.00105	0.00206
22	4.5	0.00251	0.00185	0.00130	0.00189
23	4.0	0.00230	0.00190	0.00129	0.00183
24	16.0	0.00718	0.00500	0.00253	0.00490
25	15.0	0.00545	0.00325	0.00176	0.00349
26	13.0	0.00535	0.00333	0.00159	0.00342
Average	8.08	0.00407	0.00275	0.00116	0.00266

Correlation analysis conducted between sheetwash erosion and rainfall intensity data of all the plots reveals that these two parameters are positively correlated (r = +0.55) to each other. To define the relative rates of change between sheetwash erosion and rainfall intensity, regression analysis was conducted. The average regression coefficient (b) and average constant (a) of these experimental plots stand at 0.00038 and 0.00029, respectively. The average regression line of the three plots (Fig. 8.2) reveals that in the Nana Kosi basin, 5 mm rain per hour generates about 0.00183 tonnes (i.e. 0.00038 + 0.00029 × 5) sheetwash sediment from one square kilometer area. Similarly, at different rainfall intensities the rates of sheetwash erosion per square kilometer in the Nana Kosi watershed may be estimated as presented in Table 8.3.

Table 8.3 : Estimated rates of sheetwash erosion with the help of regression equation SW = 0.00038 + 0.00029 (RI) and average regression line (Fig. 8.2).

Rainfall Intensity mm/hour	*Sheetwash Erosion (tonne/km²)*	*Rainfall Intensity (mm/hour)*	*Sheetwash Erosion (tonne/km²)*
2	0.00096	14	0.00444
3	0.00125	15	0.00473
4	0.00154	16	0.00502
5	0.00183	17	0.00531
6	0.00212	18	0.00560
7	0.00241	19	0.00589
8	0.00270	20	0.00618
9	0.00299	21	0.00647
10	0.00328	22	0.00676
11	0.00357	23	0.00705
12	0.00386	24	0.00734
13	0.00415	25	0.00763

Fluvial Processes and Degradation

Introduction

Running water as a fluid agent of denudation dominates the sculpturing of the mountain surface. The fluvial systems in which overland flow becomes organized into channel system, converging the flow into larger and longer streams. As stream transport and deposit rock material they shape a variety of landforms (Strahler and Strahler, 1983). Where slope are exceptionally steep and runoff from rain storm is exceptionally heavy, sheet erosion progresses into a more intense activity, that of "rill erosion" or 'rilling" (Plate 32, below and Plate 34) in which innumerable closely spaced channels are scored into the soil/rock in a system of long parallel lines. These rills are merely seasonal features, developed during the period of rainy season. If rills are not destroyed and they join to each other, they may soon begin to integrate into still larger channels, termed gullies (Plate 6 and 9 below). This transformation comes about as the work of active rills deepen more rapidly than their neighbours and incorporate the adjacent drainage areas. Erosive action thus is concentrated into a few large channels which deepen into steep walled canyon-like trenches whose upper ends grow progressively upslope. Both rills and gullies are seasonal phenomena of erosion which are active in the rainy season. The assessment of rill and gully erosion can be approached in two ways. Firstly, measurements can be made of the material discharged by the stream at the outlet of a gully and an attempt made to relate this transported material to the overall volume of erosion. General studies of rill and gully growth can be supplemented by more intensive studies at individual sites using erosion pins (Gregory and Walling, 1973). The perennial agent of erosion is a stream which erodes in various ways, depending on the nature of the channel materials and the tools with which the current is armed. The force of the flowing water alone, exerting impact and a dragging action upon the bed can erode poorly consolidated alluvial materials such as gravel, sand, silt and clay, a process termed hydraulic action (Strahler and Strahler, 1983). This section of the chapter includes the degradation of the study area by fluvial processes, i.e., by rills, gullies and channels and embraces identification, measurements of rills, gullies and channels, and to monitor their collective erosion at 25 different channels mouth as shown in Figure 1.1.

Rilling

The barren convex hillslopes are dissected by small rills downslope and hollows upslope (Plate 34). Apart from convex deforested hillslopes the forested convex hillslopes are subject for rilling because of the looped and scattered trees. On the hillslopes sheetwash rapidly becomes concentrated as the water is diverted round objects into very sufficient depth for considerable turbulence to entrain larger particles than sheetwash. The head of the rills are not extended all the way to the water divide which remains unrilled because the depth of overland flow is not great enough to develop rills.

Such unchannelled valleys on the upper part of the hillslope are termed as hollows (Reneau and Dietrich, 1987). Morphometry of some rills (Table 8.4) based on field measurements reveals that the width, depth and length of the rills in the Nana Kosi watershed ranges in between 0.18 and 0.80 m; 0.13 and 0.75 m; and 6.0 and 19 m, respectively. The mean length, width and depth stands at 12.9 m, 0.49 m and 0.42 m, respectively.

Table 8.4 : Mean length, width and depth of some of the rills of the Nana Kosi watershed, Central Himalaya, India

Name of Place	*Length (m)*	*Width (m)*	*Depth (m)*
Jyoli	11.0	0.70	0.15
Kotuli	7.0	0.35	0.13
Korechhina	18.0	0.80	0.22
Chinuna	6.0	0.72	0.38
Basyur	19.0	0.40	0.50
Bainskhet	15.0	0.35	0.60
Gulli	14.0	0.45	0.75
Chauna	13.0	0.18	0.60
Average	12.9	0.49	0.42

Gullying

Gullying in the Nana Kosi watershed are mainly confined where the underlying material is mechanically weak or unconsolidated. A large part of the study area composed of thick mantle of regolith (Plate 6; 9, below; 14, above; 12, below) and alluvium in Gulli, Basyur, Chinuna, Bainskhet, Chaunmunia, Pathura, and Nakuta is badly suffering from gully erosion.

Table 8.5 : Mean length, width and depth of some of the gullies of the Nana Kosi watershed, Central Himalaya, India

Name of Place	*Length (m)*	*Width (m)*	*Depth (m)*
Gulli	18.5	7.0	10.3
Basyur	10.0	10.0	8.0
Chinuna	8.5	8.0	6.0
Bainskhet	12.0	6.0	5.0
Chaunmunia	10.5	7.0	15.0
Pathura	8.5	5.0	10.0
Nakuta	13.5	7.0	10.5
Jyoli	12.0	3.0	2.5
Average	12.3	6.6	8.4

Measurements carried out in the field of some of the major gullies (Table 8.5) reveals that the gullies of the Nana Kosi watershed are very wide (mean 6.6 m, range 3.0 to 10.0 m), long (mean 12.3 m, range 8.5 m to 18.5 m) as well as deep (mean 8.4 m, range 2.5 to 10.5 m).

Stream Erosion

The work of streams consists of three interrelated activities : erosion, transportation and deposition. Erosion by a stream is the progressive removal of mineral material from the floor and sides of channel. Whether this be carved in bed rock, or in a residual or transported overburden. The undermining of the banks causes large masses of alluvium to slump into the river, where the particles are quickly separated and become part of the stream's load (Strahler and Strahler, 1983). The river is also responsible for deposition of its transported load, and hence for the formation of the plains. The most effective agent of transport is running water (hence the formerly popular concept of the normal cycle of erosion, that in which transport by running water predominates : the fluvial cycle of erosion). Thus information on the relationship between mass movement on slopes and water transport is important (Ives and Messerli, 1989). Channels of the Nana Kosi watershed are mainly carving the bed rocks but at places such as in the upper reaches in village Gulli, Bainskhet and Basyur area the channels carving residual or transported overburden.

Sediment Transport

The assessment of rill, gully and stream erosion can be approached in numerous ways (Gregory and Walling, 1973). Measurements can be made of the material discharge by the stream at the outlet of a rill, gully or channel. Alternatively, attempts may be made to document the development of the rill, gully or channel system in both section and plan by periodic surveying and to calculate the amount of material removed (Tuckfield, 1964). Stehlik (1967) has used the technique of repeated aerial photographs for demonstrating the development of these erosion phenomena. Rill, gully and channel growth can also be studied at individual sites using erosion pins. Assessment of the transport of sediment through a stream requires quantitative data on the velocities and rates of sediment movement, and the associated variations both within the channel cross-section and through time. (Gregory and Walling, 1973). Although it is possible to measure the total sediment load of a stream as one component using a turbulence flume or turbulent river's section where all transported load is in suspension, this approach is limited in application, and it is more usual to measure the components of suspended, dissolved and bed load separately. To obtain the sediment transport from entire the study area, 25 water-data stations (Fig. 1.1) have been used for sampling which receive sediment from rills, gullies and channels of the different parts of the area.

Method

One liter water was collected from each water-data station (Fig. 1.1) as sample in each month. For sampling, channel cross-section was divided into sub-sections horizontally (in case, if the width of the cross-section is more than 2 m), of two meters. Sample water was collected at 0.6 m depth from each sub-section (Ruhe, 1975). The Nana Kosi is a shallow stream, therefore, one point method was used to collect sample water at 0.6 m depth (Ruhe, 1975). Concentration of suspended as well as dissolved load in water was obtained by analyzing these samples in the Geochemical Laboratory of the Department of Geography, Kumaun University by adopting gravimetric method as follows:

$$Sq = W_2 - W_1, \text{ in mg/l}$$

where, "Sq" is concentration of suspended sediment in milligram per liter, "W_1" is the weight of the filter paper, "W_2" is the weight of filter paper with suspended particles after filtering sample water of one liter.

After removing the suspended load from the sample water, 20 ml water from each sample was evaporated in the crucible, drying it up to 100°C in oven. The remaining portion in it, is the dissolved material.

By using water discharge date (m^3/sec.) of the same stations (Table 6.4) and concentration of suspended sediment data (mg/l), the rate of suspended sediment discharge per day was obtained as follows :

$$Sq \text{ (in tonnes/day)} = 0.0864 \text{ (Q} \times \text{Sq mg/l)}$$

Similarly,

$$Dq \text{ (in tonnes/day)} = 0.0864 \text{ (Q} \times \text{Dq mg/l)}$$

where, "Dq" is dissolved load and "Q" is water-discharge in m^3/sec.

Unit of the sediment discharge in tonnes/day/km^2 was obtained as follows :

$$Squ \text{ (in tonnes/day/km}^2) = Ab/Sq$$

where, "Squ" is the unit of suspended sediment discharge in tons/day/km^2, "Ab" is the area of the entire catchments of the water data station in km^2 and "Sq" is suspended sediment in tonnes/day.

Similarly,

$$Dqu \text{ (in tonnes/day/km}^2) = Ab/Dq$$

where, "Dqu" is the unit-dissolved load discharge in tonnes/day/km^2, "Ab" is the area of the catchment and "Dq" is dissolved load in tonnes/day.

Results

Figure 8.3, A and B depict the suspended and dissolve load concentration of two study years at the mouth of the Nana Kosi watershed (i.e. Hydrological Station No. 1). Similarly, the concentration of suspended and dissolve load at 24 hydrological stations within the Nana Kosi watershed recorded in two study years have been illustrated in Figure 8.4, 8.5 and 8.6

(suspended) 8.7, 8.8 and 8.9 (dissolved). Summaries of these suspended and dissolved load graphs have been presented in Table 8.6, 8.7 (suspended) and 8.13, 8.14 (dissolved). Table 8.9 and 8.10 (suspended) and Table 8.16 and 8.17 (dissolved) contain the monthwise budget. Table 8.12 (suspended) and 8.19 (dissolved) contain the seasonwise budget of suspended and dissolved load flows from the Nana Kosi watershed.

Table 8.6 : Mean suspended sediment data of 1986-87 of 25 hydrological stations (Fig. 1.1) of the Nana Kosi watershed, Central Himalaya, India

Hydrological Station No.	*Concent-ration mg/1*	*Tonnes/day*	*Tonnes/year*	*Tonnes/km²/ day*	*Tonnes/km²/ /year*
1	80.580	21.28300	7768.295	0.386964	141.2420
2	93.350	0.09100	33.215	0.102168	37.2916
3	80.330	3.24500	1184.425	0.706986	258.0490
4	56.166	7.91000	2887.150	0.170430	62.2000
5	26.660	0.07910	28.870	0.152200	55.5500
6	44.330	0.06600	24.090	0.121600	44.3840
7	52.500	0.09880	36.062	0.049180	17.9500
8	60.580	0.26707	97.480	0.366500	133.7710
9	27.000	0.02554	9.322	0.038120	13.9160
10	120.000	0.23707	86.530	0.790220	288.4290
11	48.060	0.60603	221.199	0.054807	20.0000
12	30.250	0.06567	23.969	0.156420	57.0940
13	57.080	0.94886	346.336	0.542180	197.8950
14	71.330	0.27937	101.972	0.245010	89.4286
15	69.330	0.13047	47.622	0.301520	110.0553
16	51.000	1.32000	481.803	0.207860	75.8703
17	43.080	3.13500	1144.203	0.132600	48.3980
18	21..080	0.01360	4.946	0.052547	19.1796
19	19.250	0.01493	5.452	0.019659	7.1755
20	75.910	0.14790	53.984	0.487360	177.8860
21	30.580	0.09578	34.958	0.131240	47.9026
22	28.000	0.13399	48.906	0.297750	108.6787
23	79.980	0.10774	39.328	0.139335	50.8500
24	80.412	2.43150	887.491	0.106610	38.9100
25	74.912	0.16793	61.295	0.266620	97.3177

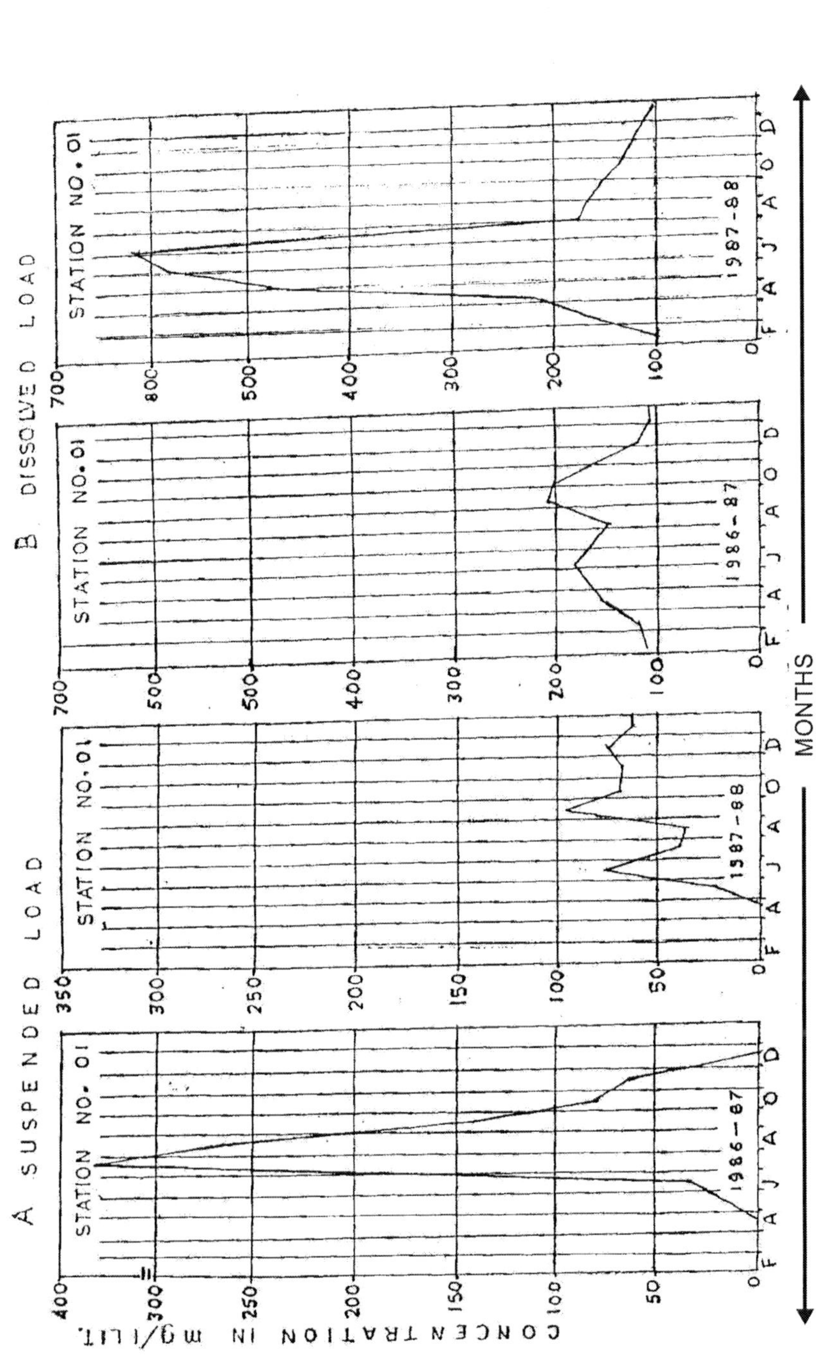

Fig. 8.3 : Suspended (A) and dissolved load (B) flow at the outlet of the Nana Kosi Watershed, Central Himalaya, India in the years 1986-87 and 1987-88

Table 8.7 : Mean suspended sediment data of 1987-88 of 25 hydrological stations (Fig 1.1) of the Nana Kosi watershed, Central Himalaya, India

Hydrological Station No.	*Concent-ration mg/l*	*Tonnes/day*	*Tonnes/year*	*Tonnes/km²/ day*	*Tonnes/km²/ year*
1	47.33	1.03200	376.680	0.13130	47.924
2	186.42	0.04578	16.711	0.05088	18.571
3	203.66	0.19348	70.620	0.04982	18.184
4	97.00	1.41240	515.526	0.03041	11.099
5	33.33	0.00313	1.141	0.00601	2.195
6	70.16	0.02462	8.986	0.04036	14.730
7	83.58	0.09480	34.602	0.04717	17.220
8	114.08	0.07943	28.990	0.11020	40.225
9	51.42	0.00545	1.990	0.00991	3.617
10	165.25	0.02284	8.336	0.07615	27.796
11	60.16	0.25200	91.982	0.23012	8.399
12	16.33	0.01688	6.161	0.04017	14.662
13	72.16	0.06008	21.929	0.03433	12.533
14	67.66	0.04150	15.148	0.03487	12.730
15	105.08	0.02202	8.052	0.05005	18.268
16	63.66	0.15581	56.872	0.02453	8.953
17	94.08	1.81710	663.234	0.07686	28.050
18	10.416	0.00180	0.655	0.00618	2.258
19	19.75	0.00218	0.795	0.00514	1.875
20	190.58	0.03983	14.538	0.07369	26.898
21	16.16	0.00369	1.348	0.00506	1.846
22	19.08	0.00951	3.470	0.02113	7.712
23	97.75	0.04907	17.912	0.04907	17.910
24	77.33	0.26981	98.481	0.04245	15.497
25	66.58	0.01325	4.836	0.02728	9.956

Analysis

Suspended Load

Results presented in the Tables 8.6 to 8.11 and Figures 8.2 and 8.3 reveal the following characteristics regarding the suspended sediment flow from the Nana Kosi Watershed :

(1) Suspended load in the water, flows in the major part of the year from the basin. Only February and March (January in case of 1986-87) are the months when concentration of suspended load in water was found zero (Fig. 8.3 A).

(2) The suspended sediment graph of the study year 1986-87 is skewed with uninodal curve having peak in the month of July, while in the drought year 1987-88 this graph has multimodal character (Fig. 8.3A).

(3) July was the month of maximum concentration of suspended load in 1986-87 when the concentration was found at 362 mg/l.

Table 8.8 : Average suspended sediment data of 1986-87 and 1987-88 (1986-88) of 25 hydrological stations of the Nana Kosi watershed, Central Himalaya, India

Hydrological Station No.	*Concent-ration mg/l*	*Tonnes/day*	*Tonnes/year*	*Tonnes/km²/ day*	*Tonnes/km²/ year*
1	63.95	11.15750	4072.4875	0.259132	94.5830
2	139.88	0.06839	24.9630	0.076524	27.9313
3	141.99	1.71924	627.5225	0.378403	138.1165
4	76.58	4.66120	1701.3380	0.100420	36.6495
5	29.99	0.04111	15.0056	0.079107	28.8724
6	57.24	0.04531	16.5380	0.080980	29.5570
7	68.04	0.09680	35.3320	0.048174	17.5850
8	87.33	0.17325	63.2350	0.238350	86.9980
9	39.21	0.01549	5.6560	0.024015	8.7668
10	142.63	0.12996	47.4330	0.433185	158.1125
11	54.11	0.42913	62.6362	0.142464	14.1998
12	23.29	0.04129	15.0708	0.098290	35.8770
13	64.62	0.50447	184.1325	0.288250	105.2140
14	69.49	0.16044	58.5590	0.139940	51.0794
15	87.20	0.07625	27.8360	0.175780	64.1618
16	57.33	0.73791	269.3370	0.116194	42.4115
17	68.58	2.47605	903.7185	0.104731	38.2240
18	15.74	0.00769	2.8006	0.029367	10.7191
19	19.50	0.00855	3.1237	0.012398	4.5253
20	132.79	0.09386	34.2609	0.280525	102.3920
21	23.37	0.04970	18.1500	0.068140	24.8745
22	23.54	0.07175	26.1880	0.159440	57.8956
23	88.86	0.07841	28.6201	0.094204	34.3800
24	78.87	1.35065	492.9850	0.074534	27.2036
25	70.74	0.09059	33.0653	0.147098	53.6369

Table 8.9 : Suspended sediment flow in per cent of different months in the study year 1986-87 at 25 hydrological stations (Fig. 1.1) in the Nana Kosi Watershed , Central Himalaya, India

Hydrological Station No.	*Feb*	*Mar*	*Apr*	*May*	*June*	*July*	*Aug*	*Sep*	*Oct*	*Nov*	*Dec*	*Jan*
1	0	0	0	1.9	3.6	37.7	27.3	14.5	8.3	6.7	0	0
2	0	0	0	0.1	2.3	33.3	28.5	19.8	9.8	6.2	0	0
3	0	0	0	0	4.6	39.6	10.5	7.9	24.8	12.6	0	0
4	0	0	0	0	6.3	56.7	14.9	10.1	3.1	8.9	0	0
5	0	0	0	0	8.3	43.6	24.5	15.9	6.2	1.5	0	0
6	0	0	0	0	42.8	11.3	15.2	14.8	10.3	5.6	0	0
7	0	0	0	0	10.6	44.3	21.4	12.6	11.1	0	0	0
8	0	0	0	0.6	6.1	37.6	29.8	18.9	7.0	0	0	0
9	0	0	0	0	3.3	37.3	25.3	18.8	12.3	3.0	0	0
10	0	0	0	1.1	8.6	65.5	11.8	7.5	5.5	0	0	0
11	0	0	0	0.1	14.9	51.9	15.9	11.9	3.4	1.9	0	0
12	0	0	0	0	4.4	34.9	33.5	27.2	0	0	0	0
13	0	0	0	0	13.5	37.9	17.4	14.6	10.2	5.9	0	0
14	0	0	0	2.2	19.5	29.2	23.4	11.5	8.2	6.0	0	0
15	0	0	0	1.5	7.9	48.4	23.9	14.5	3.8	0	0	0
16	0	0	0	0	5.8	42.8	21.2	15.1	10.1	5.0	0	0
17	0	0	0	0	8.1	52.8	18.6	11.7	6.7	2.1	0	0
18	0	0	0	0	43.8	7.3	25.6	23.3	0	0	0	0
19	0	0	0	0	3.4	51.5	25.5	19.6	0	0	0	0
20	0	0	0	0.8	7.6	43.4	24.6	15.9	7.7	0	0	0
21	0	0	0	0	6.2	36.5	29.8	27.5	0	0	0	0
22	0	0	0	0	7.1	41.3	28.4	23.2	0	0	0	0
23	0	0	0	0.3	6.6	52.9	15.7	10.8	8.3	5.4	0	0
24	0	0	0	0.1	22.0	32.7	21.7	11.9	7.2	4.4	0	0
25	0	0	0	0.1	4.4	42.4	23.3	12.7	9.4	7.7	0	0

Table 8.10 : Suspended sediment flow in per cent of different months in the study year 1987-88 at 25 hydrological station s (Fig 1.1) in the Nana Kosi watershed, Central Himalaya, India

Hydrological Station No.	*Feb*	*Mar*	*Apr*	*May*	*June*	*July*	*Aug*	*Sep*	*Oct*	*Nov*	*Dec*	*Jan*
1	0	0	0	4.4	14.3	7.3	6.6	17.7	12.5	12.3	13.5	11.4
2	0	0	0	5.7	5.9	21.9	17.4	32.2	4.6	4.4	3.7	4.2
3	0	0	0	9.0	34.7	25.2	17.1	4.7	4.9	4.4	0	0
4	0	0	0	14.5	16.3	24.0	18.0	8.7	6.8	7.5	4.2	0
5	0	0	0	0	0	45.0	22.5	15.0	12.5	5.0	0	0
6	0	0	0.8	8.9	10.6	34.5	20.4	9.5	8.3	4.7	2.3	0
7	0	0	0.9	16.8	14.9	47.8	0	11.7	7.9	0	0	0
8	0	0	0.6	1.4	5.8	47.6	32.5	7.8	2.9	1.4	0	0
9	0	0	0	0	0	75.1	0	16.6	8.3	0	0	0
10	0	0	0.7	1.9	0	50.9	44.5	0	2.0	0	0	0
11	0	0	0.4	8.5	27.2	30.4	18.1	12.7	2.7	0	0	0
12	0	0	0	0	22.9	39.9	21.4	15.8	0	0	0	0
13	0	0	0.9	8.4	18.6	31.6	17.3	9.4	8.1	5.7	0	0
14	0	0	1.2	4.9	21.4	36.9	13.5	10.4	7.3	4.3	0	0
15	0	0	0.6	1.1	7.7	45.9	34.5	8.3	1.9	0	0	0
16	0	0	0.5	9.8	25.9	30.8	16.2	13.6	2.6	0	0	0.6
17	0	0	0.1	9.7	16.8	29.8	18.6	15.8	6.2	2.2	0.8	0
18	0	0	0	0	20.0	32.0	24.0	16.0	8.0	0	0	0
19	0	0	0	0	16.0	25.3	21.2	37.5	0	0	0	0
20	0	0	0.8	1.3	4.3	41.5	40.6	7.4	2.8	1.3	0	0
21	0	0	0	0	20.2	30.9	28.3	20.6	0	0	0	0
22	0	0	0	0	24.6	28.3	26.2	20.9	0	0	0	0
23	0	0	1.5	3.4	16.6	41.7	26.4	2.5	5.4	2.5	0	0
24	0	0	0.3	3.7	11.8	42.4	19.9	11.8	4.3	3.7	0	2.1
25	0	0	0.2	1.8	0	48.8	25.6	11.5	8.4	3.7	0	0

Table 8.11 : Average suspended sediment flow in per cent at different months in the study years 1986-87 and 1987-88 at 25 hydrological stations in the Nana Kosi Watershed, Central Himalaya, India

Hydrological Station No.	*Feb*	*Mar*	*Apr*	*May*	*June*	*July*	*Aug*	*Sep*	*Oct*	*Nov*	*Dec*	*Jan*
1	0	0	0	3.1	8.9	22.5	16.9	16.3	10.4	9.5	6.7	5.7
2	0	0	0	2.9	4.1	27.6	22.9	26.1	7.2	5.3	1.8	2.1
3	0	0	0	4.5	19.6	32.4	13.8	6.3	14.8	8.6	0	0
4	0	0	0	7.2	11.3	40.7	16.4	9.4	4.9	8.2	2.1	0
5	0	0	0	0	4.2	44.3	23.5	15.4	9.3	3.3	0	0
6	0	0	0.4	4.4	28.8	22.9	17.8	12.2	9.3	5.1	1.1	0
7	0	0	0.4	8.4	12.7	46.0	10.7	12.1	9.5	0	0	0
8	0	0	0.3	1.0	5.9	42.6	31.3	13.3	4.9	0.7	0	0
9	0	0	0	0	1.6	56.2	12.6	17.8	10.3	1.5	0	0
10	0	0	0.3	1.5	4.3	58.2	28.3	3.7	3.7	0	0	0
11	0	0	0.2	4.3	21.1	41.2	17.0	12.3	3.0	0.9	0	0
12	0	0	0	0	13.6	37.4	27.4	21.6	0	0	0	0
13	0	0	0.4	4.2	16.3	34.8	17.3	12.1	9.1	5.8	0	0
14	0	0	0.6	3.5	20.4	33.3	18.4	10.9	7.8	5.1	0	0
15	0	0	0.3	1.3	7.8	47.2	29.2	11.4	2.8	0	0	0
16	0	0	0.2	4.9	15.8	36.8	18.8	14.4	6.3	2.5	0	0.3
17	0	0	0	4.8	12.4	41.3	18.6	13.7	6.4	2.0	0.8	0
18	0	0	0	0	32.9	20.6	24.8	16.9	4.8	0	0	0
19	0	0	0	0	9.7	38.4	23.3	28.6	0	0	0	0
20	0	0	0.4	1.1	5.9	42.4	32.6	11.6	5.2	0.8	0	0
21	0	0	0	0	13.2	33.7	29.1	24.0	0	0	0	0
22	0	0	0	0	15.8	34.8	27.3	22.1	0	0	0	0
23	0	0	0.7	1.8	11.6	47.3	21.3	6.6	6.8	3.9	0	0
24	0	0	0.1	1.8	16.9	37.5	20.8	11.8	5.7	4.2	0	1.2
25	0	0	0.1	0.9	2.2	45.6	24.4	12.1	8.9	5.8	0	0

Table 8.12 : Average seasonal contribution of suspended sediment flow in per cent in the study years 1986-87 and 1987-88, at 25 Hydrological stations (Fig. 1.1) in the Nana Kosi watershed, Central Himalaya

Station No.	*Summer*	*Rainy*	*Winter*
1	3.1	64.6	32.3
2	2.9	80.7	16.4
3	4.5	72.1	23.4
4	7.2	77.8	15.2
5	0	87.4	12.6
6	4.8	79.7	15.0
7	8.8	81.5	9.5
8	1.3	93.1	5.6
9	0	88.2	11.8
10	1.8	94.5	3.7
11	4.5	91.6	3.9
12	0	100.0	00
13	4.6	80.5	14.9
14	4.1	83.0	12.9
15	1.6	95.6	2.8
16	5.2	85.9	8.9
17	4.8	86.0	9.2
18	0	95.2	4.8
19	0	100.0	0
20	1.5	92.5	6.0
21	0	100.0	0
22	0	100.0	0
23	2.5	86.8	10.7
24	1.9	87.0	11.1
25	1.0	84.3	14.7

(4) In the drought year (1987-88), the maximum concentration (i.e., 101 mg/l) was found in the month of September.

(5) The mean annual concentration of suspended load in 1986-87 was found 80.58 mg/l and 47.33 mg/l in 1987-88. The average of two years stand at 63.95 mg/l.

(6) In 1986-87, about 37.7 per cent of the total annual sediment flow (i.e., 7768.3 tonnes) was carried by water in the month of July only (Fig. 8.10 A and Table 8.9).

(7) In 1987-88 (i.e.. drought year), about 17.7 per cent of the total annual sediment flow (i.e., 376.7 tonnes) was carried out by the water in the month of September (Fig. 8.10 B and Table 8.10).

(8) The contribution of different seasons in the total annual suspended flow varies from 100 per cent to 64.6 per cent in rainy season, 0 to 3.1 per cent in summer and 0 to 32.3 per cent in winter season (Fig. 8.10 C and Table 8.12).

(9) On an average 64.6 per cent of the total annual suspended sediment load flows in rainy season. Summer and winter flow contribute 3.1 per cent and 32.3 per cent, respectively (Fig. 8.10 C and Table 8.12).

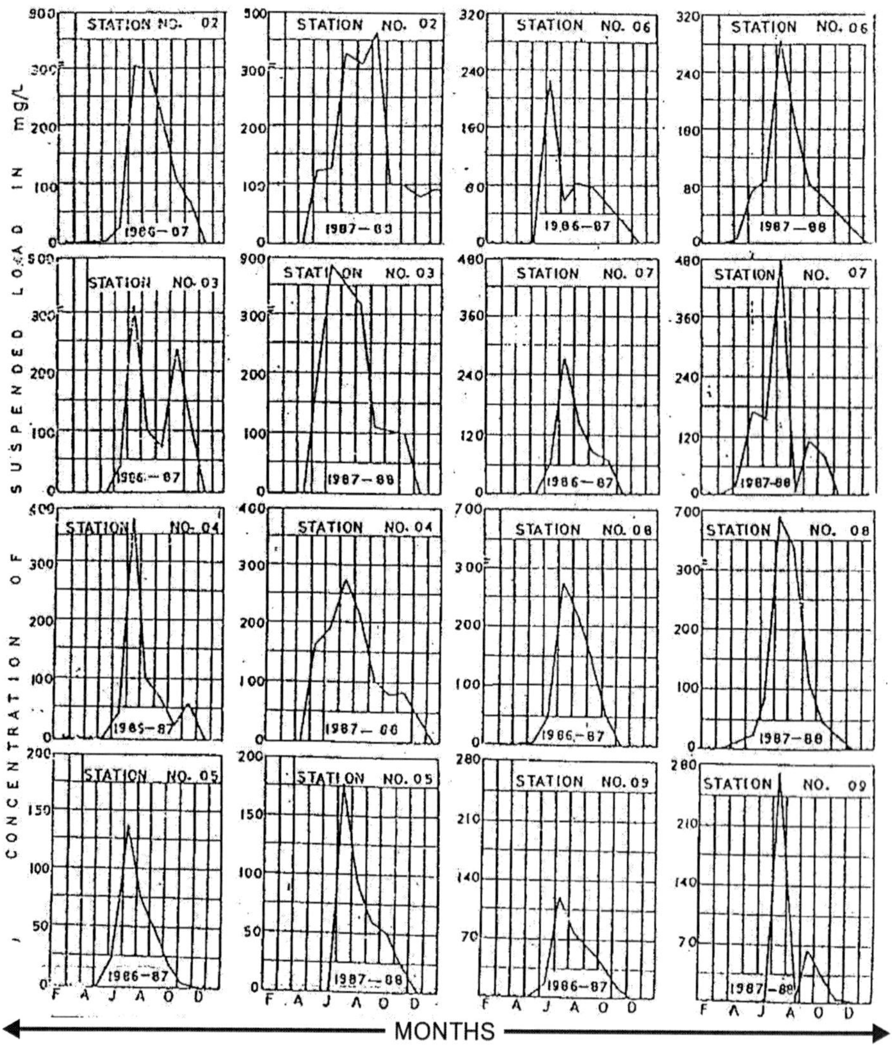

Fig. 8.4 : Suspended load graphs (1986-87 and 1987-88) of Hydrological Station No. 2 to 9 of the Nana Kosi watershed, Central Himalaya (See Fig. 1.1 for the location of hydrological stations).

(10) The spatial distribution of suspended sediment load (Fig. 8.12 A) depicts that there were three groups of suspended load flow in the study area in 1986-87 which ranges in between less than 100 tonnes/km^2 and more than 200 tonnes/km^2.

(11) In 1987-88, the suspended sediment delivery was relatively low which ranges in between less than 10 tonnes/km^2 and more than 40 tonnes/km^2 (Fig. 8.12 B).

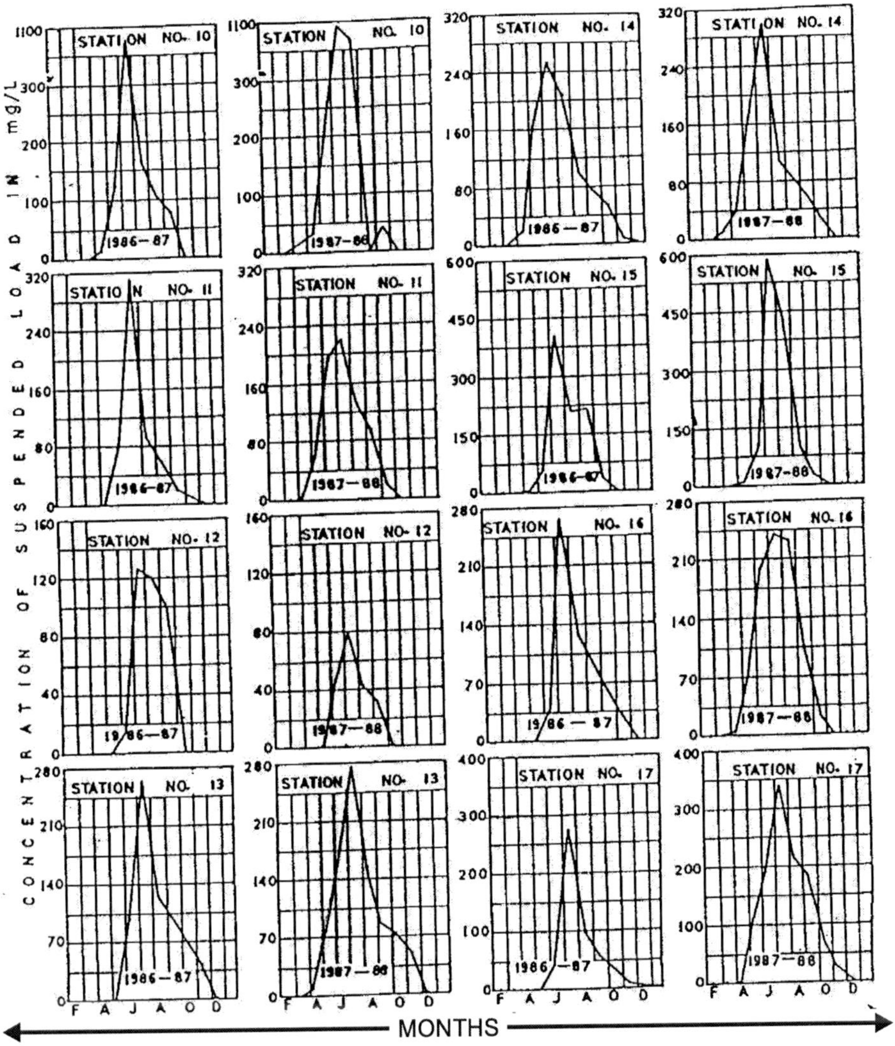

Fig. 8.5: Suspended load graphs (1986-87 and 1987-88) of hydrological station no. 10 to 17 of the Nana Kosi watershed, Central Himalaya (See fig. 1.1 for the location of hydrological stations).

(12) On an average in 1986-87, the suspended sediment from the entire catchment area was generated at the rate of 141.24 tonnes/km^2 while in 1987-88 this rate was found at 47.92 tonnes/km^2 only.

(13) On an average in during the course of the study period (1986-88), the suspended sediment from entire the catchment area was delivered at the rate of 94.58 tonnes/km^2.

(14) During the course of the study period (1986-88), 8145.075 tonnes suspended sediment was discharged from entire the catchment

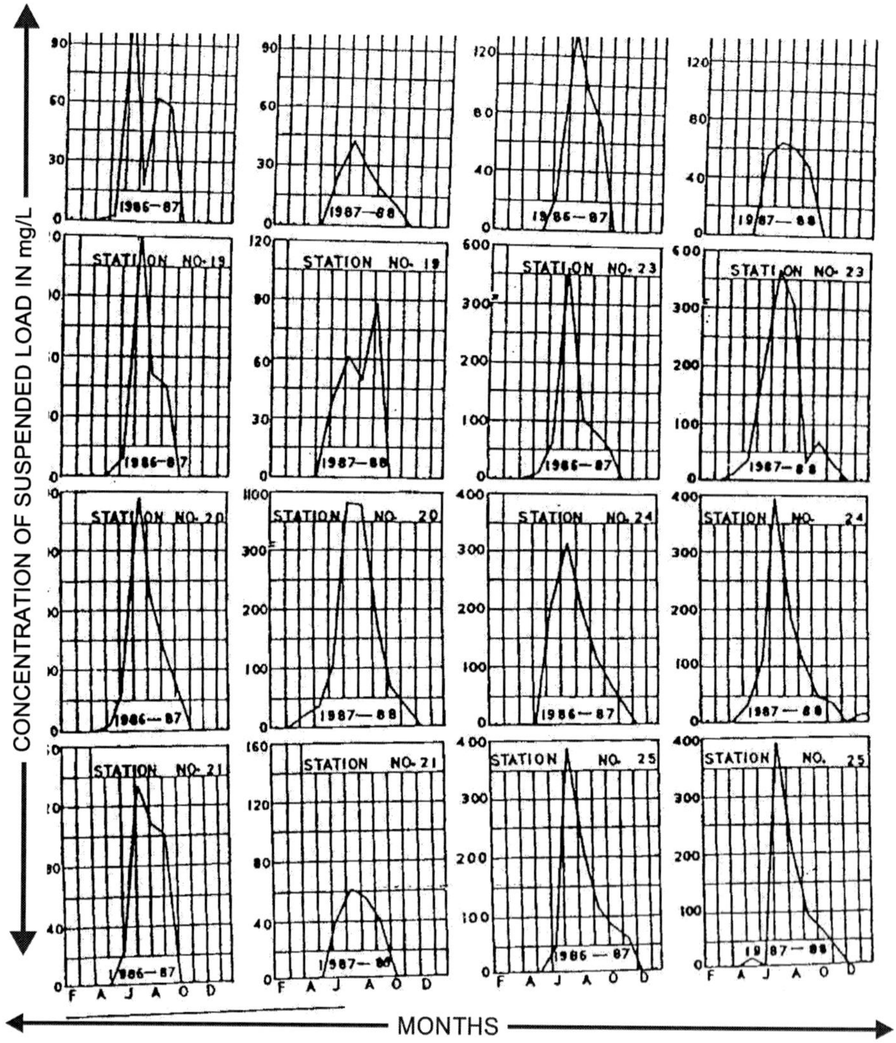

Fig. 8.6 : Suspended load graphs (1986-87 and 1987-88) of hydrological station no. 18 to 25 of the Nana Kosi watershed, Central Himalaya (See fig. 1.1 for the location of hydrological stations).

area of the Nana Kosi Watershed, wherein contribution of draught year (1987-88) was only 25.4 per cent.

Dissolved Load

Results presented in tables (Table 8.13, 8.14, 8.15, 8.16, 8.17, 8.18 and 8.19) and figures (Fig. 8.3B, 8.7, 8.8, 8.9, 8.11 and 8.12 C and D) of dissolved load reveal the following characteristics of the dissolved load flow of the Nana Kosi watershed :

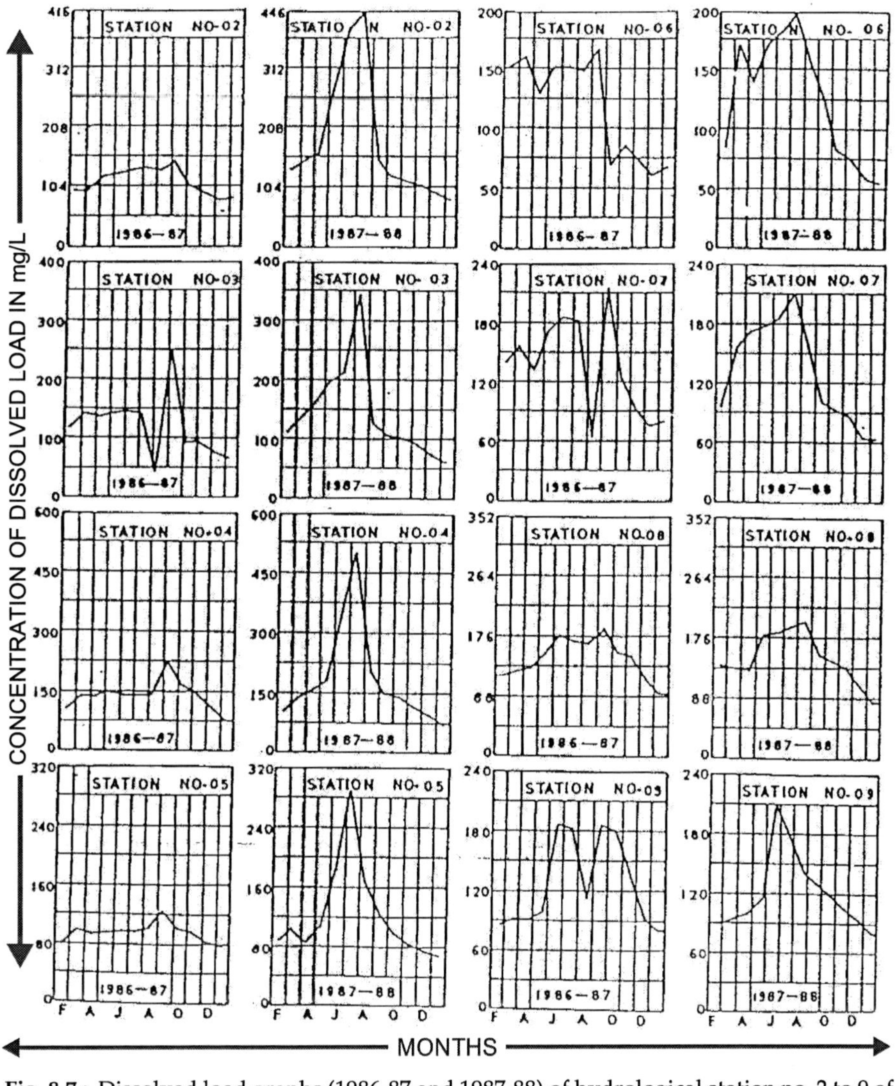

Fig. 8.7 : Dissolved load graphs (1986-87 and 1987-88) of hydrological station no. 2 to 9 of the Nana Kosi watershed, Central Himalaya (See Fig. 1.1 for the location of hydrological stations).

(1) In 1986-87, the maximum concentration of dissolved solutes in water was found in the month of September (i.e., 210 mg/l). It was found minimum (100 mg/l) in the month of January and February (Fig. 8.3 B).

(2) In 1987-88, it approached maximum in the month of June (585 mg/l) and found minimum in January and February (105 mg/l).

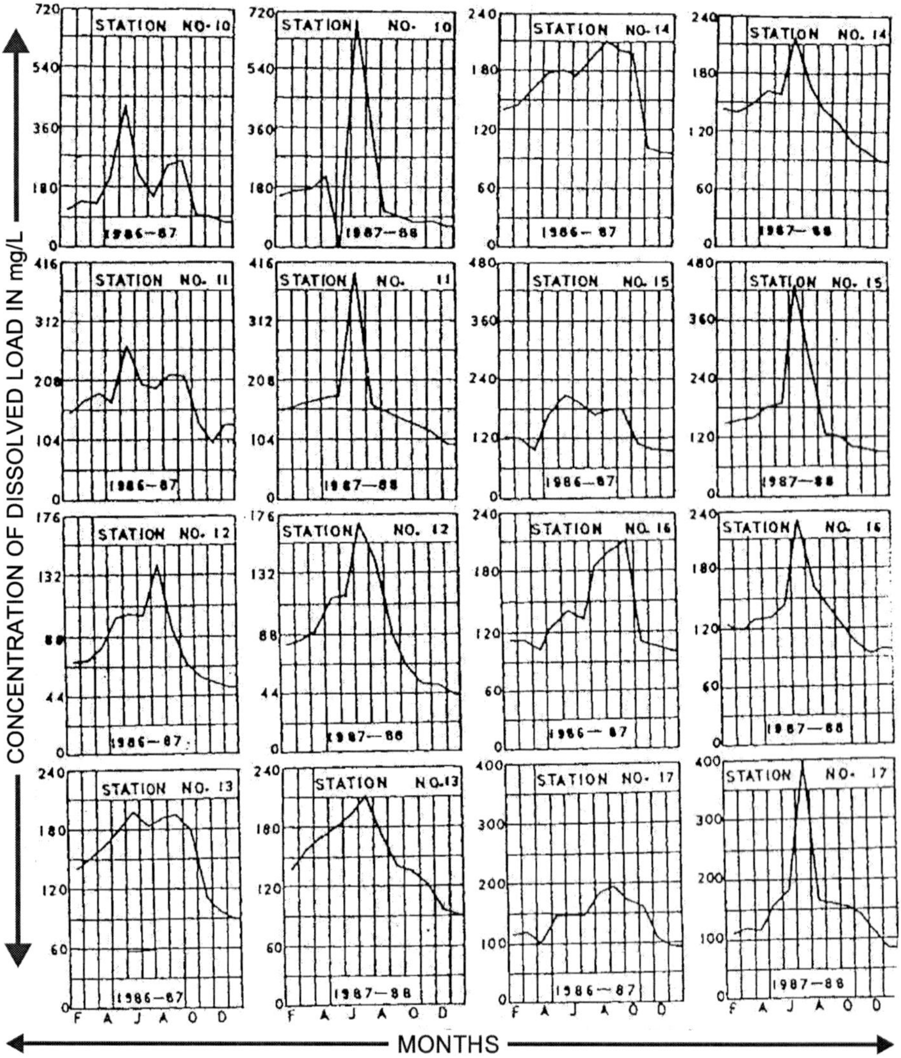

Fig. 8.8 : Dissolved load graphs (1986-87 and 1987-88) of hydrological station no. 10 to 17 of the Nana Kosi watershed, Central Himalaya (See Fig. 1.1 for the location of hydrological stations).

(3) The average dissolved concentration for the study period (1986-88) stands at 204.4 mg/l (Table 8.15). For the study year 1986-87 and 1987-88 it stand at 155.91 mg/l and 252.91 mg/l, respectively (Table 8.13 and 8.14)

(4) From entire the study area, the maximum flow of dissolved load occurred in the month of September in 1986-87 which was 11.2 per cent of the total annual flow. In this month the dissolved load

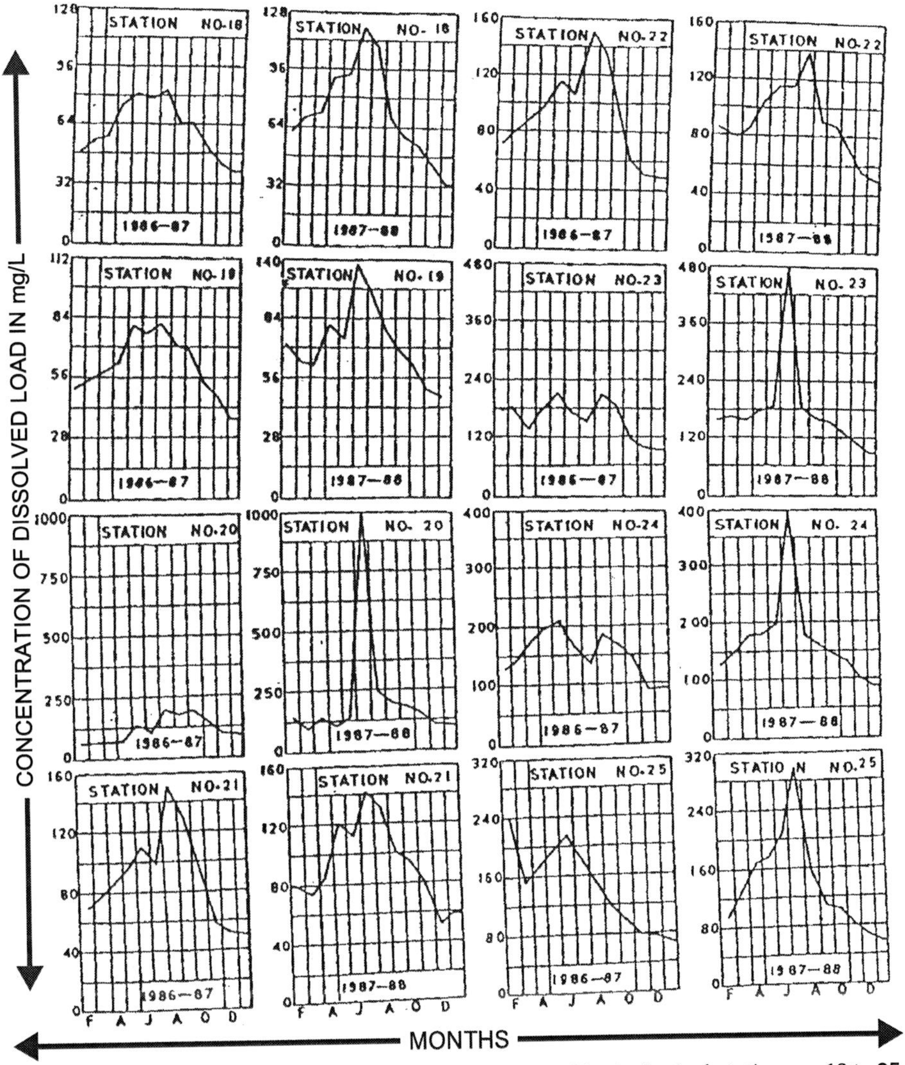

Fig. 8.9 : Dissolved load graphs (1986-87 and 1987-88) of hydrological station no. 18 to 25 of the Nana Kosi watershed, Central Himalaya (See Fig. 1.1 for the location of hydrological stations).

flow coupled with water at the rate of 65.76 tonnes/day, and dissolved load generating capacity of land to water was 1.12 tonnes/km^2/day (Fig. 8.11 A and Table 8.16).

(5) In 1987-88, maximum flow of dissolved load occurred in the month of July (20.6% of the total annual). In this month dissolved load flowed at the rate of 121.73 tonnes/day and the dissolved load generating capacity of the land was 2.21 tonnes/km^2/day (Table 8.17 and Fig. 8.11 B).

Table 8.13 : Mean dissolved load data of 1986-87 of 25 hydrological stations (Fig. 1.1) of the Nana Kosi watershed, Central Himalaya, India

Hydrological Station No.	*Concent-ration mg/l*	*Tonnes/day*	*Tonnes/year*	*Tonnes/km²/ day*	*Tonnes/km²/ year*
1	155.910	16.18700	5908.25500	0.310160	113.2084
2	113.500	0.11107	40.54000	0.123109	44.9348
3	122.916	1.44500	527.42500	0.366390	133.7323
4	145.416	8.52490	3111.58850	0.183153	66.8510
5	94.916	0.08656	31.59650	0.201879	73.6856
6	117.500	0.15665	57.17650	0.256076	93.4677
7	135.000	0.27215	99.33500	0.143867	52.5116
8	144.080	0.23885	87.17870	0.332406	121.3282
9	125.875	0.07929	28.94194	0.144166	52.6208
10	184.333	0.08242	30.08819	0.274720	100.2730
11	173.833	2.33951	853.92100	0.211365	77.1482
12	84.170	0.07635	27.86700	0.177384	64.7452
13	157.250	0.78567	286.76900	0.448389	163.6620
14	157.080	0.47365	172.88500	0.377440	137.7680
15	147.583	0.11662	42.56700	0.265030	96.7370
16	137.333	1.45130	529.73460	0.228500	83.4000
17	138.166	3.78950	1383.16700	0.160250	58.4920
18	61.416	0.02826	10.31680	0.098734	36.0379
19	61.500	0.03579	13.06300	0.047103	17.1927
20	120.416	0.10114	36.91880	0.224760	82.0390
21	89.167	0.22138	80.80500	0.443740	16.1965
22	91.583	0.20380	74.38700	0.453570	165.5511
23	11.641	0.17769	64.86050	0.150516	54.9385
24	153.900	1.74195	635.81290	0.255051	93.0938
25	142.790	0.11253	41.07580	0.178688	65.2212

(6) In the month of minimum flow, i.e., January and February, in 1986-87, only 5.8 per cent dissolved load of the total annual, flowed in water. In these months dissolved solutes flowed at the rate of 1.40 tonnes/day and the dissolved load generating capacity of land was 0.025 tonnes/km²/day (Table 8.11 A).

Table 8.14 : Mean dissolved load data of 1987-88 at 25 hydrological stations (Fig 1.1) of the Nana Kosi watershed, Central Himalaya, India

Hydrological Station No.	*Concent-ration mg/l*	*Tonnes/day*	*Tonnes/year*	*Tonnes/km²/ day*	*Tonnes/km²/ year*
1	252.916	12.000000	4380.00000	0.218180	79.6357
2	181.250	0.040408	14.74870	0.044890	16.3864
3	146.083	0.172213	62.85780	0.037407	13.6536
4	182.250	2.776870	1013.55900	0.059787	21.8224
5	121.500	0.011682	4.26382	0.020862	7.6148
6	125.750	0.045162	16.48420	0.074045	27.0266
7	132.416	0.106067	38.71460	0.052833	19.2842
8	161.250	0.082824	30.23079	0.107586	39.2691
9	122.166	0.015165	5.53540	0.042027	15.3400
10	185.417	0.021930	8.00400	0.121039	44.1790
11	172.666	0.786507	287.07500	0.071059	25.9366
12	91.250	0.016700	6.07840	0.037170	13.5653
13	150.166	0.113802	41.53790	0.065000	23.7250
14	143.916	0.55060	20.09690	0.346283	16.8934
15	177.916	0.029967	10.93790	0.068105	24.8580
16	133.000	0.269751	98.45910	0.042479	15.5048
17	158.250	1.300840	474.80700	0.055040	20.0901
18	78.583	0.009505	3.46950	0.032760	11.9580
19	75.416	0.008059	2.94175	0.010596	3.8676
20	217.750	0.041575	15.17490	0.092389	33.7221
21	93.080	0.032320	11.79000	0.044360	16.1914
22	89.750	0.038305	13.98132	0.085130	31.0736
23	185.500	0.082635	30.16200	0.070117	25.5980
24	172.750	0.571060	208.43900	0.089230	32.5701
25	139.666	0.021430	7.82200	0.034014	12.4151

Table 8.15 : Average dissolved load data of 1986-87 and 1987-88 (1986-88) of 25 hydrological stations (Fig. 1.1) of the Nana Kosi Watershed, Central Himalaya, India

Hydrological Station No.	*Concent-ration mg/l*	*Tonnes/day*	*Tonnes/year*	*Tonnes/km²/ day*	*Tonnes/km²/ year*
1	204.413	14.09300	5144.1275	0.264170	96.422
2	147.375	0.07570	27.6440	0.083900	30.660
3	134.499	0.80860	295.1410	0.201890	73.693
4	163.833	5.65100	2062.5737	0.121470	44.336
5	108.208	0.04910	17.9301	0.111370	40.650
6	121.625	0.10090	36.8300	0.165060	60.247
7	133.708	0.18911	69.0240	0.098350	35.897
8	152.665	0.16083	58.7040	0.219900	80.298
9	124.020	0.04720	17.2380	0.093090	33.980
10	184.874	0.05217	19.0430	0.197870	72.226
11	173.250	1.56300	570.4980	0.141210	51.542
12	87.710	0.04652	16.9720	0.107277	39.155
13	153.710	0.44973	164.1530	0.256690	93.662
14	150.490	0.26435	96.4900	0.211860	77.330
15	162.750	0.07329	26.7520	0.166580	60.797
16	135.170	0.86052	314.0960	0.135480	49.452
17	148.210	2.54500	928.9870	0.107640	39.291
18	69.990	0.01888	6.8930	0.065740	23.997
19	68.458	0.02192	8.0020	0.028840	10.530
20	169.083	0.07136	26.0460	0.158570	57.880
21	91.124	0.12685	46.2970	0.044360	16.194
22	90.666	0.12105	44.1842	0.269350	98.312
23	98.570	0.13016	47.5110	0.110310	40.268
24	163.330	1.15650	422.1250	0.172140	62.832
25	141.228	0.06698	24.4480	0.106350	38.818

(7) In 1987-88, the minimum dissolved flow months (January and February) contributed 3.4 per cent dissolved load in the total annual flow. In these months dissolved load flowed at the rate of 1.0 tonne/day and the dissolved load generating capacity of land was 0.01 tonnes/km²/day (Table 8.17 and Fig. 8.11 B).

(8) On an average out of the total annual flow of dissolved load about 45 per cent flows in the rainy season. The percentage of other seasons, i.e., summer and winter stand at 30.9 per cent and 24.1 per cent, respectively (Fig. 8.11 C and Table 8.19).

Table 8.16 : Dissolved load in per cent of different months in the study year 1986-87 at 25 hydrological stations (Fig. 1.1) in the Nana Kosi Watershed, Central Himalaya, India

Hydrological Station No.	*Feb*	*Mar*	*Apr*	*May*	*June*	*July*	*Aug*	*Sep*	*Oct*	*Nov*	*Dec*	*Jan*
1	5.8	6.4	8.1	9.2	9.7	9.5	8.2	11.2	10.9	8.8	6.4	5.8
2	7.4	7.4	8.8	9.1	9.5	9.9	9.6	11.6	7.7	6.9	5.8	6.3
3	8.1	9.8	9.3	9.8	10.6	9.5	3.0	16.9	6.4	6.5	5.4	4.7
4	6.4	8.2	8.3	8.9	8.3	8.1	8.3	12.8	10.3	8.8	6.8	4.8
5	6.9	8.5	7.9	8.4	8.6	8.6	8.9	10.9	8.8	8.3	7.4	6.8
6	10.6	11.5	9.2	10.7	10.7	10.5	11.7	4.9	6.3	4.9	4.4	4.6
7	8.7	9.5	8.1	10.6	11.4	11.3	4.0	13.2	7.6	5.6	4.8	5.2
8	6.9	7.4	7.5	8.8	10.3	9.9	9.6	10.6	8.8	8.5	6.3	5.4
9	5.6	6.2	6.3	6.4	12.4	12.2	7.2	12.2	11.9	8.6	5.9	5.1
10	5.4	6.8	5.8	9.4	19.2	10.3	7.3	11.3	11.9	4.6	4.4	3.6
11	7.3	8.6	9.2	8.6	12.9	9.7	9.4	10.5	9.5	5.7	4.7	4.3
12	7.3	7.4	8.2	10.2	10.4	10.3	13.8	9.4	6.9	4.9	5.4	5.8
13	7.5	8.2	8.7	9.5	10.6	9.6	10.4	10.4	9.6	5.7	5.1	4.7
14	7.4	7.8	8.4	9.4	9.6	9.3	10.3	11.4	10.6	5.5	5.3	5.1
15	7.3	7.2	6.2	9.5	11.8	10.8	9.6	10.1	10.2	6.2	5.6	5.5
16	6.9	6.9	6.2	7.8	8.6	8.3	11.2	12.4	12.8	6.6	6.3	6.0
17	6.6	6.9	6.2	8.4	8.9	8.6	10.9	11.6	10.2	9.8	6.5	5.4
18	6.5	7.3	7.5	10.4	10.9	10.5	11.6	8.8	8.5	6.9	5.8	5.2
19	6.9	7.6	7.8	8.4	10.9	10.3	10.8	9.4	9.3	7.1	6.5	5.0
20	4.8	4.9	5.3	5.6	9.8	7.2	13.8	12.4	13.2	10.3	6.9	6.2
21	6.4	7.1	8.1	8.8	10.2	9.1	14.2	12.4	9.1	5.4	4.7	4.5
22	6.3	7.2	8.4	8.8	10.4	9.5	13.1	12.2	9.4	5.5	4.7	4.5
23	9.1	9.5	7.1	9.2	11.3	9.2	7.9	10.8	9.7	6.1	5.1	5.0
24	6.9	8.2	9.6	10.7	11.3	8.9	7.3	10.1	9.2	8.1	4.8	4.9
25	14.4	8.8	9.8	9.3	12.4	10.6	8.7	6.8	5.8	4.6	4.5	4.3

Table 8.17 : Dissolved load in per cent of different months in the study year 1987-88 at 25 hydrological stations (Fig. 1.1) in the Nana Kosi Watershed, Central Himalaya, India

Hydrological Station No.	*Feb*	*Mar*	*Apr*	*May*	*June*	*July*	*Aug*	*Sep*	*Oct*	*Nov*	*Dec*	*Jan*
1	3.4	5.7	7.6	15.8	19.6	20.6	5.9	5.2	4.9	4.2	3.9	3.4
2	6.2	6.8	7.3	12.4	17.5	18.8	7.2	5.7	5.3	4.8	4.4	3.6
3	6.5	7.9	9.5	11.2	12.2	19.6	7.5	6.2	5.9	5.6	4.2	3.7
4	5.0	6.4	7.3	8.3	15.4	23.3	7.7	6.8	6.4	5.2	4.8	3.4
5	5.8	6.7	5.8	7.4	12.6	19.8	11.7	8.2	6.5	5.4	5.3	4.8
6	5.6	11.2	9.2	11.2	11.9	13.3	10.6	8.2	5.3	5.3	4.3	3.9
7	6.6	9.7	10.7	11.2	11.6	13.4	10.3	6.2	5.9	5.6	4.4	4.4
8	7.3	6.9	6.8	9.4	9.6	17.6	10.6	7.8	7.4	6.9	5.4	4.3
9	6.1	6.4	6.8	7.8	14.8	12.3	9.8	8.8	8.2	7.2	6.4	5.4
10	6.9	7.6	7.8	9.6	0	31.3	17.3	4.9	4.2	3.5	3.8	3.1
11	7.5	8.2	8.3	8.6	8.8	19.8	7.9	7.2	6.8	6.3	5.8	4.8
12	7.3	7.8	8.3	10.6	10.8	15.6	12.8	8.2	5.9	4.6	4.3	3.8
13	7.6	8.8	9.4	9.9	10.8	11.8	9.4	7.8	7.4	6.8	5.2	5.1
14	8.4	8.3	8.7	9.6	9.3	12.8	9.8	8.3	7.6	6.3	5.7	5.2
15	7.1	7.4	7.5	8.7	8.8	20.3	14.4	6.3	5.8	4.9	4.6	4.2
16	7.8	7.5	8.2	8.2	8.8	14.4	10.2	8.6	7.8	6.5	5.9	6.1
17	5.7	6.2	6.2	8.4	9.4	21.6	8.6	8.4	8.1	7.3	5.7	4.4
18	7.2	7.8	8.2	10.4	10.5	13.5	12.4	7.8	6.7	6.3	5.3	3.9
19	7.9	6.9	6.7	8.9	8.4	14.9	12.3	8.6	7.8	6.8	5.5	5.3
20	5.5	3.7	5.1	4.4	5.5	38.2	9.3	7.4	6.8	6.1	4.2	3.8
21	6.9	6.4	7.4	10.8	9.8	12.7	11.7	8.9	8.5	7.4	4.4	5.1
22	7.8	7.3	7.9	9.9	10.6	10.7	12.9	8.3	8.3	6.4	5.3	4.6
23	7.8	7.9	7.8	8.5	8.4	21.5	8.5	7.6	7.3	5.8	4.7	4.2
24	6.2	7.2	8.6	8.8	9.6	19.2	8.6	7.8	7.2	6.8	5.5	4.5
25	5.8	7.8	10.1	10.6	12.6	17.8	9.6	6.6	6.2	5.2	4.2	3.5

Table 8.18 : Average dissolved load in per cent of different months in the study years 1986-87 and 1987-88, at 25 hydrological stations (Fig. 1.1) in the Nana Kosi Watershed, Central Himalaya, India

Hydrological Station No.	Feb	Mar	Apr	May	June	July	Aug	Sep	Oct	Nov	Dec	Jan
1	4.6	6.0	7.8	12.5	14.6	15.2	7.0	8.2	7.9	6.5	5.1	4.6
2	6.8	7.2	8.2	10.7	13.5	14.3	8.4	8.6	6.5	5.8	5.1	4.9
3	7.3	8.8	9.4	10.5	11.4	14.5	5.2	11.5	6.4	6.0	4.8	4.2
4	5.7	7.3	7.8	8.6	11.8	15.7	8.1	9.8	8.3	7.0	5.8	4.1
5	6.3	7.6	6.8	7.9	10.6	14.5	10.3	9.5	7.6	6.8	6.3	5.8
6	8.2	11.3	9.2	10.9	11.3	11.9	11.2	6.5	5.8	5.2	4.3	4.2
7	7.6	9.6	9.4	10.9	11.5	12.3	7.2	9.7	6.8	5.6	4.6	4.8
8	7.1	7.1	7.2	9.2	9.9	13.7	10.2	9.2	8.1	7.7	5.8	4.8
9	5.8	6.3	6.5	7.2	13.7	12.3	8.5	10.5	10.0	7.9	6.1	5.2
10	6.1	7.2	6.8	9.5	9.6	20.8	12.3	8.2	8.0	4.0	4.2	3.3
11	7.4	8.4	8.7	8.6	10.8	14.7	8.6	8.8	8.1	6.2	5.2	4.5
12	7.3	7.6	8.2	10.4	10.6	12.9	13.4	8.8	6.5	4.7	4.8	4.8
13	7.5	8.5	9.0	9.7	10.7	10.7	9.9	9.2	8.5	6.2	5.2	4.9
14	7.9	8.2	8.5	9.5	9.4	11.1	10.0	9.8	9.1	5.9	5.5	5.1
15	7.2	7.3	6.8	9.1	10.3	15.5	12.2	8.2	8.0	5.5	5.1	4.8
16	7.3	7.2	7.2	8.0	8.8	11.3	10.8	10.5	10.3	6.5	6.1	6.0
17	6.2	6.6	6.2	8.4	9.2	15.1	9.7	10.0	9.1	8.5	6.1	4.9
18	6.8	7.5	7.8	10.4	10.7	12.2	12.1	8.3	7.6	6.6	5.5	4.5
19	7.4	7.3	7.3	8.6	9.6	12.7	11.6	9.0	8.5	6.9	6.0	5.1
20	5.1	4.3	5.2	5.0	7.6	22.7	11.5	9.9	10.0	8.2	5.5	5.0
21	6.6	6.7	7.7	9.8	10.3	10.9	12.9	10.6	8.8	6.4	4.5	4.8
22	7.0	7.2	8.1	9.3	10.5	10.1	13.2	10.2	8.8	5.9	5.2	4.5
23	8.4	8.8	7.6	8.8	9.8	15.3	8.2	9.2	8.5	5.9	4.9	4.6
24	6.5	7.7	9.2	9.7	10.4	14.3	7.9	8.9	8.2	7.4	5.1	4.7
25	10.1	8.3	9.9	9.9	12.5	14.2	9.1	6.7	6.2	4.9	4.3	3.9

Table 8.19 : Average seasonal contribution of dissolved load in per cent in the study years 1986-87 and 1987-88 at 25 hydrological stations in the Nana Kosi Watershed, Central Himalaya, India.

Hydrological station No.	*Summer*	*Rainy*	*Winter*
1	30.9	45.0	24.1
2	32.9	44.8	22.3
3	36.0	42.6	21.4
4	29.4	45.4	25.2
5	28.6	44.9	26.5
6	39.6	40.9	19.5
7	37.5	40.7	21.8
8	30.6	43.0	26.4
9	25.8	45.0	29.2
10	29.6	50.9	19.5
11	33.1	42.9	24.0
12	33.5	45.7	20.8
13	34.7	40.5	24.8
14	34.1	40.3	25.6
15	30.4	46.2	23.4
16	29.7	41.4	28.9
17	27.4	44.0	28.6
18	32.5	43.3	24.2
19	30.6	42.9	26.5
20	19.6	51.7	28.7
21	30.8	44.7	24.5
22	31.6	44.0	24.4
23	33.6	42.5	23.9
24	33.1	41.5	25.4
25	38.2	42.5	19.3

(9) The spatial distribution of dissolved load flow (Fig. 8.12 C and D) in the study area reveals that there is considerable difference in the spatial distribution of dissolved load flow of the normal (1986-87) and drought year (1987-88).

(10) In 1986-87, the study area is divisible into four zones of relatively higher flow of dissolved load than that of 1987-88.

(11) The mean rate of dissolved load flow in 1986-87 stand at 75.85 tonnes/km^2, while for 1987-88 it stand at 16.51 tonnes/km^2 only.

(12) In 1986-87, the dissolved load from entire the catchment area was generated at the rate of 113.20 tonnes/km^2 while for 1987-88 this rate was found at 79.36 tonnes/km^2.

(13) On an average during the course of the study period (1986-88), the dissolved load from entire the catchment area was delivered at the rate of 96.42 tonnes/km^2.

Estimation of Denudation Rates

Denudation (vertical lowering of the land surface) is a term used to describe the overall lowering of the landscape resulting from the erosive and transporting activities of all operating processes. Any attempt to understand the significance of rates of denudation that have been determined for the Himalayan region not only requires and appreciation of the status of mountain environmental geomorphology. In practical terms this is usually calculated as mm yr^{-1} in surface lowering averaged over entire regions, usually drainage basins, despite the fact that actual surface lowering will be extremely variable in space, as it depends upon many factors including the underlying bedrock lithologies and structures, and slope angle (Ives and Messerli, 1989). An impression of the intensity of geomorphological processes operating in the Himalayan mountains can be gained from denudation rates estimated for the region and for catchments of some of the main rivers (Table 8.20). The rates reported are high, up to five times or more higher than general estimates of erosion even in areas of steep relief (0.1-1.0 mm yr^{-1}; Saunders and Young, 1983). Despite their inherent errors the figures suggest a very dynamic geomorphological environment (Ramsay, 1986).

Stream Transport is conveniently divided into the suspended load, dissolved load and bedload. The sediment yield that is actually measured is often only the suspended sediment. Even this is difficult to measure accurately for rivers that experience enormous variations in volume over the course of the year and from year to year. This is especially characteristic of rivers of monsoonal climates where low flow in late winter and spring may be several orders of magnitude below peak rainy season discharge (Ives and Messerli, 1989). Bedload sediment have not been monitored on any Himalayan river, even under conditions of normal summer flow. An estimate is usually made for this component of the total sediment transfer in calculating the design life of reservoirs. Bedload measurement is a critical obervation since hundreds of millions of dollars have been expended on dam and reservoir construction with the design life over estimated two-three-and four fold. In this dynamic geomorphological environment, some workers successfully identified both transport and storage processes, and recognized the linkages between them. However, qualification of these elements and the development of even a preliminary sediment budget for a watershed is at a very early stage in Central Himalaya.

Hydrological station number one in Table 8.6 and 8.13 reveal that about 7768 tonnes suspended and 5908 tonnes dissolved load was discharged from the mouth of the Nana Kosi watershed in 1986-87. Thus, the total sediment discharged from the study area in 1986-87 was 13676 tonnes. On an average the total denudation (i.e., 13767 tonnes) from the

Table 8.20: Some denudation rates of the Himalayan mountains (from various sources, after Ramsay, 1986)

Location	*Denudation Rate (mm yr¹)*	*Comments*	*Research*
Himalaya	1.00	Regional	Menard, 1961
Ganges/Brahmaputra Watershed	0.70	From present rate of influx to Bay of Bengal	Curry and Moore, 1971
River Hunza Watershed	1.80	From sediment yield	Ferguson, 1984
River Tamur Watershed	5.14	From sediment yield	Seshadri, 1961*
River Tamur Watershed	4.70	From sediment yield	Ahuja and Rao, 1958*
River Tamur Watershed	2.56		Williams, 1977
River Arun Watershed	1.90	1947-60	Pal and Bagchi, 1974*
River Arun Watershed	0.51		Williams, 1977, after Das, 1968
River Sun Kosi Watershed	2.50		Pal and Bagchi, 1974*
River Sun Kosi Watershed	1.43		Williams, 1977, after Das, 1968
River (Sapta) Kosi Watershed	0.98	From suspended sediment	Schumm, 1963, based on Khosla,1953
River (Sapta) Kosi Watershed	1.00		Williams, 1977, after Das, 1968
River Karnali Watershed	1.50		UNDP, 1966
Darjeeling area**	0.50-5.00	Forested/Deforested	Starkel, 1972 a
Darjeeling area**	10.0-20.00	In catastrophic storms	Starkel, 1972 a

* Brunsden et al. (1981).

** These figures are estimstes and are not based on precise measurements.

study area was done by different processes at the rate of 248.6 tonnes/km². For 1987-88 (which was drought year) this rate stands at 86.49 tonnes/km². Values of suspended and dissolved yields from drainage basins are often used to calculate the rate of erosion or denudation within the catchment expressed as the volume of material removed per unit area within a given time. The basic calculation involved the conversion of the suspended and dissolved yields into volumes or depths of erosion per unit area and, therefore, involves values of specific gravity or density (Gregory and Walling, 1973), i.e.:

$$\text{Denudation in m}^3/\text{km}^2/\text{year or 1000 yrs} = \frac{\text{Total load (tonnes)}}{\text{Area (km}^2) \times \text{Specific gravity}}$$

The specific gravity of the sedimentary rocks stands at 2.65 (Valdiya, 1971). By using the total load of 1986-87 and 1987-88 (i.e. 13676 tonnes and 4757 tons) and specific gravity (i.e. 2.65) the rates of denudation of the

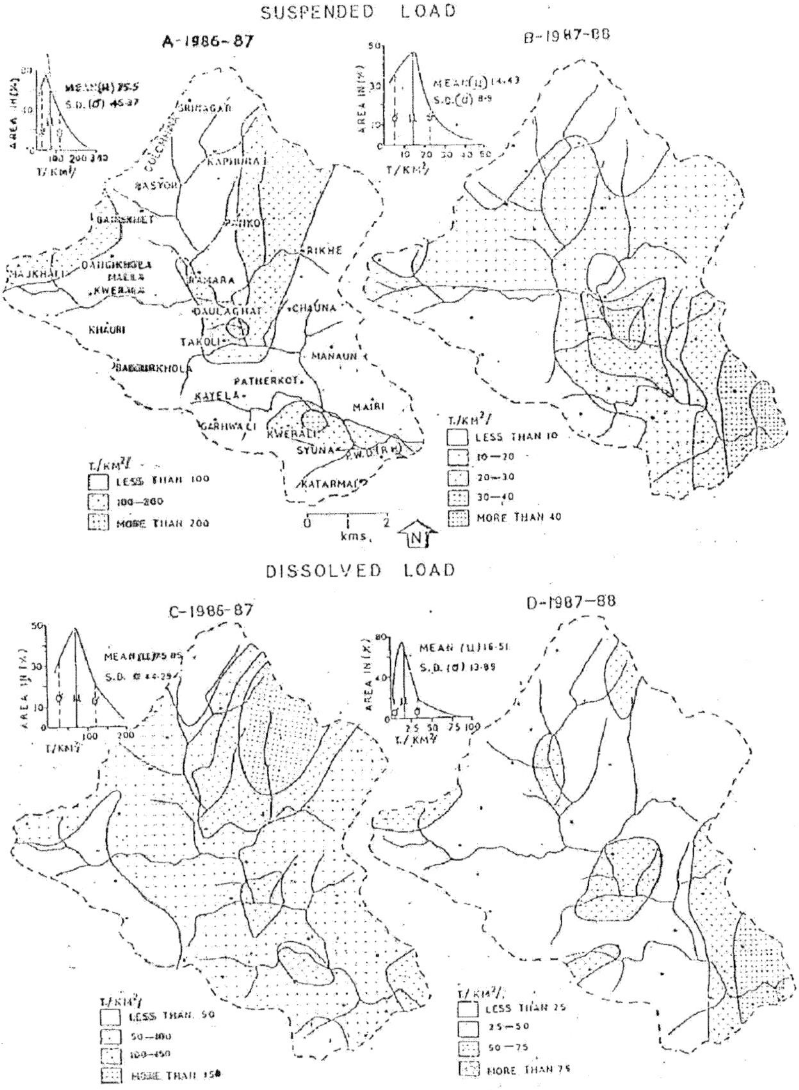

Fig. 8.10 : Spatial distribution of suspended (A and B) and dissolved load (C) and D) generating capacity of land (tonnes/km^2) to channels in the Nana Kosi Watershed, Central Himalaya during two study years.

Nana Kosi watershed were deduced for two study years which stand at 93.83 and 32.63 m^3/km^2 for 1986-87 and 1987-88, respectively. This suggests that on an average, the Nana Kosi watershed was lowered at the rate of about 0.93 mm per year in 1986-87 and 0.3 mm per year in 1987-88, i.e., in drought period.

There is some suggestions that the rates of erosion in the Himalaya are higher than was previously thought. Two decades ago the erosion rate in the Ganges basin in the Indian Himalaya was estimated at 910 mm/ 1000yr, i.e., 0.9 mm/yr^{-1} (Gregory and Walling, 1973). More recently in the Central Himalaya it has been estimated at 1.7mm/yr^{-1} (Valdiya and Bartarya, 1989 b). There are several factors that may contribute to this acceleration, including deforestation (Bartarya, 1988), poorly managed agriculture, forest fire, overgrazing and sub-standard construction of road and building on ill-suited sites. However, the actual impact of these anthropogenic activities remains poorly understood and unquantified. The existing studies reveal that the soil erosion in the Central Himalaya has been shown to be an important phenomenon and is probably higher than in most other major mountain systems.

REFERENCES

Chow, V.T. 1964 : *Handbook of applied hydrology* (ed.) McGraw-Hill, New York, pp. 1418.

Coutts, J.R.H. 1968 : Use of radioactive 59 fe for tracing soil particle movement. Pt. I. Field studies of splash erosion. *J. Soil. Sci.,* 19, pp. 24-311.

De Poley, J. 1967 : *Erosion pluvial all congo occidental. Isotopes in Hydrology,* I.A.E.A. Vienna, pp. 291-300.

Ellision, W.D. 1950 : Splash erosion in pictures. *J. Soil and water conser,* 5, pp. 71-74.

Emmett, W.W. 1965 : The vigil network; methods of measurement and a sample of data collection. *Internet. Assoc. Sci. Hyd.* Pub., 66, pp. 89-106.

Geib, H.V. 1933 : A new type of installation for measuring soil and water losses from plots. *J. Ame. Soc. Agronomy,* 24, pp. 229-240.

Gregory, K.J. and Walling, D.E. 1973 : Drainage basin forms and process. A Geomorphological Approach, Arnold, London, pp. 1-465.

Kazo, B. and Klimes-Szmik, A. 1962 : A method of artificial sprinkling for the investigation of the process of erosion. Internet. *Assoc. Sci. Hyd. Pub.,* 59, pp. 52-61.

Mcqueen, I.S. 1963 : *Development of a hand portable rainfall—simulator Infiltrometer.* U.S. Geol. Surv. Circular, p. 482.

Osborne, B. 1953 : Field measurements of soil splash to evaluate ground Cover. *J. Soil and Water Conser,* 8, pp.

Reneau, L.S. and Dietrick, E.W. 1987 : The importance of hollows in debris flow studies, examples from Marin Country, Califor. *Geol. Soc. of Ame. Reves. in Enginee. Geol.* 7, pp. 165-180.

Ruhe, R.V. 1975 : *Geomorphology, geomorphic processes and surficial geology.* Houghton Mifflin Co., Boston, pp. 60-266.

Schick, A.P. 1967 : Suspended sampler, Revue de Geomorph. *Dynamique,* 17, pp. 170-172.

Selby, M.J. 1980 : A rock mass strength classification for geomorphic purposes with tests from Antarctica and New Zealand. *Zeitschrift fur geomorphologie,* 24, pp. 31-51.

Stehlik, O. 1967 : On methods of measuring sheetwash and rill erosion. Revue de Geomorph. *Dynamique*, 17, p. 176.

Strahler, A.H. and Strahler, A.N. 1977 : *Geography and man's environment*. John Wiley & Sons, New York, p. 216

Touckfield, C.G. 1964 : Gully erosion in the New Forest, Hampshire. *Ame. J. Sci.*, 262, pp. 795-807.

Valdiya, K.S. 1971 : *Bhoovigyan; Kuchh Jwalant Samasyayen*. Uttar Pradesh Hindi Granth Academy, Lucknow, p. 16.

Van Doren, C.A., Stauffer, R.S. and Kidder, E.H. 1950 : Effect of contour farming on soil loss and runoff. *Soil Sci. Soc. Ame. Proc.*, 15, pp. 113-417.

Wooldridge, D.D. 1965 : Tracing soil particle movement with fe-59. *Soil Sci. Soc. Ame. Proc.*, 29, pp. 469-472.

9

Mass Movement Processes and Degradation

Everywhere on the earth surface, gravity pulls continually downward on all materials. Bedrock is usually so strong and well supported that it remains fixed in place. A hillslope, however, may become too steep in certain places through removal of rock at its base, as a result, bedrock masses may break free and fall or slide to new position of rest. In case where huge masses of bedrock are involved, the result may be catastrophic in loss to life and property in the path of slide. The type of gravity pull causes environmental or geomorphological hazard in mountainous regions. Thus, "the various kinds of downslope movements occurring under the pull of gravity are collectively termed mass-wasting" (Strahler and Strahler, 1977). The term implies that gravity is the sole important force and that no transporting medium such as wind, flowing water, ice or molten lava is involved (Bloom, 1979).

Geomorphological processes active in mountain environments include, weathering, frost action, glaciation, mass movement surface erosion, creep, solution processes, fluvial action, effect of wind and anthropogenic activities. These phenomena are well described in a number of texts (e. g. Fairbridge, 1968; Carson and Kirkby, 1972; Slaymaker and McPherson, 1972; Ives and Barry; 1974; Price, 1981). In the Himalayan context it is as well to emphasize the distinctions between surface erosion, fluvial action and mass-movement, since they are frequently confused. Surface erosion includes rainsplash, sheetwash, and the effect of wind, and is primarily a product of sparse or reduced vegetation cover. Fluvial action involves riling, erosion gullying, sediment transport and deposition by flowing water confined to channels, or during floods. Mass movement processes (synonymous with mass wasting) includes all gravity induced movements except those in which material is carried by a transporting medium such as water, air or ice. In practice, processes sometimes arbitrary (Fairbridge, 1968). Nevertheless, it is important that policy-makers appreciate the differences between these three general categories of erosion. They have fundamentally different causes and consequences and whereas surface erosion is controllable, mass wasting often is not (at an economic price). Gullying can sometimes be checked by structural measures, but is best prevented before initiation by minimizing uncontrolled runoff (Ramsay, 1986).

Gregory and Walling (1973) have advocated that mass movement must included within a study of the slope phases of fluvial processes both for the purposes of comparison of its efficiency with sheet and gully erosion, and in its capacity as a supplier of material to the stream at the base of slope. On the gentle configuration of surface, this source of supply is unimportant. A study on mass-wasting in United States (Emmett, 1965) has shown that it constitutes less than one per cent of the amount contributed by sheet erosion. However, in areas with steep and unstable slopes such as in Gisborne and East Coast area of New Zealand, and in the San Gabriel Mountains of southern California, mass-movement provides a major sediment source (Campbell, 1955, Krammes, 1965).

Many measuring techniques have been developed to measure various forms and processes of mass-wasting (Rapp, 1960; Young, 1960 and 1969; Williams, 1957; Everett, 1962; Miller and Leopold, 1963; Krammes, 1965; Campbell, 1966; Hadley, 1967; Kirkby, 1967; Emmett and Leopold, 1967; Selby, 1968; Rudberg, 1967; Benedict, 1970; Hutchinson, 1970; Prior, *et al.*, 1971; Prior and Stevens, 1971; Luckman, 1971 *et al.*). Gregory and Walling (1973) have suggested that these mass-wasting processes require long-term monitoring to obtain their rate of flow. The fundamental aim of this section is to identify and to measure some of the morphometric parameters of mass-wasting forms of the Nana Kosi watershed. The geomorphological study observe many characteristic morphological features, caused by mass-movements. These are genetically tectonically controlled landforms, because the mass-wasting forms are generally confined along the tectonic zones, i.e., the zones of reverse and transverse faults. These mass-wasting forms of the study area may be classified into two major groups. These are various types of (i) landslides which include block-glide, rockfall, debris-fall, creeping and slumping, and (ii) debris flow.

Landsliding

According to Bloom (1979), the mass-wasting, wherein a mass of rock or weathered debris moves downhill along discrete shear surface is defined as a slide. The word landslide is frequently extended to include all rapid forms of slide or fall. Sub-categories of slide include block-glide, rockfall, debris fall, creeping and slumping.

Block-glide—The most simple form of slide is block-glide. In the study area these are confined on the downthrown blocks of the reverse faults, discernible particularly along the Patharkot-Kayela Reverse Fault (Plate 4 and 5). The geomorphic observations reveal the distribution of block-glides within the Nana Kosi watershed which reveal that there is a series of old block-glides along reverse faults. Table 9.1, based on field measurements, contains the average size of blocks, slope of the scarp and other environmental factors such as geology of scarps and vegetation etc. It reveals that the average diameter of blocks stands at 15 m. These blocks are detached from steeply inclined scarps (40°) due to vertical uplift along the fault planes composed of mica-schist. The average vegetation canopy upslope the scarps is 33.1 per cent while the down slope cover is 25.9 per cent (Table 9.1). It implies the 7.2 per cent vegetation killing down slope is mainly due to block-gliding in the Nana Kosi watershed.

Rock-Fall—Rock-fall in the Nana Kosi watershed occurs where a steeply sloping rockface is characterized by well jointed rock (Plate 5, above and 10 below). Such type of falls are confined along transverse faults such as discernible particularly near Golchhina (Plate 5, above). The rockfalls are frequently available in Kesta, Chauna, Patharkot, Kathpuria, Jyoli and Katarmal area of the Nana Kosi watershed.Table 9.2 based on field measurements, contains some morphometric, geologic and vegetation characteristics of these rockfalls. The average sediment size of these rockfalls is found 1.8 m which ranges in between 1.0 and 3.5 m. The mean outfall slope of these rockfall is 23° which ranges in between 15° and 32°. The rock-fall in the study area are confined mainly on the hillslopes, composed of quartzites.

Table 9.1 : Morphometric parameters, geology and vegetation characteristics of some of the major block-glides of the Nana Kosi watershed, Central Himalaya, India

Place	*Average diameter of Blocks (m)*	*Slope of scarp (°)*	*Vegetation cover upslope (%)*	*Vegetation cover down slope (%)*	*Rock type of scarp block-glide*
Mauh	22.80	40	15.0	10.0	Mica-schist
Bari	18.50	45	30.0	20.0	Mica-schist
Patharkot	10.60	35	5.0	1.0	Mica-schist
Kathpuria	13.50	35	45.0	40.0	Mica-schist
Gazol	16.00	40	50.0	35.0	Mica-schist
Kesta	14.00	45	45.0	41.0	Mica-schist
Kwerali	12.00	35	30.0	20.5	Mica-schist
Charpathar	13.50	40	45.0	40.0	Mica-schist
Average	15.00	40	33.1	25.9	Mica-schist

Debris Fall—Largely crushed or well jointed scarps of quartizites are subject to continuous debris fall relatively of finer sediment (Plate 5, below). Apart from the rocks, the thick mantle of regolith are also subject for debris fall (Plate 13, below and 27, above). Large fans of such debris falls are discernible in the northwest facing Katarmal hillslope (Plate 6) and near Korichhina where the quartzites have been largely crushed and fragmented (Plate 10, below) by Jyoli and Korichhina faults, respectively. Table 9.3 based on field measurements, contains the morphometric parameters, geology and vegetation characteristics of some of the debris falls of the Nana Kosi watershed. It reveals that the average debris size of debris falls in the Nana Kosi watershed stands at 6.37 cm which ranges in between 3 cm and 11 cm. These debris falls having a mean slope 19.37° are continuously receiving debris from steep (33°) upslope scarps. The major (66.5%) part on upslope of the scarps of debris falls are devoid of vegetation. The vegetation cover upslope these scarps ranges in between 18 and 35 per cent only (Table 9.3).

Table 9.2 : Morphometric parameters, geology, and vegetation characteristics of some of the major rockfalls of the Nana Kosi Watershed, Central Himalaya, India

Place	*Average sediment size (m)*	*Outfall slope (°)*	*Upslope (°)*	*Vegetation cover upslope (%)*	*Rock type of rockfall*
Kesta	1.5	30	35	65.0	Quartzites
Charpathar	1.6	32	35	65.0	Quartzites
Chauna	1.4	20	25	30.0	Quartzites
Golchhina	1.2	15	25	25.0	Mica-schist/quartzites
Katarmal	1.8	25	20	30.0	Quartzites
Patharkot	1.0	25	25	20.0	Mica-schist
Jyoli	1.5	20	25	30.0	Quartzites
Barameel	3.5	15	20	40.0	Mica-schist/quartzites
Sukhiyathol	3.0	25	25	50.0	Mica-schist/quartzites
Kathpuria	2.5	20	25	60.0	Quartzites
Korichhina	1.5	23	25	45.0	Quartzites
Average	1.8	23	26	41.4	Quartzites

Creeping—The imperceptible and non-accelerating downslope movement of soil or rock is known as creep (Bloom, 1979). The geomorphic consequences of such imperceptible and non-accelerated downslope movement of soil as well as rocks are not commonly available in the Nana Kosi watershed which lies in the least tectonically active zone of the Himalayas (Valdiya, 1985). But at places there are sharp evidences of gradual creeping of rocks on either sides of the river banks where the stream is deeply incised into the bedrock. The large tension cracks on either side of the Nana Kosi river, downstream Gewapani (Plate 17, above and 18, below) are caused by gradual creeping of river banks due to valley deepening by channel. Such type of gradual creeping of rocks requires long-term monitoring to obtain the rate of creeping (Gregory and Walling, 1973).

Table 9.3 : Morphometric parameters, geology and vegetation characteristics of some of the debris falls in the Nana Kosi watershed, Central Himalaya, India

Place	*Average sediment size (m)*	*Outfall slope (°)*	*Upslope (°)*	*Vege-tation cover upslope (%)*	*Rock type*
Katarmal	4.50	15.0	25	20.0	Quartzites
Pathura	3.00	20.0	36	25.0	Mica/quartzites
Jyoli	4.00	18.0	32	30.0	Mica/quartzites
Korichhina	6.50	22.0	38	15.0	Quartzites
Sukiyathol	7.00	25.0	35	20.0	Quartzites
Chinuna	5.50	20.0	33	18.0	Mica/quartzites
Kesta	9.50	15.0	35	35.0	Mica-schist
Gulli	11.00	20.0	30	25.0	Mica/quartzites
Average	6.37	19.4	33	33.5	Mica-schist/quartzites

Table 9.4 : Morphometric parameters, geology and vegetation characteristics of some of the debris flows of the Nana Kosi watershed, Central Himalaya, India

Place	*Length (m)*	*Width (m)*	*Vegetation cover up-slope (°)*	*Rock type*
Bari	2.0	1.5	10	Mica-schist/quartzites
Ghingrani	3.0	1.5	15	Quartzites
Ban	2.8	1.0	20	Mica-schist/quartzites
Kakari	1.5	1.0	25	Quartzites
Kathpuriya	5.5	2.5	10	Quartzites
Bangsar	3.5	2.0	30	Quartzites
Chinuna	8.0	3.5	30	Quartzites
Basur	10.5	3.7	25	Mica-schist/quartzites
Korichhina	11.0	3.8	30	Mica-schist/quartzites
Nakuta	8.5	3.0	35	Mica-schist/quartzites
Average	5.63	2.35	23.0	Mica-schist/quartzites

Slumping—Slump is the form of slide most common in thick, homogeneous, cohesive materials such as clay (Bloom, 1979). In the Nana Kosi watershed slump are confined not only on clay soil but they are frequently available in the areas of thick colluvial deposition (Plate 6, above) and areas of thick regolith mental in the central and upper part of the watershed particularly at Bainskhet, Nakuta, and Chinuna.

Debris Flow

Below the hillcrest the adjacent hill slopes in the Nana Kosi watershed are covered by a thin sheet of soil—specially in the small unchannel valleys or hollows and below convex and sometimes planner slopes. This thin sheet of fine material is accumulated on the hillslopes by sheet erosion during the rainy season. Table 9.4 contains some morphometric characteristics of the debris flow cones of the study area. It reveals that the average length of the debris flow cones stands at 5.63 m, having maximum length 11 m near Korichhina and minimum length 1.5 m near Kakari. On an average the debris flow cones are 2.35 m wide, the maximum (3.8 m) and minimum (1.0 m) width was recorded near Korichhina and Kakari, respectively. There is no marked relationship between debris flow cones and upslope vegetation cover as well as with geology (Table 9.4).

The ubiquity of landslides and other catastrophic slope failures throughout the Himalayan mountain system has been not only widely reported but viewed with alarm because it assured to be the direct consequence of land-use changes over recent decades. Seismicity is undoubtedly important but lack of adequate earthquake records precludes any quantification of its influence. Frequently, the triggering mechanism is a catastrophic rainstorms with a long recurrence interval such as the Central Himalayan landslides disaster of September 1993 or somewhat smaller event such as the next monsoon storms. Mass movement processes are not usually directly related to man's activities. Consequently, intervention by man to reduce mass wasting can be very expensive with less clearcut results. Carson (1985) concludes that flooding and sedimentation problems in India and Bangladesh are a result of the geomorphic character of the rivers and man's attempts to control the rivers.

Anthropogenic Processes and Degradation

Human activities have played an important role in degrading the landforms of the Nana Kosi watershed. These all activities may be divided into two groups, i.e., technogenetic and anthropogenic activities.

Technogenetic Processes

The geomorphic investigation observed some technogenitic landforms of the Nana Kosi watershed which includes roads, quarrying, settlements, bridges and watermills etc. Among these, road construction is the most important technogenic process which is creating various environmental deteriorations in the study area in particular and the Himalaya in general. This process has been studied in detail.

Road Construction and Environmental Degradation–A Review—Recent investigations in road induced hazards (Haigh, 1979 a, 1979 b, 1984 a and 1984 b; Valdiya, 1985; Haigh, *et al.*, 1988; Moseley, 1980) have demonstrated that road construction has played a significant role in imbalancing the landscape ecology and have created severe environmental deterioration of physical as well as cultural landscapes. Near Nelson (New Zealand), Moseley (1980) found that the road system contributed 750-800 cubic metre/kilometer/year debris to the local sediment budget. At Mussoori of Central Himalaya, Haigh (1979 a) found that the road construction have contributed 5-10 per cent increase in watershed sediment yield. According to Valdiya (1985) the construction of 44,000 km long roads in the Himalayan region have generated 2650×10^6 m^3 of debris and each year every kilometer of these roads produce 550 cubic meters of bebris by landslides and rockfall, so that every year 24×10^6 m^3 of sediment slide down the slopes-killing vegetation smothering springs and chocking mountain springs and streams. Variations in above annual rate are noticeable. The annual rate of sediment generation as reported by Border Road Organization, is as high as 724 cubic metres/kilometer on Jammu-Srinagar Highway of Kashmir, 591 cubic metres/kilometers on the Arunachal Pradesh highways, and 411 cubic metres/kilometer on the Tanakpur-Tawaghat road of Kumaun Himalaya (Haigh *et al.*, 1986).

Variables which correlate with accelerated landslide activity were studied in detail by Haigh, *et al.*, (1988) in two hill roads at Almora and Nainital. The study reveals that cumulatively 32 per cent of the roadcut is affected by rockfall and 27 per cent by the slumping of rock or regolith. Correlation and discriminant analyses suggest that rock falling may be predictable from measures of the frequency of enlarged joints in the roadcut supported by members of an interrelated complex of variables including slope angle, roadcut height, apparent dip, rock strength, and upslope vegetation cover. Direct measures of environmental instability, such as the underminig of the road bed by erosion, were also shown to have value. However, the study found few useful environmental indicators of slumping. A positive relation between slumping and tree cover upslope may reflect the fact that forest survives as a relict land use in locations which are underdeveloped because of their instability. The roadcut through reserved forest (viz., Kilbury road in Nainital) on a northeasterly slope has an average width of 6.2 m, angle 74°, 7.7 m high roadcut carved into weak slates and shale. Rock dip is 34° to the west and southwest. Slope angle upslope of the road is 39°, slope angle down slope is 46°. A total of 39 per cent of the road bed receives debris from rockfall and about 38 per cent from slumping. Undermining by erosion is a problem for 69 per cent of the road bed, 50 per cent of which is supported by a retaining wall. Upslope of the road, 87 per cent of the ground is covered by vegetation. The tree canopy shades 57 per cent of the ground surface. By contrast, down slope, ground cover is only 35 per cent and the tree canopy shades just 36 per cent of the ground surface (Haigh, *et al.* 1988).

The Almora Bypass passes through a more disturbed environment to the west of the Almora ridge. For most of its length, this road passes through agricultural fields and suburban development. On an average the Bypass is 7.4 m wide and it has a 64°, 5.7 m high roadcut. This is carved into hard schist and quartzites. The rock dip is at 18° towards the northeast. The road crosses the upper part of the hillside so that the slope angle upslope of the road (22°) is less than the down slope (37°). A quarter of the road bed receives debris from rockfall and 18 per cent is affected by slumping. Undermining by erosion is a problem for 48 per cent of the road bed, 45 per cent of which is supported by a retaining wall. Upslope of the road, 61 per cent of the ground is covered by vegetation. The tree canopy is 14 per cent down slope, in the area affected by outfalls of shovelled road clearance debris. Only 56 per cent of the ground is covered by vegetation and the tree canopy is just 8 per cent. Thus, the study of Haigh *et al.*, (1988) concludes that road derived debris has had the more serious impact on the reserved forest lands on the steep, fragile, slopes between Nainital and Kilbury. Here, ground vegetation down slope of the road is only 40 per cent and the tree canopy only 63 per cent of that upslope. The more disturbed suburban environment of Almora By-pass, with its more gentle slopes, stronger rocks and many fewer landslides have suffered less. However, even here road debris has had an impact on the vegetation cover down slope. Ground vegetation is 92 per cent but tree cover only 57 per cent of that upslope of the road.

Road Induced Sediment in the Nana Kosi Watershed—Following Haigh, *et al.*, (1988) two hillroads, viz., the Someshwar-Majkhali and Kathpuria-Daulaghat (Fig 1.1) of the Nana Kosi Watershed were surveyed in the field by a team of four workers under the Channel Network Capacity Project armed with tape measures, compass, and abney level. Because of the steep and unstable character of the hillside and roadcut, all measurement were of necessity, recorded from the surface of the roadbed. Records were collected at each 200 m benchmark for the entire 3 km of Someshwar-Majkhali road and 5.6 km. reach of Kathpuria-Daulaghat Road. This created two small samples of 15 and 28 cases respectively.

The following variables were measured at each benchmark : roadcut height (RH), roadcut angle (RA), upslope (US), rockdip (RD), true bearing of dip (TBD), joint density (JD), schistocity (SCH), roadcut aspect (RAP), tree cover up (TCU), ground cover up (GU), soil cover up (SC). Apart from these, each individual landslide within each 200 m zone of road were surveyed. The following variables were measured direct at each landslide; scar length (SL), scar width (SW), scar depth (SD), scar angle (SA), outfall

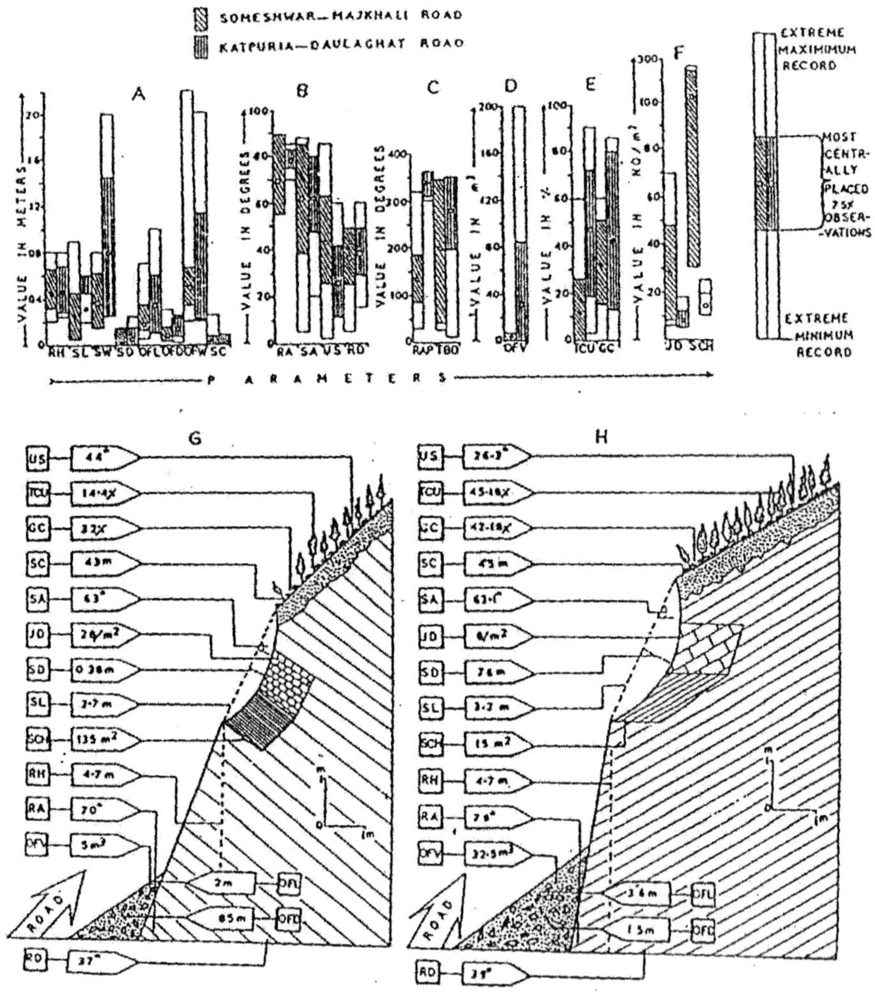

Fig. 9.1 : Compound bar diagrams of the roadcut and road induced landslides parameters along Someshwar-Majkhali and Kathpuria-Daulaghat roads surveyed in 1986 and 1987 (A to F); and the roadcut and road induced landslides models of Majkhali-Someshwar (G); and Kathpuria-Daulaghat (H) roads of the Nana Kosi Watershed, Central Himalaya (RH) roadscut height, SL- scar length SW- scar width, SD- scar depth, OFL- outfall length, OFD- outfall depth, OFW- outfall width, SC- soil cover, RA- roadcut angle, SA- scar angle, US-up slope , RD- rock dip, RAP- roadcut aspect, TBD- true bearing of dip, OFV- outfall volume, TCU- tree cover up, GC- ground cover up, JD- joint density, SCH- Schistosity).

length (OFL), outfall depth (OFD), outfall width (OFW), and outfall volume (OFV).

Among all these a few variables could not always be measured directly and then had to be estimated from base line established on the road bed. These include roadcut height (RH), depth of soil (SC), vegetation cover upslope (VCU) and ground cover upslope (GCU).

Results—Table 9.5 and 9.6 provide descriptive statistics for each variable collected, tabulated for each road way. Figure 9.1 A to F, depicts the diagrammatic illustration of all these variables. Figure 9.1 G and Figure 9.1 H are the models of roadcut and the road induced landslide of Majkhali-Someshwar and Kathpuria-Daulaghat roads respectively. These are based on the mean of measured variables (Table 9.5 and 9.6).

Table 9.5 : Statistical parameters of the road induced landslides and associated environmental factors along 7 km long Someshwar-Majkhali Road in the Nana Kosi watershed, Central Himalaya, India

Name of Parameters	*Symbol used*	*Mean*	*Standard Deviation*	*Extreme Maximum Record*	*Extreme Minimum Record*
Road cut Height (m)	RH	4.70	1.60	8.0	2.00
Road cut Angle (°)	RA	70.00	23.00	90.0	55.00
Scar Length (m)	SL	2.70	1.80	9.0	0.50
Scar Width (m)	SW	3.80	2.40	8.0	1.50
Scar Depth (m)	SD	0.38	0.27	1.5	0.15
Scar Angle (°)	SA	63.00	25.00	85.0	5.00
Outfall Length (m)	OFL	2.00	1.50	7.0	1.20
Outfall Depth (m)	OFD	0.85	0.65	3.0	0.30
Outfall Width (m)	OFW	5.00	1.60	22.0	2.00
Outfall Volume (m^3)	OFV	5.00	1.90	15.0	0.52
Up Slope (°)	US	44.20	10.90	85.0	2.00
Rock Dip (°)	RD	37.00	11.90	55.0	5.00
T. B. of Dip (°)	TBD	200.00	160.00	345.0	25.00
Joint Density (m/m^2)	JD	28.00	20.00	70.0	6.00
Schistosity (no/m^2)	SCH	135.00	111.00	260.0	30.00
Road cut Aspect (°)	RAP	134.70	51.10	320.0	30.00
Tree Cover Up (%)	TCU	14.40	12.00	60.0	20.00
Ground Cover (%)	GC	32.00	20.25	60.0	15.00
Soil Cover (m)	SC	0.43	0.26	25.0	0.01

The roadcut and landslide model of Majkhali-Someshwar road (Fig. 9.1 G) reveals the following :

1. This road is constructed mainly along steep antidip slope (44°) composed of highly jointed (24 joints/m^2) and steeply dipping (37°) mica-schist, interbedded with quartzites at places.
2. 14.4 per cent area upslope the road is covered by tree canopy and 32 per cent of the surface is covered by ground cover.
3. The road has angle 70°, 4.7 m high road cut and crosses the upper course of the southwestern facing hillside.

Table 9.6 : Statistical parameters of the road induced landslides and associated environmental factors along 9 km long Kathpuria-Daulaghat Road in the Nana Kosi watershed, Central Himalaya, India

Name of Parameters	*Symbol used*	*Mean*	*Standard Deviation*	*Extreme Maximum Record*	*Extreme Minimum Record*
Road cut Height (m)	RH	4.78	1.99	8.0	2.5
Road cut Angle (°)	RA	79.00	4.05	85.0	70.0
Scar Length (m)	SL	3.28	1.27	6.0	2.0
Scar Width (m)	SW	8.12	6.31	20.0	2.5
Scar Depth (m)	SD	0.76	0.74	2.5	0.1
Scar Angle (°)	SA	63.12	17.85	80.0	20.0
Outfall Length (m)	OFL	3.62	2.43	10.0	1.0
Outfall Depth (m)	OFD	1.55	0.79	2.5	0.2
Outfall Width (m)	OFW	6.80	4.53	20.0	2.0
Outfall Volume (m^3)	OFV	32.55	50.67	200.0	0.2
Up Slope (°)	US	26.37	15.15	60.0	0.0
Rock Dip (°)	RD	39.00	10.34	60.0	15.0
T. B. of Dip (°)	TBD	283.12	88.05	350.0	10.0
Joint Density (m/m^2)	JD	8.12	3.95	18.0	5.0
Schistosity (no/m^2)	SCH	14.60	4.73	25.0	10.0
Road cut Aspect (°)	RAP	341.25	17.63	360.0	300.0
Tree Cover Up (%)	TCU	45.18	26.70	90.0	3.0
Ground Cover (%)	GC	42.18	29.40	80.0	0.0
Soil Cover (m)	SC	0.45	0.23	0.9	0.1

4. The mean landslide scar depth, length and angle along this road stands at 0.38 m, 2.7 and 63° respectively.
5. The mean length, depth and width of the outfall along this road at 2.0 m, 0.85 m and 5.0 m respectively.
6. The mean volume of the outfall along this road stands at 5 cubicmeters.

Along this 3 km long road, as many as 34 landslides were recorded. Thus, on this road, the frequency of landslide outfall, having a mean volume of 5 cubic meters, was found 11 per km. During the course of the construction of this road, about 48×10^4 cubic meters sediment was extracted and slide down the slopes. At present, each kilometer is generating 54.20 cubic meters sediment each year by landsliding along the roadcut during monsoon rain.

The model of roadcut and road induced landslide of Kathpuria-Daulaghat road (Fig 9.1 H) reveals the following :

1. This road is constructed mainly along dip slope (26.3°) composed of relatively less jointed (8 joints/m^2) mica-schist, interbedded with quartzites at places.

2. 45.18 per cent area upslope the road is covered by tree canopy and 42.18 per cent of the surface is covered by ground cover.
3. The road has an angle of 79° and 4.78 m high roadcut.
4. The mean landslide scar depth, length and angle along this road stand at 0.76 m, 3.28 m and 63.12° respectively.
5. The mean length, width, and depth of the outfall along this road stand at 3.62 m, 6.8 m and 1.55 m respectively.
6. The mean volume of the outfall along this road stands at 32.55 cubic meters.

Along this 5.6 km long road, the total number of outfalls were recorded 16. Thus, on this road the frequency of landslide outfall, having a mean volume of 32.55 cubic meters is 5.6 per km. During the course of the construction of this road, 32×10^4 cubic meters sediment was extracted and slide down the slope (Plate 1). At present each kilometer road is generating 75.55 cubic metres sediment each year during monsoon rains by landsliding.

In terms of frequency of landslides, it is higher (i.e., 11 no/km) in Majkhali-Someshwar road constructed along highly jointed antidip slope, than that of the Kathpuria-Daulaghat road (i.e., 5.6 no/km) constructed on the dip slope of the same rocktype. But in terms of volume of landslide outfalls, it is more than 6 times higher in the Kathpuria-Daulaghat road (32.5 cubic meters) constructed along dip slope than that of the Majkhali-Someshwar road (5 cubic meters) construction along anti-dip slopes. Thus, the road constructed along the antidip slope is relatively more stable than that of the road constructed along dip slope.

The network of roads in the Nana Kosi watershed is 58.5 km long (Fig. 1.1). With the help of the above roadcut surveys, it can be deduced that during the period of road construction about 13689×10^4 cubic metres debris was removed from the hillsides of the Nana Kosi Watershed at the rate of 234×10^4 cubic metres per kilometre. Each year every kilometre of these roads produces about 64.87 cubic metres of debris by landsliding and rockfall during monsoon rains which slide-down the hillslopes killing vegetation smothering springs and chocking streams (Plate 1).

Anthropogenic Processes

According to Valdiya (1985), the deforestation resulting from overgrazing by an explosively large population of cattle, and reckless exploitation of forest for fuel, timber and industries has reduced the protective vegetal cover to mere 35 per cent of surface areas of the Central Himalaya, thus exposing about 65 per cent area to the erosive forces. These rapid anthropogenic processes are leading to drying-up of springs and consequent dwindling of water resources on the one hand, excessive runoff flowing down streams on the other causing floods. Such imbalance or disequilibrium in landscape ecology of the Himalaya is mostly man induced or is caused by scientific ignorance about the consequences of disequilibrium landscape ecology or sometimes by human negligence also. However, there is a great paucity of numerical data in the Himalayas which could define and correlate the role of anthropogenic activities in transformating the natural systems (Rawat, 1988 a). To overcome this problem, Rawat (1988 a), formulated a research strategy to monitor, quantify and analyse various ecological imbalances induced by man. Preliminary results of his experimental study in the micro catchments of the Kumaun Himalaya, reveal that about 50% changes in waterflow capacity are man induced. In the month of the heaviest rainfall, i.e., July (under identical geological and geomorphological character, and climatic input), agricultural land has the maximum capacity to generate water discharge (i.e., 8738.3 m^3/km^2/day) coupled with maximum flow of suspended (i.e., 1.571 tons/km^2/day) and dissolved (i.e., 2.151 tons/km^2/day) load, while oak mixed forest land has the minimum capacity to generate water discharge (i.e., 487.2 m^3/km^2/day), coupled with minimum flow of suspended (i.e., 0.066 ton/km^2/day and dissolved (i.e., 0.40 ton/km^2/day) load. In the driest month, i.e., April, the flow capacity of the same land is quite opposite. Agricultural land generates the minimum water discharge (i.e., 180.0 m^3/km^2/day) without suspended material, coupled with dissolved load (i.e., 0.680 ton/km^2/day), while the oak mixed forest land generates the maximum water discharge (i.e., 307.6 m^3/km^2/day) without suspended material coupled with dissolved load (i.e., 0.017 ton/km^2/day). Rawat (1988 a) has further advocated that sediment flow data of the experimental catchments indicate that the intensity of suspended and dissolved load flow has been increased up to approximately 24 and 5.5 times higher, respectively in the agricultural land than that of the forested land due to anthropogenic processes.

Apart from the anthropogenic transformation of channel networks, experimental studies in the small plots of different land use on the hill slopes in the Central Himalaya (Rawat, 1988 b) have suggested dramatic changes in surface runoff on the hillslopes. The study reveals that geological, climatic and topographic conditions being the same, the least disturbed forest land produces the minimum surface runoff (3.2%) of the total rainfall. The greatly disturbed agricultural land produces the maximum surface runoff (20% of the total rainfall). In the barren land the surface runoff was 10.38 per cent. Thus, the study concludes that human activities have increased the quantity of surface runoff on the hillslopes by a factor approximately seven times greater than natural culminations of this phenomenon is acceleration of mass-movements and frequent floods. It is evident that a significant proportion of the rainfall goes waste as flood water without replenishing the ground water resources that is, without recharging the spring (Rawat, 1988 b). The fundamental aim of this section is to define the role of anthropogenic processes, viz., agriculture and deforestation, in the channel network capacity and sheet wash erosion on the hillslopes of the Nana Kosi watershed.

Anthropogenic Impact on Channel Network Capacity—To define the role of anthropogenic processes in the channel network capacity, stratified sampling procedure (Cochran, 1977) has been employed in two stages. The study area, viz., the Nana Kosi watershed was divided into two major land type units, i.e., forested and deforested. Micro drainage basins (having hydrometric station) from each stratum were selected. All those drainage basin were avoided which stretch on more than one stratum. Thus, nine such micro drainage basins are available in the study area out of which 5 are forested and 4 are deforested. To minimize the variations within these two major stratums, they were restratified into substrata as follows (Table 9.7).

(A) Forested—pine forest (P), Oak mixed forest
(B) Deforested—Mixed type having both barren and Agricultural land (M), Agricultural land (A)

Table 9.7 : Landuse pattern in the different micro sample basins of the Nana Kosi Watershed, Central Himalaya

Sam-ple No.	*Area*	*Forest*		*Barren*		*Agriculture*		*Land type*	
	km²	*km²*	*%*	*km²*	*%*	*km²*	*%*		
P_1	0.42	0.42	100	—	—	—	—	Forested	Pine
P_2	0.73	0.73	100	—	—	—	—		
P_3	0.45	0.45	100	—	—	—	—		
O_1	0.29	0.29	100	—	—	—	—		Oak Mixed
O_2	0.76	0.76	100	—	—	—	—		
M_1	0.77	—	—	0.25	32.58	0.51	67.42	Deforested	Mixed
M_2	0.44	—	—	0.13	30.68	0.30	69.32		
A_1	0.30	—	—	—	—	0.30	100		Agri-cultural
A_2	0.45	—	—	—	—	0.45	100		

Thus, all the nine sample drainage basins were classified (Fig. 9.2) into two major and four minor strata as per their landuse pattern. Table 9.7 contains the area of these sample catchments and their landuse pattern. Geologically, these all the sample catchments are composed of mica-schist interbedded with quartzites at places and geomorphologically they are identical.

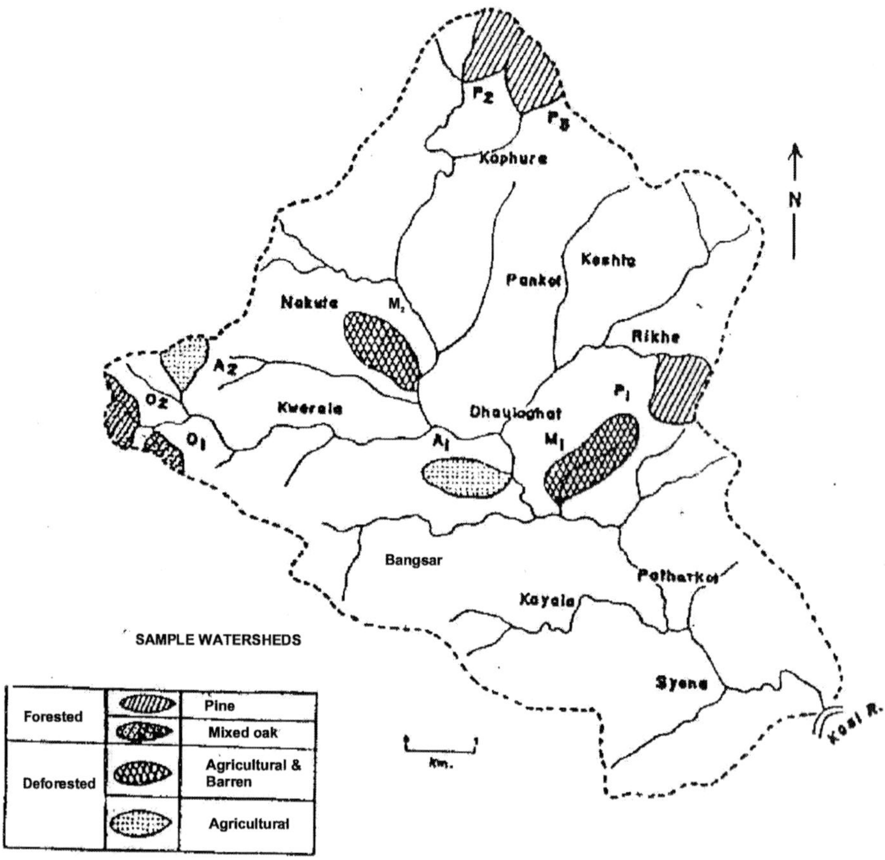

Fig. 9.2 : Distribution of the selected micro sample watersheds of different landuse pattern in the Nana Kosi Watershed, Central Himalaya, India

Table 6.2, 6.3, 6.4, 8.6, 8.7, 8.8, 8.13, 8.14 and 8.15 contain the summary of water discharge, suspended and dissolved load data of all the water data stations of the Nana Kosi watershed. By selecting the data of sample basins from these tables, summary table of sample catchments were prepared for two study years, i.e., 1986-87 (Table 9.8) and 1987-88 (Table 9.9). These tables contain summary of water discharge suspended and dissolved load data of each sample in different years. A brief description of these water discharge, suspended load and dissolved load data is presented below.

1. Water Discharge—Table 9.8 reveals that in 1986-87, the water discharge from the sample catchments found in between 0.00851 to 0.01475 m^3/sec. in pine, 0.00679 to 0.01653 m^3/sec. in oak mixed, 0.00806 to 0.01788 m^3/sec. In deforested mixed and 0.0089 to 0.00469 m^3/sec. in agricultural

Table 9.8 : Summary of water and sediment characteristics in forested and deforested micro-catchments in the Nana Kosi Watershed, Central Himalaya, India (1986-87)

Water and Sediment Discharge	*Land Type*								
	Forested					*Deforested*			
	Pine			*Oak- mixed*		*Mixed*		*Agricultural*	
	Sample No.			*Sample No.*		*Sample No.*		*Sample No.*	
	P_1	P_2	P_3	O_1	O_2	M_1	M_2	A_1	A_2
Water discharge									
m^3/sec	0.00851	0.01475	0.01010	0.00679	0.01653	0.01788	0.00806	0.00469	0.00890
m^3/day	1129.044	1274.260	1700.710	586.450	1428.190	1544.830	695.750	421.410	769.070
m^3/day/km^2	1750.54	1768.99	1989.53	2022.26	1879.20	1968.50	1580.83	1106.76	1709.04
Suspended sediment flow									
Mg/lit	30.25	30.58	28.00	21.08	19.25	60.58	69.33	120.00	75.91
Tons/day	0.06600	0.09577	0.13400	0.011360	0.01490	0.26707	0.13040	0.23707	0.14790
Tons/day/km^2	0.1564	0.1312	0.2980	0.0530	0.0197	0.3665	0.3015	0.7902	0.4873
Dissolved load									
Mg/lit	64.17	69.17	91.60	61.42	61.50	144.08	147.60	184.33	190.42
Tons/day	0.0763	0.2214	0.2040	0.0283	0.0358	0.2390	0.1200	0.0824	0.1464
Tons/day/km^2	0.1774	0.0444	0.4535	0.0987	0.0471	0.3324	0.2650	0.2747	0.3250

Table 9.9 : Summary of water and sediment characteristics in forested and deforested micro-catchments in the Nana Kosi Watershed, Central Himalaya, India (1987-88)

Water and Sediment Discharge	Land Type								
	Forested					Deforested			
	Pine			Oak- mixed		Mixed		Agricultural	
	Sample No.			Sample No.		Sample No.		Sample No.	
	P_1	P_2	P_3	O_1	O_2	M_1	M_2	A_1	A_2
Water discharge									
m^3/sec	0.001957	0.00433	0.00452	0.00433	0.00314	0.00544	0.00170	0.00120	0.00186
m^3/day	168.26	369.05	390.83	374.11	271.30	467.82	149.25	103.70	160.80
m^3/day/km^2	400.63	505.55	868.52	1290.04	356.97	610.50	332.35	345.70	357.30
Suspended sediment flow									
Mg/lit	16.33	16.16	19.08	10.42	19.75	114.08	105.08	165.25	190.58
Tons/day	0.01700	0.00369	0.00951	0.00179	0.00218	0.02943	0.02202	0.02284	0.03983
Tons/day/km^2	0.04020	0.00506	0.02113	0.00620	0.00514	0.03820	0.05005	0.07615	0.07369
Dissolved load									
Mg/lit	185.42	93.08	89.75	78.58	75.42	161.25	177.92	285.45	278.75
Tons/day	0.0219	0.0323	0.0383	0.0095	0.0081	0.0828	0.0299	0.0296	0.0448
Tons/day/km^2	0.12110	0.04436	0.08510	0.03300	0.01060	0.10758	0.06811	0.09860	0.09950

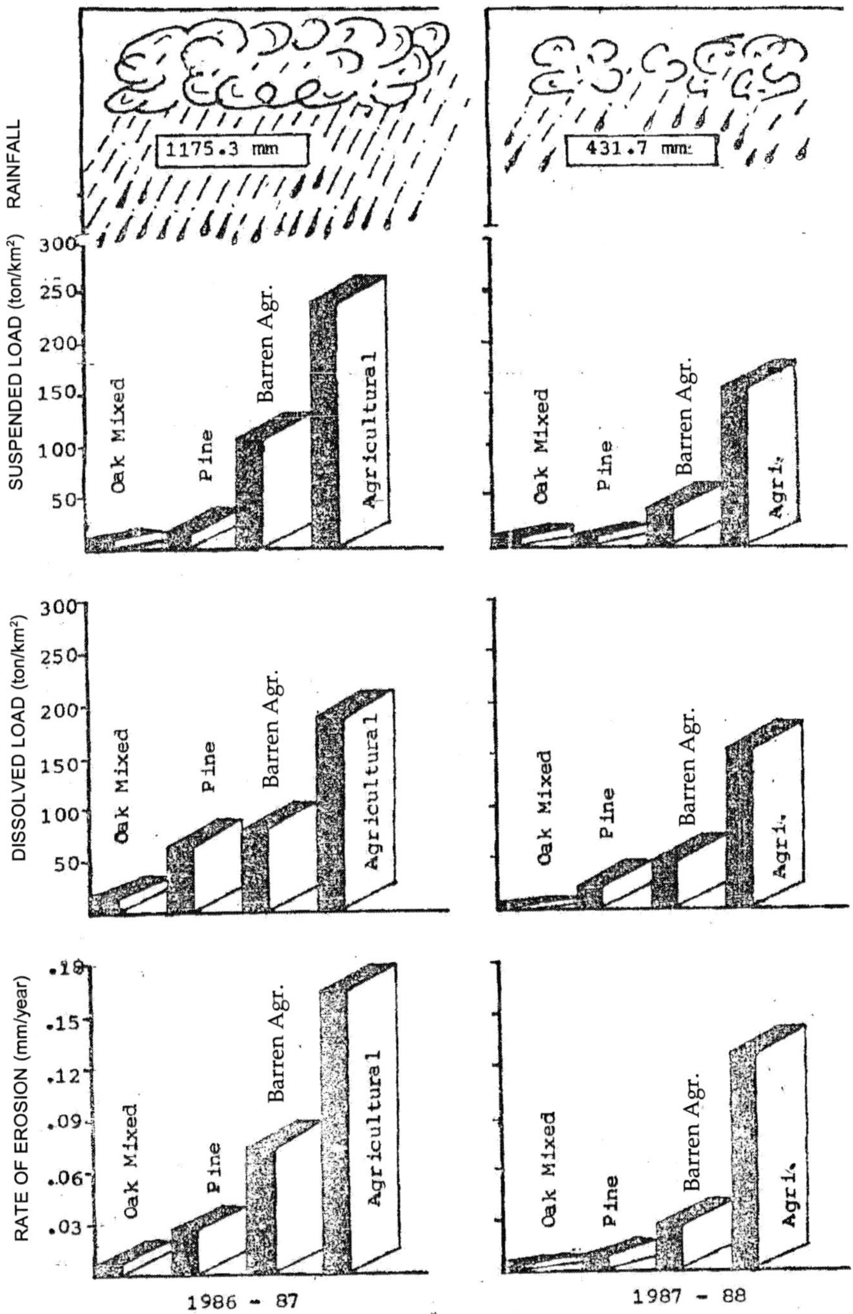

Fig. 9.3 : Suspended and dissolved sediment yield and soil erosion rates in different landuse pattern, under identical geological and geomorphological character and climatic input in the Nana Kosi Watershed, Central Himalaya, India

catchments. The water generating capacity of land to channels of these catchments was found 1879.2 to 2022.26 $m^3/km^2/day$ in oak mixed, 1750.54 to 1989.53 $m^3/km^2/day$ in pine, 1580.83 to 1968.50 $m^3/km^2/day$ in deforested mix and 1106.76 to 1709.04 $m^3/km^2/day$ in agricultural land in 1986-87 (Table 9.8).

Table 9.9 contains that in 1987-88 (i.e., drought year) the water discharge from sample catchments found in between 0.001947 to 0.00452 m^3/sec. in pine, 0.00314 to 0.00433 m^3/sec in oak mixed, 0.0017 to 0.00544 m^3/sec in deforested mixed and 0.0012 to 0.00186 m^3 sec. in agricultural catchments. The water generating capacity of land to channels of these catchments was found 356.97 to 1290.09 $m^3/km^2/day$ in oak mixed, 400.63 to 868.52 $m^3/km^2/day$ in pine, 332.35 to 610.50 $m^3/km^2/day$ in deforested mixed, and 345.70 to 357.30 $m^3/km^2/day$ in agricultural land in the drought year, i.e., 1987-88 (Table 9.9).

Table 9.10 : The mean water generating capacity of sample catchments in the Nana Kosi Watershed, Central Himalaya, India

Landuse type	*Water Discharge*					
	1986-87		*1987-88*		*1986-88*	
	$m^3/km^2/day$	*Ratio*	*$m^3/km^2/day$*	*Ratio*	*$m^3/km^2/day$*	*Ratio*
Forested						
Oak-mixed	1950.040	1.00	823.500	1.00	1386.770	1.00
Pine	1836.353	0.94	591.566	0.72	1213.660	0.87
Deforested						
Mixed	1774.660	0.91	471.425	0.57	1123.040	0.81
Agriculture	1407.900	0.72	351.500	0.45	879.700	0.63

The mean water generating capacity of land to channels of these sample catchments, as presented in Table 9.10 reveal the following characteristics regarding the water generating capacity of different types of land to channels of the Nana Kosi watershed.

1. In both the study years (i.e., 1986-87 and 1987-88), the maximum water generating capacity of land to channels was found in oak mixed catchments which was recorded 1950.04 $m^3/km^2/day$ in 1986-1987 and 823.50 $m^3/km^2/day$ in the drought year (1987-88).
2. In both the study years, the minimum water generating capacity of land to channels was found in the agricultural catchments which was recorded 1407.09 $m^3/km^2/day$ in 1986-87 and 351.5 $m^3/km^2/day$ in drought year (1987-88).

3. In the catchments of the pine forests, the water generating capacity of land to channels was recorded 1836.353 $m^3/km^2/day$ in 1986-87 and 591.566 $m^3/km^2/day$ in 1987-88.
4. In the deforested mixed type land this capacity was found 1774.7 $m^3/km^2/day$ in 1986-87 and 471.4 $m^3/km^2/day$ in 1987-88.
5. Thus, under identical geological and geomorphological character and climatic inputs the water generating capacity of the agricultural land has been reduced 1.38 (1986-87) to 2.34 times (1987-88) than that of the oak mixed forest land. On an average (1986-88) the oak mixed forest land has about 1.6 times higher water generating capacity than that of the agricultural land.

With the help of above data, it can be concluded that the anthropogenic processes (i.e., agriculture and deforestation) have played a significant role to reduce the water generating capacity of land to channels. The ratio of water generating capacity of different lands (Table 9.10) suggests that, if the water generating capacity of land to channels is one in Oak mixed forest land, it is 0.94 in pine forest land, 0.91 in deforested mixed type land and 0.72 in agricultural land in the Nana Kosi watershed.

2. ***Suspended Sediment*** : Table 9.8 reveals that in 1986-87, the concentration of suspended sediment from the stream of sample catchments was found in between 28.00 to 30.58 mg/l in pine, 19.25 to 21.08 mg/l in oak mixed, 60.58 to 69.33 mg/l in deforested mixed and 75.91 to 120.00 mg/l in agricultural catchments. The suspended sediment generating capacity of land to channels of these catchments was found 0.4873 to 0.7902 $ton/km^2/day$ in agricultural, 0.3015 to 0.3665 $ton/km^2/day$ in deforested mixed, 0.1312 to 0.298 $ton/km^2/day$ in pine and 0.01965 to 0.053 $ton/km^2/day$ in oak mixed land in 1986-87 (Table 9.8).

Table 9.9 contains that in 1987-88 (i.e., drought year) the concentration of suspended sediments in the streams of sample catchments was found in between 16.16 to 19.08 mg/l in pine, 10.42 to 19.75 mg/l in oak mixed 105.08 to 114.08 mg/l in deforested mixed and 165.25 to 190.58 mg/l in agricultural catchments. The suspended sediment generating capacity of land to channels of these catchments was found 0.07369 to 0.07615 $ton/km^2/day$ in agricultural, 0.0382 to 0.05005 $ton/km^2/day$ in deforested mixed, 0.00506 to 0.0402 $ton/km^2/day$ in pine and 0.00514 to 0.0062 $ton/km^2/day$ in oak mixed forested land in the drought year, i.e., 1987-88 (Table 9.9).

The mean suspended sediment generating capacity of land to channels of these sample catchments as presented in Table 9.11, reveals the following characteristics regarding the suspended sediment generating capacity of different types of lands to channel of the Nana Kosi watershed.

Table 9.11 : The mean suspended sediment generating capacity of sample catchments in the Nana Kosi Watershed, Central Himalaya, India

Landuse type	*Suspended Sediment*					
	1986-87		*1987-88*		*1986-88*	
	ton/km²/day	*Ratio*	*ton/km²/day*	*Ratio*	*ton/km²/day*	*Ratio*
Forested						
Oak-mixed	0.03632	1	0.00567	1	0.02099	1
Pine	0.19520	5.37	0.02213	3.90	0.10866	4.85
Deforested						
Mixed	0.33400	9.20	0.04412	7.78	0.18906	9.00
Agriculture	0.63875	17.58	0.07492	13.21	0.35683	16.99

1. In both the study years (i.e., 1986-87 and 1987-88), the maximum suspended sediment generating capacity of land to channels was found in agricultural catchments, which was recorded 0.63875 ton/ km^2/day in 1986-87 and 0.07492 ton/km^2/day in the drought year (1987-88).
2. In both the study years, the minimum suspended sediment generating capacity of land to channels was in the oak mixed catchments which was recorded 0.03632 ton/km^2/day in 1986-87 and 0.00567 ton/km^2/day in drought year (1987-88).
3. In the catchments of the deforested mixed type, the suspended sediment generating capacity of land to channels was recorded 0.334 ton/km^2/day in 1986-87 and 0.04412 ton/$km^{2/}$day in 1987-88.
4. In the pine forested catchments this capacity of land was found 0.1952 ton/km^2/day in 1986-87 and 0.02213 ton/km^2/day in 1987-88.
5. Thus, under identical geological and geomorphological character and climatic inputs the suspended sediment generating capacity of the agricultural land has been increased 17.58 (1986-87) to 13.21 (1987-88) times higher than that of the oak mixed land. On an average (1986-88), the agricultural land has about 17 times higher suspended sediment generating capacity than that of the mixed forest land.

With the help of above data, it can be concluded that the anthropogenic processes (i.e., agriculture and deforestation have played a significant role to increase the suspended sediment generating capacity of land to channels. The ratio of suspended sediment generating capacity of different land (Table 9.11) suggests that, if the suspended sediment generating capacity of land to channels is one in oak mixed forest land, it is 4.85 in pine forest land, 9.00 in deforested mixed type land and 0.72 in agricultural land in the Nana Kosi Watershed.

3. Dissolved Load—Table 9.8 reveals that in 1986-87, the concentration of dissolved load flow from the streams of sample catchments found in between 84.17 to 91.60 mg/l in pine, 61.41 to 61.50 mg/l in oak mixed land, 144.08 to 147.60 mg/l in deforested mixed land and 184.33 to 190.42 mg/l in agricultural catchments. The dissolved load generating capacity of land to channels of these catchments was found 0.1774 to 0.4535 ton/km²/day in pine forest, 0.04710 to 0.0987 ton/km²/day in oak mixed forest, o.2650 to 0.3324 ton/km²/day in deforested mixed type and 0.2747 to 0.325 ton/km²/day in agricultural catchments in 1986-87 (Table 9.8).

Table 9.9 contains that in 1987-88 (i.e., drought year) the concentration of dissolved load in the streams of sample catchments found in between 185.42 to 193.08 mg/l in pine, 75.416 to 78.583 mg/l in oak mixed, 161.25 to 177.916 mg/l in deforested mixed and 278.75 to 285.45 mg/l in agricultural land. The dissolved load generating capacity of land to channels of these catchments was found 0.04436 to 0.1211 ton/km²/day in pine forest, 0.0106 to 0.0330 ton/km²/day in oak mixed forest, 0.06811 to 0.107586 ton/km²/day in deforested mixed and 0.0986 to 0.0995 ton/km²/day in agricultural land in the drought year, i.e., 1987-88 (Table 9.9).

Table 9.12 : The mean dissolved load generating capacity of sample catchments in the Nana Kosi Watershed,Central Himalaya, India

Landuse type	*Dissolved Load*					
	1986-87		*1987-88*		*1986-88*	
	ton/km²/day	*Ratio*	*ton/km²/day*	*Ratio*	*ton/km²/day*	*Ratio*
Forested						
Oak-mixed	0.07290	1.00	0.02180	1.00	0.04735	1.00
Pine	0.22510	3.08	0.08352	3.83	0.15431	3.25
Deforested						
Mixed	0.29870	4.09	0.08785	4.02	0.19327	4.08
Agriculture	0.29981	4.10	0.09910	4.54	0.19945	4.21

The mean dissolved load generating capacity of land to channels of these sample catchments as presented in Table 9.12, reveals the following characteristics regarding the dissolved load generating capacity of different types of lands to channels of the Nana Kosi watershed :

1. In both the study years (i.e., 1986-87 and 1987-88, the maximum dissolved load generating capacity of land to channels was found in agricultural catchments which was recorded 0.29981 ton/km²/day in 1986-87 and 0.09910 ton/km²/day in the drought year (1987-88).
2. In both the study years, the minimum dissolved load generating capacity of land to channels was found in the oak mixed catchments

which was recorded 0.0729 ton/km^2/day in 1986-87 and 0.0218 ton/km^2/day in drought year (1987-88)

3. In the catchments of the deforested mixed type land the dissolved load generating capacity of land to channels was recorded 0.2987 ton/km^2/day in 1986-87 and 0.087848 ton/km^2/day in the drought year (1987-88).
4. In the pine forested catchments this capacity of land was found 0.2251 ton/km^2/day in 1986-87 and 0.08352 ton/km^2/day in 1987-88.
5. Thus, under identical geological, geomorphological character and climatic inputs the dissolved load generating capacity of the agricultural land has been increased 4.10 (1986-87) to 4.54 (1987-88) times higher than that of the oak mixed land.
6. On an average (1986-88) the agricultural land has about 4.2 times higher dissolved load generating capacity than that of the oak mixed forest land (Table 9.12).

With the help of above data, it can be concluded that the anthropogenic processes (i.e., agriculture and deforestation) have played a significant role to increase the dissolved load generating capacity of land to channels. The ratio of different land (Table 9.12) suggests that, if the dissolved load generating capacity of land to channels is one in oak mixed forest land, it is 3.25 in pine forest land, 4.08 in deforested mixed and 4.21 in agricultural land in the Nana Kosi Watershed.

Anthropogenic Impact on Sheetwash Erosion

It has been discussed in Chapter 8, during the experimental period 1986-87 the total rainfall 140.2 mm (average intensity 8.03 mm/hour) generated sheetwash sediment at the rate of 0.00265 ton/km^2 (Table 8.2). Considerable variations in the sheetwash erosion were recorded from three small plots having different landuse patterns, namely forest (15.5 m^2), barren (8.5 m^2) and agriculture (11 m^2) having fairly uniform geology, climate and topography on 19° hillslopes in the Nana Kosi watershed (Table 8.1). A brief discussion of sheetwash erosion from these experimental landuse plots is presented below :

Sheetwash Erosion in the Forest Land

Table 8.1 contains the total amount of sheetwash erosion (in grams) of 26 storms of rain of different amount from the forested experimental plot (15.5 m^2). It suggests that sheetwash erosion ranges in between 0 to 73.6 grams at 1.5 to 15 mm rainstorms. Summary of these field data (Table 8.2) reveals that, on an average forested hillslope in the Nana Kosi watershed generated sheetwash sediment at the rate of 0.001155 tons/km^2 (or 1.15 kg/km^2) at 140.2 mm rainfall (average intensity 8.03 mm/hr). To define the relative rates of change between rainfall intensity and sheetwash erosion in the forest land, regression analysis was conducted by using data presented in Table 8.3. The regression model diagramatically illustrated in Fig. 8.2, expresses the statistical relationship between rainfall intensity and sheetwash erosion on forest land of the Nana Kosi watershed as follows :

$$SE = 0.00019 + 0.00014\ (RI),\ \text{in tons/km}^2$$

where, "SE" is sheetwash erosion and "RI" is rainfall intensity in mm/hour.

The regression model reveals that a unit increase in rainfall intensity, increases sheetwash erosion at the rate of 0.00033 ton/km^2 or 0.33 kg/km^2 (i.e., SE = 0.00019 +0.00014 x 1 mm). Similarly, the rate for different units of rainfall intensity may be obtained. Table 9.13 contains estimates of the sheetwash erosion for the forest land at different rainfall intensities based on this regression model.

There are very small differences between estimated (Table 9.13) and observed values (Table 8.2) of sheetwash erosion for the forest land. For example, the estimated rate of sheetwash erosion at 30 mm/hour rainfall stands at 0.00439 ton/km^2 (Table 9.13) and the observed value stands at 0.00475 ton/km^2 (Table 8.2).

Table 9.13 : Estimated rates of sheetwash erosion on different land use terrain in the Nana Kosi Watershed, Central Himalaya, India (Based on regression models).

Rainfall intensity (mm/h)	*Forest*	*Barren*	*Agricultural*
	SE = 0.00019 + 0.00014 (RI)	*SE = 0.00053 + 0.00028 (RI)*	*SE = 0.00042 + 0.00046 (RI)*
1	0.00033	0.00080	0.00090
2	0.00040	0.00110	0.00140
3	0.00061	0.00137	0.00180
4	0.00075	0.00165	0.00226
5	0.00100	0.00190	0.00270
6	0.00103	0.00221	0.00318
7	0.00117	0.00249	0.00364
8	0.00131	0.00277	0.00448
9	0.00145	0.00305	0.00456
10	0.00160	0.00330	0.00500
20	0.00300	0.00610	0.00960
30	0.00439	0.00893	0.01422
40	0.00579	0.01173	0.01882
50	0.00750	0.01450	0.02340

Sheetwash Erosion in the Barren Land

Table 8.1 contains the total amount of sheetwash erosion (in grams) of 26 rainstorms of different amount from the barren experimental plot (8.5 m^2). It suggests that sheetwash erosion ranges in between 8.9 to 87.1 grams at 2.0 to 15 mm rainstorms. Summary of these field data (Table 8.2) reveals that, on an average barren hillslope in the Nana Kosi watershed generated sheetwash sediment at the 0.002754 ton/km^2 (or 2.75 kg/km^2) at 140.2 mm total rainfall (average intensity 8.03 mm/hour). To define the relative rates of change between rainfall intensity and sheetwash erosion in the barren land, regression analysis was conducted by using the data presented in Table 8.2. The regression model, diagrammatically illustrated in Fig. 8.2, expresses the statistical relationship between rainfall intensity and sheetwash erosion on barren land of the Nana Kosi watershed as follows:

$$SE = 0.00053 + 0.00028\ (RI),\ \text{in tons/km}^2$$

where, "SE" is sheetwash erosion and "RI" is rainfall intensity in mm/ hour.

The regression model reveals that a unit increase in rainfall intensity, increases sheetwash erosion at the rate of 0.0008 ton/km^2 or 0.8 kg/km^2 (i.e., SE + 0.00053 + 0.00028 x 1mm). Similarly, the rate for different units of rainfall intensity may be obtained. Table 9.13 contains estimates of the sheetwash erosion of the barren land at different rainfall intensities based on this regression models.

There are very small differences between estimated (Table 9.13) and observed values (Table 8.2) of sheetwash erosion for the barren land. For example, the estimated rate of sheetwash erosion at 6 mm/hour rainfall stands at 0.00221 ton/km^2 (Table 9.13) and the observed value stands at 0.00215 ton/km^2 (Table 8.2).

Sheetwash Erosion in the Agricultural Land

Table 8.1 contains the total amount of sheetwash erosion (in grams) of 26 rain storms of different amount from the agricultural experimental plot (11 m^2). It suggests that sheetwash erosion ranges in between 32.8 to 178.8 grams at 1.5 to 15 mm rainstorms. Summary of these field data (Table 8.2) reveals that, on an average agricultural hillslopes in the Nana Kosi watershed generated sheetwash sediment at the rate of 0.00404 ton/km^2 (or 4.04 kg/km^2) at 140.2 mm rainfall (average intensity 8.03 mm/hour). To define the relative rates of change between rainfall intensity and sheetwash erosion in the agricultural land, regression analysis was conducted by using data presented in Table 8.2. The regression model, digrammatically iillustrated in Figure 8.2, expresses the statistical relationship between rainfall intensity and sheetwash erosion on agricultural land of the Nana Kosi watershed as follows :

$$SE = 0.00042 + 0.00046\ (RI), \text{ in ton/km}^2$$

where, "SE" is sheetwash erosion and "RI" is rainfall intensity in mm/hour.

The regression model reveals that a unit increase in rainfall intensity, increases sheetwash erosion at the rate of 0.0009 ton/km^2 or 0.90 kg/km^2 (i.e., SE = 0.00042 + 0.00046 x 1 mm). Similarly, the rate for different units of rainfall intensity may be obtained. Table 9.13 contains the estimates of the sheetwash erosion for the agricultural land at different rainfall intensities based on this regression models.

There are very small differences between estimated (Table 9.13) and observed values (Table 8.2) sheetwash erosion for the agricultural land. For example, the estimated rate of sheetwash erosion at 6 mm/hour rainfall stands at 0.00318 ton/km^2 (Table 9.13) and the observed value stands at 0.00298 ton/km^2 (Table 8.2).

Thus, the study of sheetwash erosion on three experimental plots of different types of landuse but identical geomorphological and geological character, and climatic inputs in the Nana Kosi watershed suggests the following :

(1) Under identical geological, geomorphological character and climatic inputs the most disturbed land, i.e., agricultural land is generating about 3.5 times (0.00407 ton/km^2) higher sheetwash erosion than that of the undisturbed forest land (0.00116 ton/km^2).

(2) Under identical geological, geomorphological character and climatic input the agricultural land is generating about 2.4 times higher (0.00407 ton/km^2) sheetwash erosion than that of the relatively less disturbed barren land (0.00275 ton/km^2).

(3) The regression model (Fig. 8.2) depicts the significant differences in the slope of the regression lines on different types of land. The regression slope is the lowest (b = 0.00014) in forest land which reveals that a unit increase in rainfall intensity increases very small amount of sheetwash erosion (i.e, 0.00033 ton/km^2, Table 9.13). The regression slope is maximum in the agricultural land (b = 0.00046) which reveals that a unit increase in rainfall intensity increases 0.0009 ton/km^2 sheetwash erosion which is about three times higher than of the undisturbed forest land. The regression slope (b = 0.00028 in the barren land is higher than the undisturbed forest land but is lower than the most disturbed agricultural land. On the barren land a unit increase in rainfall intensity increases 0.0008 ton/km^2 sheetwash erosion which is about more than two

times higher than that of the forest land but is lower than agricultural land.

With the help of the above data, it can be deduced that anthropogenic processes i.e., agriculture and deforestation, have played a significant role to increase the sheetwash erosion on the hillslopes. Thus, under identical geological, geomorphological character and climatic input, the ratio of sheetwash erosion on the forested, barren and agricultural hillslope of the Nana Kosi watershed stand at 1.0 : 2.4 : 3.5 respectively.

REFERENCES

Benedict, J.B. (1970) : Downslope soil movement in a Colorado Alpine Region; Rates, processes and climatic significance. *Arctic and Alpine Res.*, 2, pp. 165-226.

Bloom, A.L. (1979) : *Geomorphology : A systematic analysis of late Cenozoic landforms.* Prentice Hall of India Pvt. Ltd., New Delhi, pp. 163-196.

Campbell, A.P. (1966) : Measurement of movement of an earth-flow. *Soil and Water,* 2(3), pp. 23-24.

Campbell, D.A. (1955) : Down to the sea in slips. N.Z. Soil Conservation and rivers control. *Council Bulletin* 5, Wellington.

Cochran, W.C. (1977) : *Sampling techniques.* Wiley Eastern Ltd. New Delhi, pp. 18-48.

Emmett, W.W. (1965) : The vigil network; methods of measurement and a Sample of data collection. Internat. *Assoc. Sci. Hyd. Pub.*, 66, pp. 89-106.

Emmet, W.W. and Leopold, L.B. (1967) : On the observation of soil movement in excavated pits. Revue de Geomorph. *Dynamique,* 17, p. 157.

Everett, K.R. (1962) : Quantitative measurement of soil movement. *Geol. Soc. Amer. Special paper,* 73, pp. 147-148.

Gregory, K.G. and Walling, D.E. (1973) : *Drainage basin form and processes.* London, Edward Arnold, pp. 1-407.

Hadley, R.F. (1967) : On the use of holes filled with colored grains. Revue de Geomorph. *Dynamique,* 17, pp. 158-159.

Haigh, M.J. (1979a) : Landslide sediment accumulation on the Mussoorie-Tehri Road, Garhwal Lesser Himalaya. *Indian Jourl. Soil Conserv.*, 7 (1), pp. 1-4.

Haigh, M.J. (1979b) : Environmental geomorphology of the Landour-Mussoorie area, *U.P. Himalayan Geol.*, 9, pp. 657-688.

Haigh, M.J. (1984a) : Landslide Prediction and Highway Maintenance in the Lesser Himalaya, India. *Zeitshrift fur Geomorphologie,* NF Sb. 51, pp. 17-38.

Haigh, M.J. (1984b) : Prediction and morphology of road induced landslides in the Himalaya. Case study from Central Himalaya. In *Rural Development in the Himalaya : Problem and Prospects (ed.)* Joshi, S.C. *et al.* Gyanodaya Prakashan, Nainital, pp. 176-206.

Haigh, M.J., Rawat, J.S. and Bartariya, S. (1986) : Environmental correlates of landslide frequency along new highway in the Central Himalaya, Preliminary results, Presented in the Internat. *Sym. on Geomorphic processes in Environments with strong seasonal contrasts,* Spain, Sept. 1986.

Haigh, M.J., Rawat, J.S. and Bartariya, S. (1988) : Environmental correlations of landslide frequency along new highways in the Himalaya, Preliminary results. Intdisp. *Journ. Soil Sci. Hydro. Geomorph.* CATENA 15, pp. 539-553.

Hutchinson, J.N. (1970) : A coastal mudflow on the London clay cliffs at Beltinge *North Kent Geotechnique,* 20, pp. 412-438.

Kirkby, M.J. (1967) : Measurement and theory of soil creep. *Jourl. Geol.,* 75, pp. 359-378.

Krammes, J.S. (1965) : *Seasonal debris movement from steep mountainside slopes in southern California.* U.S. Deptt. of Agri. Miscellaneous Pub., 970, pp. 85-88.

Luckman, B.H. (1971) : The role of snow avalanches in the evolution of Alpine tatlus slopes. In slopes, form and process. Comp. D. Brunsden. Institute of British Geographers, Special Pub. 3, pp. 93-110.

Miller, J.P. and Leopold, L.B. (1963) : Simple measurements of morphological changes in river channels and hillslopes. In *Changes of Climate,* UNESCO Arid Zone Research Series, XX, pp. 421-427.

Moseley, M.P. 1980 : Impact of forest road erosion in the Dart Valley, Nelson, *New Zealand. Jour. of Forestry,* 25(2), pp. 184-198.

Prior, D.B. and Stephens, N. (1971) : A method of monitoring mudflow movements. *Engineering Geol.,* 5, pp. 239-246.

Prior, D.B., Stephens, N. and Douglas, G. R. (1971) : Some examples of mudflow and rockfall activity in northeast Ireland. In slopes, form and process. Comp. D. Brunsden, Institute of British Geographers, Special Pub., 3, pp. 129-140.

Rapp, A. (1960) : Recent development of mountain in slopes in Karkevagge and surrounding northern Scandinavia. *Geogr. Ann.,* 42, pp. 73-200.

Rawat, J.S. (1988 a) : Water resources and burning hydrological problems of Kumaun. In *Kumaun Land and People (ed.)* K.S. Valdiya, Gyanodaya Prakashan, Nainital, pp. 201-212.

Rawat, J.S. (1988 b) : Anthropogenic transformation of channel network capacity : An experimental study in Kumaun Himalaya. *Proc. Ind. Natn. Sci. Acad.,* 54 (4), pp. 605-615.

Rawat, J.S. (1988c): Channel network capacity and geochemical properties of water of the Nana Kosi Basin, Kumaun Lesser Himalaya, India. Dept. Geog., Kumaun Univ., Almora, D.S.T. Project, Final Report, pp. 1-146.

Rudberg, S. (1967) : On the use of test pillers. Revue de Geomorph. *Dynamique,* 17, pp. 164-165.

Selby, M.J. (1968) : Cones for measuring soil creep. Journ. Hyd. (NZ), 7, pp. 136-137.

Strahler, A.H. and Strahler, A.N. (1977) : *Geography and man's environment.* John Wiley and Sons., New York, p. 216.

Valdiya, K.S. (1985) : Accelerated erosion and landslide prone zones in the Central Himalayan Region. In *Environmental Regeneration in Himalaya* (ed.) J.S. Singh, Gyanodaya Prakashan, Nainital, pp. 12-38.

Williams, P.J. (1957) : Some investigations into solifluction features in Norway. *Geog. Journ.* 123, pp. 42-58.

Young, A. (1960) : Soil movement by denudation processes on slopes. *Nature,* 188, pp. 120-122.

Young, A. (1969) : Present rate of land erosion. *Nature,* 244, pp. 851-853.

PART D

MANAGEMENT STRATEGIES AND CONCLUSIONS

10

Watershed Management Strategies

The increasing population and the need to provide a better quality of life to hill people, the pressure on land and water resources is tremendous in the Himalayan region. The watersheds are under constant threat of mass wasting and erosion caused by natural processes, deforestation, unscientific agricultural practices and other developmental activities. It is significant, therefore, that the management and development activities must be based on principles of watershed management. It is estimated that about 70-80 per cent of the hill population depends on land and other natural resources for their livelihood support system. Therefore, watershed management in the hills is of paramount importance. As a consequence of degradation, the Central Himalayan region is facing acute shortage of drinking water, depletion of groundwater resource, increased soil erosion, lower productivity of land and loss of biodiversity. The proper treatment and conservation of these resources are possible only through watershed management for overall sustainable development of the region. The ecological restoration of the natural environment should be taken up to rejuvenate and conserve land and water resources. Natural processes of degradation is inherent in the watersheds due to earth's structure, framework and dynamics which have to be well understood in terms of various quantified dynamic and static elements of earth and atmosphere and their constant interactions which define the natural upgrading and degrading processes of the watersheds.

Environmental Deterioration in Himalaya

Existing State

The Himalaya "is being denuded of its soil cover and is being deeply dissected as a result of quickened pace of erosion in the catchments of the myriads of streams and rivers—the average rate of erosion being of the order of one millimeter per year, which is five times faster than it was in past 40 million years. The rivers are carrying incredibly large amounts of sediment, generated by widespread and frequently devastating landslides, rockfalls and slumping. Deforestation results from overgrazing by an explosively large population of cattle, and reckless exploitation of forests for fuel, timber and industries, has reduced the protective vegetal cover to a mere 35 per cent of the surface area, thus, exposing about 65 per cent area to the erosive forces. Construction of roads has caused colossal destruction of forests and triggered profound erosion in the vulnerable areas. The recurrent landslides on these roads have further aggravated the deterioration of the mountain terrain" Valdiya (1985).

Regarding the degraded landscape ecology of the fragile Himalaya, Valdiya has further remarked that the impact of erosion in the Himalayan region has been profound and far reaching. The loss of vegetal cover has reduced the capacity of mountain slopes to absorb and infiltrate rainwater, leading to drying-up of springs and consequent dwindling of the water resources in the one hand and excessive-runoff flowing downstreams are the other, causing floods with regular periodicity in the Indo-Gangetic plains where 40 per cent of the Indian population is concentrated. These phenomena threaten to initiate desertification of the once green and beautiful Himalaya and cause irreparable flood-damage in the fertile plains of North India.

The importance of land and water for meeting the human needs is recognized by ancient Indian scriptures. Adverse effects of watershed degradation are serious in both uplands and low lands. Accelerated soil erosion from degraded uplands affects the people and ecosystem in low lands. The Himalayan watersheds have been witnessing severe degradation and environmental problems, among which heavy sedimentation, floods and water shortage are the prominent ones. In a degraded watershed steep bed gradient of channels causes high runoff velocities with associated heavy sediment flow, which flushes out with the discharge. The mountain terrain is characterized by different sizes watersheds with geologically sensitive and unstable soil profiles. Rapid geomorphological changes due to active tectonics are evident. The ecological sensitivity is further lent by the steep and hilly terrain, and high bimodal rainfall, out of which approximately 80 per cent is received between Mid-June to Mid-September annually. It is during these times that landslides become an acute problem. Increased pressure of human and livestock population causing deforestation and improper land use have caused a steady process of degradation especially that of land and water resources. The mountainous specificities and fragilities of the Himalaya are important from climate, resource conservation considerations. The conservation of natural resources in the Himalayan region is an issue of utmost concern for sustainale development and improving the livelihood of local inhabitants.

Serious weaknesses

Postulating the Hypothesis of Himalayan environmental degradation Ives (1985) has suggested :

"There are number of serious weaknesses, however, first, not account is taken of the natural circumstances of the overall Himalayan Ganga Plain System. It is generally, understood that this largest of the world's mountain ranges, in a geological sense, is youthful and active; tectonic uplift continues, and the Ganga Plain is the product of the erosion of the mountains. Thus, it is necessary to differentiate between natural sediment transfer and deposition and that which is induced by human activities. Second, little information is available about rates of soil erosion in different slopes, at different altitudes, under different vegetation cover types and under different landuse practices. Does the sediment, which is destroying the capacity of major hydro-electric projects, come from the Siwaliks, the Mahabardt Lek the middle Mountains, the greater Himalaya, or the trans-Himalaya, or from the Terai itself? Third little reliable data is available about fuelwood consumption. Incidentally, that published data on per capita fuelwood consumption varies by factor of 27. How much forest remains and what is its quality? Is the demand for fuel-wood a primary factor in deforestation?" In a recent study, Bajrachara (1983) argues that the fuel-wood demand is irrelevant, and that the primary cause is the need for more agricultural land for growing subsistence crops. In this context, it is sobering to realize that despite the so-called "green revolution" average crop yields have actually declined over the last two decades." Although, the resources are abundant, their excessive, ruthless, unscientific and unauthorized exploitation is being a serious threat for long-term sustainability of the Himalayan ecosystem, the concerted efforts are required to improve agricultural productivity, conserve natural resources and to maintain ecosystems on a long-term sustainable basis.

Environmental Degradation in the Nana Kosi Watershed

The Nana Kosi watershed was lowered at the rate of 0.96 mm per year in 1986-87 and 0.30 mm per year in 1987-88. The present investigation has provided abundant geomorphological evidence to indicate that the environment of the Nana Kosi is degrading fastly. The indicator of this fact may be grouped in five categories :

(1) Frequently available hazards of mass-movement or zones of geomorphic damages (Chapter-nine).
(2) Anthropogenic transformation of hillslope erosion (Chapter-nine).
(3) Anthropogenic transformations of channel erosion (Chapter-nine).

(4) Anthropogenic transformation of water flow in channels (Chapter-nine).
(5) Anthropogenic transformation of water generating capacity of land to channels (Chapter-nine).

Thus, the damage to the ecological balance of the Nana Kosi watershed is mostly man induced or is caused by human negligence.

Watershed Management Strategies

Watershed managment basically refers to analysis, protection, repair, utilization and maintenance of watersheds for optimum control and conservation of land and water with due regard to various other resources. To conserve precious resources like, land and water and to maintain and enhance the productivity of the system, proper formulation, implementation, monitoring and evaluation of watershed management programmes are required. It has to be kept in mind that watershed management programmes are basically interdisciplinary in nature and no single agency or department can successfully achieve the objectives of watershed management. The planning for environmental management and sustainable development for a hill region essentially revolves around its watersheds. The watershed, a manageable geomorphic and hydrologic unit encompasses apart from water, forests, agriculture, livestock and other associated components. A watershed based development approach thus necessitates accounting for complex and interrelated multidisciplinary factors. It involves creation of a complex data base both spatial and non-spatial.

However, there is a great paucity of numerical data in the Himalaya which could (i) define and correlate the role of anthropogenic activities in transforming natural ecosystems; and (ii) could recommend sound strategies for the regeneration of disturbed ecological system. To overcome this problem, we are in need of an action oriented multi-disciplinary research strategy to monitor, quantify and analyse the ecological imbalances (Rawat, 1988), and to initiate land reclamation works to manage the environment.

This research strategy has four requirements :

(1) To employ drainage basin as a unit for environmental management and watershed development.
(2) Need to develop watershed consciousness.
(3) Need to conduct operation research to define the state of environment.

(4) Need to introduce watershed management programmes through action projects.

Watershed as a Unit for Environmental Management and Economic Development

A drainage basin may be defined as the area which contributes water to a particular stream or set of streams (Lepold, *et al.*, 1964). It is also known as a drainage area, catchment area and watershed of a particular stream. It is widely recognized as a fundamental unit in the geomorphological milieu and also is being used as a basic unit for ecological research (Curry, 1976) and environmental management (Myers, 1976; Warshall, 1976; Simons, *et al.*, 1982; Swanson, *et al.*, 1982) because : (i) it is a limited convenient and usually clearly defined and unambiguous topographic unit, available in a nested hierarchy of sizes on the basis of stream ordering (Chorley, 1969); (ii) it provides the best way to measure precipitation and solar radiation inputs, and outputs of drainage (Lee, 1964); (iii) basin provide opportunity to estimate the amount of erosion because measurement of river flow and by knowing the area of the drainage basin and by assuming a diversity of material, rate of land erosion over the whole catchment may be deduced (Gregory and Walling, 1979); (iv) it is easy to estimate the volume of material which has accumulated in the reservoir and if the date of construction of the reservoir is known, this can also provide the basis for and estimate of land erosion rate (Gregory and Walling, 1979); (v) the study of deposits within the basin or at the basin mouth can provide considerable information about the environmental processes and about chronology of events which occurred in the past (Gregory and Walling, 1979); (vi) drainage basins are mini-biospheres of earth and the first extension of mind to the environment (Warshall, 1976); (vii) drainage basins focus on the monitoring of water and land the process where by landscape is moulded, soils are moved around and nutrients cycled to plants and us (Warshall, 1976). Thus, it is obvious that *a watershed has form, processes, system of processes and life.*

Need to Develop Watershed Consciousness

Warshall (1976) has described the word 'watershed'. According to him "Sceadu" the Anglo-Saxon word became "shade" (the parting of sunlight from darkness). Shade sought for and found light-built structures like lean-tos and arborbs, transformed into shed. Sceadu= shed, the light building of shatter/storage as in; wagorished, woolshed, woodshed. But sounds play on each other and nouns and verbs change hats. To shedblood became bloodshed hardly a building. In the United States "to shed water" became "watershed" "to shed water" over the surface of the land. Thus, hillslopes are like cheeks shedding tears into rivers that pour into the sea. Watershed is the total area of the waterflow in land, not just the boundary line dividing flow. In this way water shed is "an area of land which drains water, sediment and dissolved materials to a common outlet at same point along a stream or river" (Warshall, 1976).

Watershed Character

Quantitative expression of drainage basin characteristics was introduced by Horton (1932, 1945), who suggested the drainage basin geometry in the form of stream hierarchy. This was further modified by Strahler (1964). Rawat (1985) has advocated that the veins of the watershed, viz., streams have their certain laws. Watershed is constituted of five different factors (Doornkamp and King, 1971) :

(1) the size,
(2) the dissection
(3) the shape,
(4) the stream length, and
(5) the relief.

Association among the morphometric parameters of these factors is another important character of the drainage basin. Regarding the association among these drainage basin factors, it is postulated that an increase in the size factor of the drainage basin corresponds to an increase in the dissection and relief factors, and a decrease in shape and length factors and vice-versa (Rawat, 1985).

Watershed System

Watershed receives a continuous energy supply from different sources (Fig. 6.3). The watershed loose energy through the water and sediment loss. The erosion cycle, hydrological cycle, biogeochemical cycle are the product of the interaction among energy supply and energy loss parameters (Rawat, 1985 and 1987) of the watershed system.

Energy Input and Output of Watershed

There are two main sources of energy supply (i.e., input in a watershed system), i.e., climate above the surface and the endogenetic processes below the surface (Fig. 6.3). The endogenetic forces are constructive processes by which the initial forms of the landform is constructed. On these initial landforms various kinds of landforms develop which are controlled by climatic processes. The watershed looses energy (output) by evaporation and transpiration and by various denudational and biological processes. The environment and the form of the watershed is a function of all these inputs and outputs and controlled by the characteristics of the drainage basin such as geomorphology, geology, vegetation, soils, man and animal etc.

Input-output Balance of the Watershed

Equilibrium (balance) between input and output of a watershed means—no environmental deterioration, no environmental pollution, or healthy environment.

Thus, "an equilibrium state is one in which the many variables of a watershed system are dynamically balanced" (Curry, 1976). When the total watershed remains in the physical balance nutrients like water and soils are detained longer on land. The soils, retain more moisture further retaining water and simultaneously, encouraging life. The build up soils have increased nutrients storage sites and the biochemical cycle looks more, keeping the chemicals as richer lingering life before, like every thing, we stream on out to sea to sky to land to sea...." (Warshall, 1976).

In a balanced watershed system (Curry, 1976) "a hillslope profile is a product of a balance between runoff, infiltration, and erosion". All of these are modified by the degree of soil development since that in turn controls what grows on the hillside and thus, controls runoff, infiltration and erosion. Soil development is in turn determined by the age and stability of the surface. Age and stability are in part, a function of the history of runoff, infiltration and erosion at the site, which are themselves in turn a function of the history of climate and biotic activities on the hillside. Each integrally intertwined loop rests within a larger loop and all determine the state of equilibrium. Upset of the balance can be compensated only to a certain point and then disequilibrium occurs.

Disequilibrium State of Watershed

Describing the disequilibrium state of watershed, Curry (1976) has remarked that the planner must be familiar with disequilibrium through the interactive reactions in a watershed, Runoff intensity usually increases, thus, causing erosion of hillslopes. Simultaneously, flood waters reach watercourses faster due to denser and more effective integration of rills and ephemeral channels on the hillslopes and flood heights increase. Increased sedimentation and increased flooding lead to increased lateral erosion of stream channels that must change their channel geometry to accommodate a greater percentage of sediment load to water discharge.

This result in a shallower stream channel flowing at a somewhat steeper gradient like the Nana Kosi. A shallower channel cuts adjacent hillslpoes downstream. These undercut hillslopes are steeper and thus, erode faster, thus further adding insult to injury in the already sediment chocked streams. Depositional channels result that plug free-flowing watercourses with braided changing streams, and side slopes continue to ravel and erode until the slope steepness is once again reduced to an equilibrium profile that extends to the drainage divides. In this fashion, a headwater change in biota can effect a change in the shape of the whole watershed below it (Curry, 1976).

Thus, before managing the environment of a watershed, the managers should be well aware about the "watershed consciousness" i.e., about its life, way, structure, system, inputs, outputs and input-output interactions etc. There is a gap in the Himalayan management works carried out by government as well as by various public organizations. Managers (governments, inhabitants and other public organizations) are not familiar with the various aspects of the watershed which have been discussed in this section.

Operation Research

Management works to regenerate to conserve or to preserve the environment are in vain without the operation research. It is just like a medical treatment of a person without diagnosing his health. Operation research means monitoring/quantifying the energy of the drainage basin system, and to construct the energy gain (input) and energy loss (output) budget which could highlight the state of the drainage basin system, i.e., (i) equilibrium state or (ii) disequilibrium state.

The fundamental aim of the management works is to bring the system in equilibrium or balanced state of environment, therefore, the management work should be started after defining the state of the system. Managing the environment means healing the wounds and treatment of various types of land diseases. Before starting treatment (or management) of a disease, operation research is needed to find out its cause(s) and effects in the entire systems. Then only the disease can be rooted out from the entire system. To regenerate the environment—specifically of the fragile Himalaya, multidisciplinary operation research through holistic approach (Bhandari, 1987) is the first hand need which could suggest that way the watershed systems is in disequilibrium state? Which part of this watershed system is not operating properly? Either the disequilibrium is caused by excesses energy supply or paucity of energy etc. Rawat (1987) has presented a detailed account of strategies and concept regarding such operation research by considering drainage basin as a natural laboratory (Fig. 6.3).

Watershed Management Programmes through Action Projects

To manage and develop the watershed means to provide an ecologically sound economic base for the watershed; bureaucratically, to maximize the long-term productivity of the drainage basin and optimize to social and economic well-being of the basin residents; and scientifically, a combination of environmental repair and economic development. For this purpose the Nana Kosi watershed in particular and the Himalayan watersheds in general, require action projects composed of a variety of interactive programmes :

(1) *Administrative Programme* : Purpose-coordination, administration and communication, technical services are required; prepare an environmental atlas of the basin.
(2) *Study* : Conduct an intensive, basin-wise research study of relationships between precipitation, stream flow, sediment yield and landuse practices.
(3) *Watershed Repair Programme* : Purpose—reduce suspended material carried by streams, to a definable minimum through watershed repair and revegetation as follows :

    (a) Preparation of problem slopes for reseeding, includes restoration of original drainage patterns, tracing construction of check-dams and retaining walls of local materials.
    (b) Restoration of drainage patterns as required.
    (c) Restoration of metalled, unmetalled and bridle-paths and foot-paths.
    (d) Initial reseeding of bare surfaces with perennial grasses.
    (e) Replanting of local vegetation (scrubs, bushes, fodder plants and other plants) as appropriate.
    (f) Storage of surface runoff by construction of small tanks on upland hillslopes.
    (g) Minimize stream bank erosion through restoration of vegetal cover of problem slopes.
    (h) Plant stream-bank, stream side vegetation as required to restore cover and reduce water temperature
    (i) Road maintenance work with special emphasis on adequate culverting and elimination of culvert outfall gullies.
    (j) Establishment of an inter-basin nursery for propagation of native plants for special purpose to meet out the requirement of fodder and erosion control.
    (k) Study project—cost-effectiveness studies and reports on the techniques and methods used on the action project.

(l) Dissemination of methods applicable for use in other parts of the Himalayas.

Conservation and Management Strategies of Land and Water Resources of the Nana Kosi Watershed

Soil and water are critical natural resources. The careful management of these resources is essential to food security and environmental protection. When use in sustainable ways, soil and water produce the food, forestry and other products that we all depends upon. Degradation of watershed resources and environment threatens the livelihood of rural people of Himalayan watersheds. As population continue to rise the pressure on watershed resources lead to leave a barren environment. There is an urgent need of the formulation of management strategies for the land and water resources of the HImalayan region in general and Nana Kosi watershed in particular.

Formulation of the conservative strategies for land and water requires :

(i) Detailed mapping of land unit systems and knowledge of their environmental parameters to obtain the class of physical limitations of land and to categorise the land capability class,
(ii) Monitoring of waterflow capacity of channels to define their water potentiality in lean period and to study their anthropogenic transformation.

The present applied geomorphic investigation of the Nana Kosi watershed is an attempt to fulfil these requirements.

Land Units, Physical Limitations and Land Capability

The author has classified the Nana Kosi watershed into 11 different land units (Table 10.1). The environmental characteristics of these land unit systems (Table 10.1) were partially obtained from the geomorphic map and partially by field surveying. With the help of the land unit systems and their environmental parameters, the basin may be divided into 6 classes of physical limitations (Table 10.2). These classes of physical limitations provide a sound base for the land capability classification of the Nana Kosi watershed which may be divided into 6 categories (Table 10.2).

Management of Land Having None/Minor Physical Limitation

This is the best quality land and may be categoried as class-I land of the basin. The middle level terraces, i.e., T_4, T_5, and T_6, (Plate 15 above, 16, 3 above) fall under this category. The environmental characteristics of this land are presented in Table 10.1, which revels that this is level land having a layer of transported soil, i.e., fine alluvium. The physical environment favours their maximal utilization.

Unfortunately, such fertile pockets of the basin are without irrigation facilities. The fertility status of this land can be raised by introducing :

(i) Irrigation facilities as proposed in Figure 10.1;
(ii) Farmers to take new methods of farming and land management; and
(iii) Some land reclamation works to check the degradation of this land by gully and rill erosion (Table 10.1).

Management of Land Having Minior Physical Limitations

This is class II land which included high level (T_7, T_8, T_9, T_{10}, and T_{11}; Plate 2, Plate 9 above) and low level (T_1, T_2, and T_3; Plate 15 below) terraces and wet land of alluvial fans. The high level terraces are flat areas of without alluvium. These are capped by very thin sheet of colluviums. The low level terraces are flat surfaces of mainly coarse alluvium. The class-II land is being degraded fastly by pluvial rill and gully erosion. These terraces are mostly used for cultivation (Plates 15 and 21 below) but at places this class of land having minor physical limitations is barren (Plate 32). The land unit, alluvial fan are very small pockets of useful wetland, locally known as "simar". This land unit is being used for the cultivation of rice but most of these fans are in barren condition. It is recommended that :

(i) the low level terraces of class-II land near the villages should be used to grow vegetables by introducing irrigation facilities and all the barren land of the low level terraces should be used for cultivation of crops;
(ii) the high level terraces of class-II land should be used for cultivation, wherever this is in barren condition;
(iii) in both, the high level and low level agricultural terraces of class-II land—new method of farming and land management should be introduced; and
(iv) all the alluvial fans should be used for the cultivation of vegetables/ rice/fodder/fruits and bamboo as applicable.

Table 10.1 : Land Units, their environmental characteristics and general class of physical limitations in the Nana Kosi Watershed, Central Himalaya

Land Units	Relative Relief				Slope Steepness				Slope Form				Material type			Soil depth					Soil texture				General class of Physical Limitations (Contd.....) →
	Low	Moderate	High	Very High	Flat/gentle	Moderate	Steep	Very Steep	Horizontal	Concave	Convex	Straight Planner	Alluvium	Colluviums	Rocks	Good	Moderate	Restricted	Poor	None	Fine	Medium	Coarse	Very Coarse	
Scarped land				x				x				x			x					x					Extremely severe
Triangular facet			x –	x			x –	x				x			x				x			x			Very severe
Landslide deposit		x –	x			x –	x			x		x		x					x					x	Extremely severe
Hollows	x –	x				x				x				x				x			x				Severe
Convex hill			x				x				x				x				x			x			Severe
Sheetflow fans	x					x				x				x		x						x -	x		Some
High level terraces	x				x				x					x					x			x			Minor
Middle level terraces	x				x				x				x			x					x				None / minor
Low level terraces	x				x				x				x			x							x		Minor Severe
Alluvial fans	x –	x			x –	x				x			x			x					x				Minor
Floodplains	x				x				x				x				x						x –	x	Extremely severe

(contd.)

Table 10.1 (*contd.*)

Land Units	Liability to Erosion																	General class of Physical Limitations (Contd.....)
	Mass Movement				Pluvial erosion			Rill erosion				Gully erosion				Channel erosion		
	.None	.Moderate	.Small	.Severe	.Moderate	.Small	.Severe	.None	.Moderate	Small	Severe	.None	.Moderate	.Small	Severe	.None	.Moderate	.Small	.Severe	.	
Scarped land				x	x				x			x				x			x		Extremely severe
Triangular facet				x			x				x	x				x					Very severe
Landslide deposit				x			x				x				x			x -	x		Extremely severe
Hollows		x					x	x				x				x					Severe
Convex hill				x			x				x	x				x					Severe
Sheet flow fans			x				x				x				x				x		Some
High level terraces	x					x			x			x				x					Minor
Middle level terraces		x			x					x					x	x					None / minor
Low level terraces		x			x						x				x	x					Minor Severe
Alluvial fans		x			x				x										x		Minor
Flood plains	X				x			x							x				x		Extremely severe

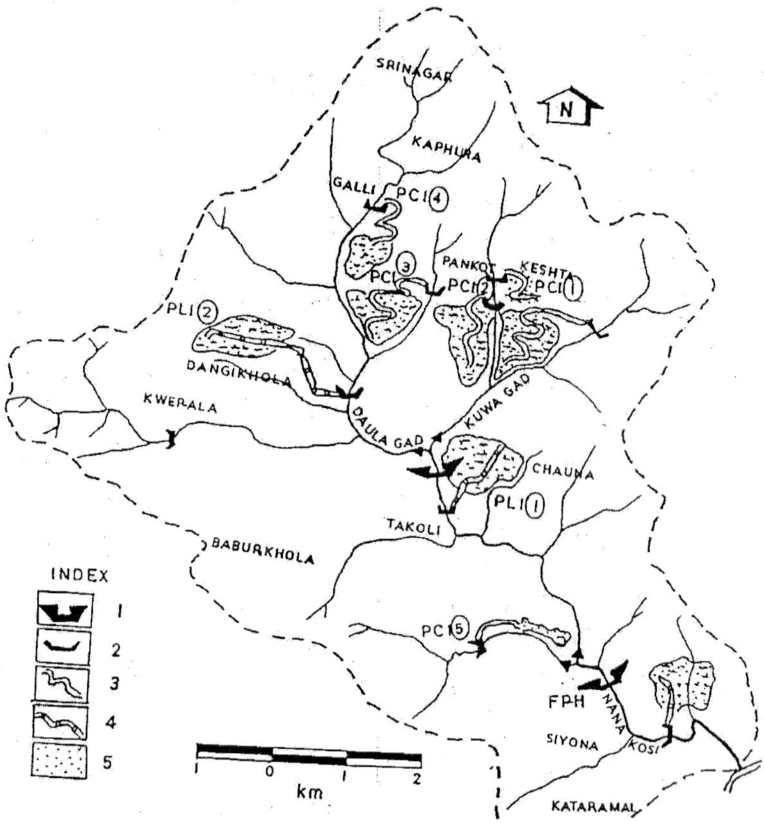

Fig. 10.1 : Proposed plan for the utilization of channels water of the Nana Kosi Watershed, Central Himalaya. 1- Proposed sites for mini-micro hydle Plants, 2- Proposed sites for check-dams, 3- Proposed canals, 4-Proposed sites for lift irrigation, 5- Proposed command area (irrigation), i.e., Class-I, & II land.

Table 10.2: Major and Minor land units within different general classes of physical limitations, and land capability categories in the Nana Kosi Watershed, Central Himalya.

General Class of Physical limitations	*Land system Units*	*Land Category Class*
None/minor	Middle Level Terraces (T_4, T_5, T_6)	I
Minor	High Level Terraces (T_7, T_8, T_9, T_{10}, T_{11}) Low Level Terraces (T_1, T_2, T_3) and Alluvial Fans	II
Some	Sheetwash Fans/cones	III
Severe	Convex Hills and Hollows	IV
Very severe	Triangular Facets	V
Extremely severe	Floodplains, Landslides (block gliding, rockfall, Debris fall and debris flow) and Scarped Land	VI

Management of Land Having Some Physical Limitations

A considerable part of the Nana Kosi watershed have some physical limitations. It includes the areas of sheetwash fan/cones. The sheetwash fans have gentle to moderate concave slope and are composed of medium to coarse colluvium. This land has moderate liability for mass-movements and severe liability for pluvial, rill, gully and at places channel erosion (Table 10.1). This land may be categorized as class-III land (Plate 14). Both erosion and waterlogging impose serious limitations on this land. Utility of this category of land can be improved if erosion is controlled and suitable drainage methods are introduced to combat waterlogging (Fig. 10.2)

Management of Land Having Severe Physical Limitations

Two land units of the basin,i.e., convext hillslopes and hollow (Fig. 6.1, A, B, & C) have severe physical limitations. The steep convex hills have a very thin layer of medium to coarse colluvium and has liabilities for severe mass-movements, pluvial and rill erosion (Table 10.1). The hollows have more or less the same limitations, except small liabilities for rill and gully erosion where hollows on convex hills are barren, they should be used for intensive afforestation works-supported by some construction works where applicable to control the areas of severe mass-wasting. Where these land units are under cultivation (Plate 1 above, Plate 30 below) these require intensive implementation works for their management and to control erosion as illustrated in Fig. 10.2.

Management of Land Having Extremely Severe Physical Limitations

Four land units of the Nana Kosi watershed, viz., scarped land, floodplains, landslides (blockgliding, rockfall, debris fall) and debris flow have extremely severe physical limitations. It is recommended that :

(i) these land units should be banned for any constructional works related to development,
(ii) action project should be induced to plant the stream-bank and floodplains;
(iii) construction works, as applicable—such as construction of brest wall or retaining walls should be induced to control the mass-wasting processes of these geologically damaged areas; and
(iv) these geologically damaged areas should be immediately replanted for their stabilization by local grass/scrubs and plants as applicable.

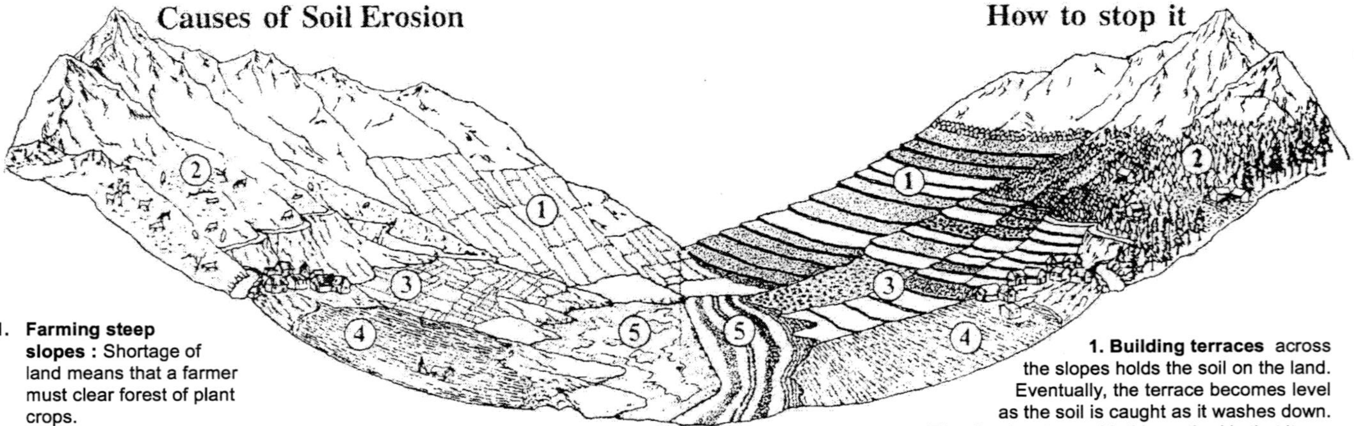

Causes of Soil Erosion

1. **Farming steep slopes :** Shortage of land means that a farmer must clear forest of plant crops.
2. **Overgrazing :** If vegetation is grazed down to the roots faster than it can grow back, the soil is more easily washed away. This happens when the number of animals allowed to graze freely is greater than the land can support.
3. **Overcropping :** Shortage of land means that a farmer cannot leave land fallow for several years before replanting. Nutrients needed to protect the soil are no longer replaced and the soil erodes more easily.
4. **Bad farming practices :** Leaving a field bare during the rains. or ploughing up and down the slopes rather than across them, will accelerate erosion.
5. **Result :** Soil and water run down valley ruining fields.

How to stop it

1. **Building terraces** across the slopes holds the soil on the land. Eventually, the terrace becomes level as the soil is caught as it washes down. (The disadvantage with this method is that it can mean taking up to ten per cent of land out of production).
2. **Trees and grasses can be planted** on the grazing lands, and the areas closed off to allow the plants to regenerate. Animals can be kept in stalls, rather than being allowed to graze freely. The grass can then be cut selectively by hand once it is fully grown, and brought to the animals in their pens. This reduces the likelihood of overgrazing, and raises the productivity of grazing land.
3. **Investment for research** into how to improve yields will allow the farmer to produce more in one year and so leave his land fallow the next.
4. **More investment in a government extension service** would allow trained experts to provide farmers with advice on improved farming practices.
5. **Result :** Good farmland preserved.

Fig. 10.2 : Hypothetical Model showing the causes of soil erosion and their remedies in the hillslopes (*Source* : *Vanishing Earth,* 1987).

Water Management Strategies

There are two major potentialities for the utilization of the water of the Nana Kosi streams, i.e., development of "Mini-Micro-Hydle Plant" and development "Irrigation facilities"

Mini-Micro-Hydel Plant

The dwindling reserves of fuel in the Himalaya, the diminishing resources of crude oil of country reserves and the increasing price suggests need to explore the alternative energy resources. Mini-micro hydel plant is a clear source of energy which can be extensively developed in the regions of easily available hill stream with low maintenance of operational problems (Sharma, *et al.*, 1987). Site testing for mini-micro hydel plants in different part of Kumaun (Sharma, *et al.*, 1987) have suggested that the general requirements for mini-micro-plants are good water potential in lean period (i.e., more than 0.05 m^3/sec), sufficient water head and hard stream bed.

An observation of the preliminary water discharge data of different streams (Fig. 6.4, 6.5 and 6.6) suggests that there are 2 sites, where the Nana Kosi stream have sufficient (more than 0.05 m^3/sec). water potential in the lean month to operate min-micro hydel plants (Fig. 10.1). It is recommended at least one mini-micro hydle plant should be constructed near the centre of Nana Kosi watershed at downstream the confluence of Kua Gad and Daula Gad as shown in Figure 10.1. The water flow capacity of the Nana Kosi stream at this proposed site is 0.069 m^3/sec in the lean months which is higher than the minimum required capacity (i.e., 0.05 m^3/sec).

Irrigation

As it has been already discussed that the class I and II land of the basin, having none to minor physical limitations is badly suffering from irrigation facilities, and streams of the basin are carrying large amount of sediment during rainy season—causing floods. To solve both the problems, Fig. 10.1 presents some proposed sites for the construction of checkdams to control the sediment flow and to provide irrigation facilities to class-I and class-II land of the basin through lift and canal irrigation. It is recommended that this proposed plan should be executed by the coordination between Irrigation and Soil conservation departments or by the G.B. Pant Institute of Himalayan Environment and Development, Kalarmal, Almora.

Construction of low cost checkdams in gullies, e.g., stone checkdams, earth-fill dams, and planting grasses and shrubs in gullies and on channel banks all will have a positive impact on soil and water erosion in the watershed. Scarcity of water was found to be causative factor of land and forest degradation. Thus different kinds of cost effective waterharvesting and water-use efficiency technologies may be introduced. The stored water may sufficient to meet short-term need. Adequate water resources for future generations are a great concern in the area. Water shortage for domestic purposes is a pressing problem in and around the study area. The situation is aggravated during the dry season. Water scarcity can be mitigated to some extent by introducing rainwater harvesting practices and improving the efficiency of water use.

REFERENCES

Bajracharya, D. 1983 : Deforestation in the food/fuel Context : historical and political prospective from Nepal. *Mount. Res. Develop.*, 3 (3), pp. 227-240.

Bhandari, R.K. 1987 : Need for a holistic approach. *In Hindustan Times*, Sept. 13, 1987.

Chorley, R.J. 1969 : The drainage basin as a fundamental geomorphic unit. In *Introduction to Fluvial Processes*, Chorley, R.J. (ed.), Methuer and Co. Ltd., Great Britain, pp. 30-52.

Curry, R.R. 1976 : Watershed form and processes the elegant balance. *The Co-Evolution Quarterly*, Issue No. 2. pp. 14-21.

Doornkamp, J.C. and King, C.A.M. 1971: *Numerical analysis in geomorphology*, London, p. 9

Gregory, K.J. and Walling, D.E. 1979 : *Drainage basin form and processes, a Geomorphological approach*. Edward Arnold Ltd. Great Britain. pp. 1-60.

Horton, R.E. 1932 : Drainage basin Characteristics. *Trans. Amer. Geophys. Union*, 13, pp. 350-361.

Horton, R.E. 1945 : Erosional development of streams and their drainage basins, hydrophysical approach to quantitative morphology. *Geol. Soc. Amer. Bull.*, 56, pp. 275-370.

Ives, J.D. 1985 : Himalayan environmental regeneration an overview; what are the problems and how can they be tackled? In *Environmental Regeneration in Himalaya*, Singh, J.S. (ed.). Central Himalayan Environment Association, Gyanodaya Prakashan, Nainital, pp. 1-10.

Lee, R. 1964 : Potential insulation as a topo-climatic characteristics of drainage basins. *Bull. Internat. Associ. Sci.* Hydrology, pp. 14-30.

Leopold, L.B., Wolman, M.G. and Miller, J.P. 1964 : *Fluvial processes in geomorphology*, Freeman, San Francisco, pp. 1-522.

Myers, G. 1976 : Healing the land; The Redwood Creek Renewal Project. *Co-Evolution Quarterly*, Issue No. 2, pp. 74-77.

Rawat, J.S. 1985 : The drainage basin as a unit for physical environmental studies. In : *Environmental Regeneration in Himalaya*, Singh, J.S. (ed.). Central Himalayan Environment Association Gyanodaya Prakashan, Nainital, pp. 427-433.

Rawat, J.S. 1987 : Modelling of water and sediment budget; Concepts and strategies. Geomorphological models; Theoretical and empirical aspects CATENA, *A Cooper. Jour. Internat. Soc. Soil Sci.* (W. Germany), 10, pp. 147-159.

Rawat, J.S. 1988 : Channel network capacity and geochemical properties of water of the Nana Kosi watershed, Kumaun Lesser Himalaya, Deptt. of Geography, Kumaun Univ., Almora, D. S. T. Project, Final Report, pp. 1-167.

Sharma, S.K., Pant, B.K. and Durgapal, M.C. 1987 : Result from initial site testing for mini-micro hydel plants and Himalayan mills in Kumaun region-I. *Him, Rs. Develpment*, 6, I & II, pp. 50-52.

Simon, D.B., Li, R.M., Ward, J.T. and Shiao, Y.L. 1982 : Modelling of water and sediment yields from forested drainage basins. In *Sediment Budget and Routing in Forested Drainage Basin*, Swanson, *et al.* (eds.), U.S. Deptt. of Agro Gen. Tech. Report, PNW-141, pp. 24-38.

Strahler, A.N. 1964 : Quantitative geomorphology of drainage basin and Channel networks. In *Handbook of applied hydrology*, Chow, V.T. (ed.), McGraw Hill, New York, pp. 4-39-4-76.

Swanson, F.J., Janda, R.J., Dunne, T. and Swanston, D.N. 1982 : Sediment budgets and routing in forested drainage basins, General Technical Report, PNW, 141, pp. 1-165.

Valdiya, K.S. 1985 : Accelerated erosion and landslide prone zones in The Central Himalayan Region. In : *Environmental Regeneration in Himalaya*, Singh, J. S. (ed.), Central Himalayan Environment Association, Gyanodaya Prakashan Nainital, pp. 12-38.

Vanishing the Earth, 1987 : Vanishing the earth. An International Broadcasting Trust Viewers guide to the BBC/TVE Co-Production, pp. 4-5.

Warshall, P. 1976 : Streaming Wisdom. *Co-Evolution, Quarterly Issue* No. 12, pp. 4-10.

11
Conclusions

South of the extremely rugged topography, viz., the Great Himalaya, and north of the highly dissected terrain of Siwalik Hills, lies the Lesser Himalayan terrain. The Nana Kosi watershed lies in the central part of the Lesser Himalayan terrain of the Indian Central Himalaya. The watershed stretches in between 29°37′30" and 29°43′40" N latitudes, and 79°31′ and 79°37′40" E longitudes, and encompasses an area of 55 km^2. The watershed is far away from the zones of geodynamically sensitive and severe mass-movements and erosion which are mainly concentrated along the Main Central Thrust in the north, Main Boundary Fault in the south and along active transverse faults. Thus, geodynamically the area lies in the most stable zone of the Himalaya which is known as a zone of moderate erosion and landsliding.

Tectonically, the watershed lies in the Crystalline unit, known as Almora Nappe. Lithologically, a large part of the watershed is composed of the rocks of Gumalikhet formation. i.e., mica-schist, garnetiferous mica-schist, weathered mica-schist interbedded with quartzites at places. A negligible part of the basin is composed of the rocks of Kalmatia-Kapharkhan formation, i.e., greywack quartzite with very common lentils of graphite. Structurally, the basin falls on the southern flank near the axis of synformal Almora Nappe, and is complexly folded and faulted.

Climatically, the basin falls into cool temperate climatic region of the Himalaya. The climatic records at Almora (about 12 km south of the basin) reveal that in the months of December and February the average temperature never rises more than 10°C, January is the coldest month (average 8°) and June is the hottest month (average 24.1°C). The average annual temperature stands at 17.8°C. The rainfall records show that it is a region of moderate rainfall, where the average annual rainfall stands at 997 mm. July is the month of heaviest rainfall (average 262 mm). About 76.33 per cent of the total annual rainfall is contributed by summer monsoon. The Natural vegetation of the basin is mainly "Chir" pine. At few places, specifically on the northern and northeastern hillslopes "Chir" pine is remarkably mixed with "Banj"(*Quercus incana*); "Burans"

(*Rhododendron arboretum*) and "Kaphal" (*Murica supidea*). About 31.24 per cent (i.e., 17.18 km^2) area of the total basin falls under vegetation cover.

The Nana Kosi is a fifth order stream which comprises of as many as 360 first, 80 second, 17 third and 5 fourth order streams. The stream composition of the basin follows Horton's Law of Stream Number which reveals that stream order and number of streams have inverse geometric relationship (r= -.75). The mean stream length of the first, second, third, fourth and fifth order streams stand at 0.49 km, 0.99 km, 3.20 km and 8.5 km respectively. The length of the total stream networks is 236.90 km. The bifurcation ratio of the different order streams shows constant nature (range 3.4 to 5.00). The drainage density, stream frequency and drainage texture of the basin stand at 3.28 km/km^2, 8.42 no./km^2 and 2.80 respectively. The circularity ratio, i.e., 0.56, suggests that the basin is largely distorted.

The absolute and relative relief ranges in between 1180 m and 1900 m (mean 1578 m ± 435 m), and 75 m and 450 m (mean 161 m ± 92 m). The distribution of absolute and relative relief tend to be normally distributed. The hypsometric curve and hypsometric integral (HI = 60.45) indicates that 39.65 per cent area of the basin has been eroded by various degradation processes and the drainage basin is passing through young stage of geomorphic development. The mean average slope of the basin stands at 15°.

There are number of morphological features which are genetically tectonic. These include scarps, abandoned valleys polycyclic terrace scarps, waterfalls and rapids. All these tectonic landforms are associated with regional uplift, northeastern tilting of the basin, and reverse and transverse faulting. Several episodes of erosion and deposition caused by successive uplift have produced multiple terraces at different levels. Multitier scarps of these terraces indicate that the Nana Kosi terraces are polygenetic and suggest regional uplift of the basin since the formation of the oldest terrace. From the configuration of terrace scarps, total uplift in order of 140-245 m is concluded since the formation of the oldest terrace. These multitier terraces of the basin also suggest that the regional uplift is successive rather than continuous. The relative height of terrace scarps increases downstream which indicate the diverging tendency of terraces. The height of the oldest terrace (T_{11}) stands at 245 m near mouth, 140 m near reach. Similarly, the height of the other level terraces increases downstream. Thus, diverging tendency of terraces from reach to mouth suggest the northeastern tilting of the basin. Judging from the mode of deformation of these terrace surfaces, it can be suggested that tilting has been continuing through the formation of the oldest terrace surface. The vertical scarps on either side of the Nana Kosi watershed are also caused by the regional uplift and shows the diverging tendency from upstream to downstream due to the northeastern tectonic tilting. There are as many as six major faults in the basin. These faults were identified and marked with the help of the geomorphic features such as fault scarps, triangular facets, waterfalls, block-gliding, rockfall, fault aprons and the geological features such as shattering, crushing and shearing of rocks.

The variation of rock types with different structural characters and to different capacities to resist erosion (geomorphologically known as "petrovariance") has played a significant role in the development of landforms of the basin. The control of petrovariance in the development of landforms of the basin has grasped in two-ways, i.e., by examining and comparing the landforms of different rocktypes and by examining the rock structure of the landforms. The study reveals that the bed-rock lithologies have a profound effect on different morphometric variables. There is considerable differences between morphometric variables of the mica-schist, and between weathered mica-schist, and quartzites. The weak and less resistant mica-schist and weathered mica-schist are characterized by the high value of drainage density (3.2 to 4.1 km/km^2) and stream frequency (7.7 to 12.5 no./km^2), and low value of basin area (0.13 to 0.08 km^2) and stream length (0.41 to 0.33 km). While the relatively hard and more resistant quartzites show low value of drainage density (2.4 km/km^2) and stream frequency (3.2 no./km^2), and high value of basin area (0.20 km^2) and stream length (0.49 km).

Joints, the secondary structural features of rocks have also played a significant role in the development of the landforms at places in the basin. The hard quartzites rocks are highly jointed than that of the mica-schist. Even within the quartzites there is much variations in the joint density due to differential movements. Quartzite on the fault plane is largely jointed which is susceptible to continuous debris flow and produce small debris cones of finer sediment. Adjacent to the fault plain, i.e., fault zone, the quartzites is relatively less jointed which is not prone for continuous debris flow, but is subject for rockfall when the closely spaced joint planes are saturated by water during monsoon rains. The closely spaced joint planes produces debris cones of coarse sediments widely space joints on the mica-schist along the fault plane produces block-glidings and sometimes rockfall of very coarse materials.

The watershed is characterized by various "pluvial" landforms. Hollows, i.e., concave outportions of hillslopes not occupied by channels, and sheetwash fans and cones composed of fine material are commonly availavle pluvial landforms of the watershed. The hollows are 3 to 20 m apart along the hillslopes, resulting in a frequency of 7 hollows axis per km^2. There are as many as 140 sheetwash fan/cones in the watershed and their frequency stands at 1.2 per km^2. The experimental study of sheetwash erosion reveal that the hillspurs of the basin generates sheetwash debris at the rate of 0.00266 ton/km^2. In 1986-87 sheetwash sediment was generated at the rate of 0.0191 ton/km^2 at 1000 mm rain input. In 1987-88 (which was the drought year) the sheetwash debris was generated at the rate of 0.0082 ton/km^2 at 431.7 mm rain input. It is deduced that about 1.05 ton sediment in 1986-87 and 0.45 ton sediment in 1987-88 was mobilized on the hillslopes by sheetwash erosion in the entire watershed. Under identical geological, geomorphological character and climatic inputs, the most disturbed land (agriculture) is generating about 3.5 times (0.00407 ton/km^2) higher sheetwash erosion sediment than that of the undisturbed forest land (0.00116 ton/km^2). Agricultural land is generating about 2.4 times higher (0.00407 ton/km^2) sheetwash erosion sediment than that of the relatively less disturbed barren land (0.00275 ton/km^2). The ratio of sheetwash erosion on the forest, barren and agricultural hillslopes of the watershed stands at 1.0 : 2.6 : 3.5 respectively.

The major fluvial landforms of the watershed are eleven flights of erosional and deposional river terraces, small alluvial fans, narrow patches of floodplains (1-7 m wide), small point bars at places caused by lateral migration of meanders. The length, amplitude and mean radius of the Nana Kosi river meanders ranges in between 189-218 m, 71-103 m and 34-50 m, respectively.

The mean water discharge of the Nana Kosi river is 1.032 m^3/sec. It was drastically reduced more than three times in the drought year 1987-88. In this year, the mean water discharge was found 0.255 m^3/sec. only. About 46 to 64 per cent of the total annual water discharge flows in one month only, i.e., July. In this month the mean waterflow capacity approaches maximum, i.e., 5.645 m^3/sec (1986-87) to 2.272 m^3/sec (1987-88). April is the driest month which contributes 0.44 per cent water only of the total annual runoff. In this month the waterflow drops up to 0.22 m^3/sec. On an average 82.2 per cent of the total annual waterflow, flows in the rainy season. Summer and winter flows contribute 10.9 and 6.9 per cent respectively. The average ratio of water generating capacity of the land of the Nana Kosi Watershed to channels stands at 380621.45 m^3/km^2/ year. In the drought year (1987-88) it was found at 169441.39 m^3/km^2.

In 1986-87, the suspended sediment from the entire watershed was generated at the rate of 141.24 tons/km^2, while the drought year, i.e., 1987-88, this rate was found at 47.92 tons/km^2 only. During the course of the study period (1986-88) about 8145 tons suspended sediment was delivered. On an average (1986-88) the suspended sediment from the entire basin was delivered at the rate of 94.58 tons/km^2.

In 1986-87, the dissolved load from entire the catchment was generated at the rate of 113.20 tons/km^2, while in 1987-88 this rate was found at 79.36 tons/km^2 only. During the course of the study period (1986-88), the dissolved load from entire the catchment area was delivered at the rate of 96.42 tons/km^2.

On an average the watershed was lowered at the rate of 0.93 mm per year in 1986-87 and 0.30 mm per year in 1987-88 (drought year).

Under identical geological and geomorphological character and climatic inputs, the suspended sediment generating capacity of the agricultural land has been increased 17.58 (1986-87) to 13.21 (1987-88) times higher than that of the oak mixed land. On an average (1986-88), the agricultural land has about 17 times higher suspended sediment generating capacity than that of the oak mixed forest land. Thus, it can be deduced that anthropogenic processes have played a significant role to increase the suspended sediment generating capacity of land to channels. The ratio of suspended sediment generating capacity of different land suggest that, if the suspended sediment generating capacity of land to channels is one in oak mixed forest land, it is 4.85 in pine forest land, 9.00 in deforested mixed type land and 17 in agricultural land. Similarly, under identical geological, geomorphological character and climatic inputs, the dissolved load generating capacity of the agricultural land has been increased 4.10 (1986-87) to 4.54 (1987-88) times higher than that of the oak mixed land. On an average (1986-88) the agricultural land has about 4.2 times higher dissolved load generating capacity than of the oak mixed forest land. Thus, it can be deduced that the anthropogenic processes have played a significant role to increase the dissolved load generating capacity of land to channels. The ratio of different land suggest that, if the dissolved load generating capacity of land to channels is one in oak mixed forest land, it is 3.2 in pine forest land 4.08 in deforested mixed and 4.21 in agricultural land.

The watershed is characterized by many characteristic morphological features, caused by mass-movements. Genetically, these are tectonically controlled landforms, because the mass-wasting forms are confined along the tectonic zones, i.e., the zones of the reverse and transverse faults. The mass-wasting forms of the study area may be classified into two major groups. These are (i) various types of landslides which include block-gliding, rock fall, debris fall, creeping and slumping, and (ii) debris flows.

Roads, settlements, quarrying, bridges and watermills are the major technogenic landforms in the watershed. Among these, road is the most important technogenic process which is creating various environmental deteriorations in the study area. The networks of these road within the watershed is 58.5 km. During the period of road construction about 13689×10^4 cubic metres of debris was removed from the hillsides of the watershed at the rate of 234×10^4 m^3 per kilometre. Each year every kilometre of these road produces about 64.87 m^3 of debris by landsliding and rockfall during monsoon rains which slide down the hillslopes, killing vegetation, smothering springs and chocking streams.

The above geomorphic characteristics of the Nana Kosi watershed indicate that ecologically the watershed is not in a balanced or equilibrium state. An equilibrium state is one in which the many variables of a watershed system are dynamically balanced. When the total watershed remains in physical balance, nutrients like water and soils are detained longer on land. The soils retain more moisture further retaining water and simultaneously, encourage life. A hillslope profile is the result of balance between runoff, infiltration and erosion. All these are modified by the degree of soil development since that in turn controls what grows on the hillside and thus, controls runoff, infiltration and erosion. Soil development is in turn determined by the age and stability of the surface.

In the Nana Kosi watershed there is no balance in watershed system. Runoff intensity is very high which cause very high erosion on the hillslopes. Simultaneously, floodwater reach watercourses faster due to denser and more effective integration of rills and ephemeral channels on the hillslopes, and flood heights increases. Increased sedimentation and increased flooding lead to increased lateral erosion of stream channels that must change their channel geometry to accommodate a greater percentage of sediment load to water discharge. In such a disequilibrium system of the Nana Kosi watershed, a headwater change in biota is largely effective change in the ecological systems of the whole watershed below it.

The study provides some regeneration strategies for such an imblanced ecological system. The regeneration strategies reveal that :

1. the watershed should be considered as a natural laboratory by the planner, decision-makers and scientists for the environmental management;
2. there is a great need to develop watershed consciousness (among the local inhabitants, planners, land managers, and decision-makers) that it has form, processes and water resources and systems like a living organism; ordinarily treated, the system is like the veins of a leaf, broadly viewed the watershed is like the entire leaf;
3. managing the environment means healing the wounds of land or treatment of land diseases; before starting the treatment (or management works) of a disease, "operation research" or "environmental impact analysis" is needed to find-out causes of disequilibrium state of the entire system, and

4. to bring back in natural condition to the watershed, various watershed repair programmes should be started by initiating action projects within the watershed, it should be noted that no action project should be granted before conducting environmental impact analysis or operation research within the watershed.

Apart from the above general strategies for environmental regeneration the investigation also includes some specific conservative strategies for the management of (i) different categories (I to VI) of lands having different class of physical limitations, and (ii) water resources of the Nana Kosi watershed.

Bibliography

Chow, V.T., Maidment, R.D. and Mays, L.W. 1988 : *Applied Hydrology.* McGraw Hill Book. New York & Paris, p. 1-527.

Cooke, R.U. and Doornkamp, J.C. 1978 : *Geomorphology in Environmental Management,* Oxford Calarendon Press, pp. 14-20.

F.A.O. 1986 : Strategies, approaches and systems in Integrated Watershed Management. F.A.O. Conservation Guide 14, Food and Agriculture Organization of the U.N. Rome, p. 1-232.

Gurjar, R.K. and Jat, B.C. 2008 : *Geography of Water Resources.* Rawat Publications. New Delhi, p. 1-448.

Haigh, M.J., Rawat J.S., Bartarya, S.K. and Rawat, M.S. 1993 : Factors affecting landslide morphology along new highways in the Central Himalaya. Transactions, Japanese Geomorphological Union, *Japan No. 14-2,* p. 99-123.

Haigh, M.J. Rawat J.S., Bartarya, S.K. and Rawat, M.S., 1993b : *Natural Hazards, Netherlands. No. 8,* p. 153-170.

Haigh, M.J., Rawat J.S. and Rawat, M.S. 1995 : Interactions between Forest and Landslide activity along new highways in the Kumaun Himalaya, Forest Ecology and Management, *Netherlands. No. 78,* p. 173-189.

Haigh, M.J., RAwat J.S., Bartarya, S.K. and Rawat, M.S. 1992 : Analysis of Landslides sites, Kolbury Road, Kumaun Himalaya, India, *Current Science.* Vol. 62, No. 1, p. 518-22.

Pandey, B.P., Arya, K.L., Pant, C.C. and Sharma, A.K.I., 2002 : *Watershed Management in Himalaya : Concept and Strategy* (eds.) Watershed Management Directorate, Uttarkhand. Gyanodaya Prakashan, Nainital-263001.

Rawat, J.S. and Rawat, M.S., 1994a : Accelerated erosion and denudation in the Nana Kosi Watershed, Central Himalaya, India. Part I : Sediment Load. *Mountain Research and Development,* Vol. 14, No. 1, p. 25-38.

Rawat, J.S. and Rawat, M.S., 1994b, 1994 : The Nana Kosi Watershed Central Himalaya, India Part II. Human Impacts on Stream Runoff. *Mountain Research and Development,* Vol. 14, No. 3, p. 25-260.

Rawat, M.S., Rawat J.S. and Haigh, M.J. 1992 : Sediment discharge from a Himalayan pine forested headwater. In : *Environmental Regeneration in Headwaters* (eds. Joseph Krecok and M.J. Haigh). Prague, Czech Republic, p. 182-187.

Rawat, M.S., Rawat J.S. and Haigh, M.J. 1995 : Patterns of headwater sediment yield from Himalayan pine forest In : *Hydrological Problems and Environmental Management in Highlands and Headwaters* (eds.) Joseph Krecek et al.) Oxford & IBH Publishing Co. Pvt. Ltd. New Delhi, p. 364-393.

Rawat, M.S. and Haigh, M.J. 1998 : Rainy season runoff and sediment yields of forested and non-forested catchments in Kumaun Himalaya, In : *Proceedings of the 8th International Soil Conservation Conference on Soil and Water Conservation : Challenges and Opportunities* (eds. L.S. Bhushan, I.P., I.P. Abrol and M.S. Ramamohan Rao). Oxford and IBH Publishing Co. Pvt. Ltd., New Delhi, Vol. 2, p. 1458-1465.

Rawat, M.S., Haigh M.J., Krecek, J. and Rawat, J.S. 1999 : Dissolved load of a Central Himalayan forest headwater in an experimental catchment India. In : *Biogeochemistry of Rivers in Tropical South and Southeast Asia* (eds. Ittekkot, V. *et al.*) SCOPE, MiH. Geol. Palaont. Inst. Univ. Hamburg, Helt 82, Sonderband Marz, p. 1-297.

Rawat, M.S. 2000 : Integrated Watershed Management : An Alternative Development Strategy for the hills of Uttaranchal. In : *Regional Economic Problems and the Dynamics of Change* (ed. D.C. Pandey). Anamika Publishers & Distributors (P) Ltd., New Delhi p. 73-96.

Saxena, H.M. 2006, 2006 : *Environmental Studies.* Rawat Publications, New Delhi, p. 1-234.

Sharma, H.S. 1991 : *Indian Geomorphology : Selected papers from the 2nd Conference of the Indian Institute of Geomorphologists on environmental Geomorphology* (ed.) Concept Publishing Company, New Delhi, p. 1-358.

Sharma, H.S. 2001 : *Perspectives in Geomorphology* (ed. 4 vols.), Concept Publishing Company, New Delhi.

Sharma, H.S. 2002 : Status of Water resources and management for sustainable development. Paper presented in Indian Science Congress 2001. *Rajasthan Review.*

Valdiya, K.S. 1998 : *Dynamic Himalaya.* Educational Monographs. Jawaharlal Nehru Centre for Advanced Scientific Research. Universities Press (India) Limited Hyderabad. p. 1-178.

Valdiya, K.S. 2004 : *Geology, Environment and Society.* Universities Press (India) Limited. Hyderabad pp. 1-228.

Vishwas, S.K. and Gupta, A., 2001 : *Introduction to Geomorphology.* Orient Longman Limited, Hyderabad.

Index